P9-DXN-266

Spirit
of NOVA SCOTIA

Seagull (Refer to entry 67, page 71)

Acknowledgements

Richard Henning Field

Throughout Canada, works of fine and folk art lie undiscovered or unstudied even though they are records of our heritage, the expressions of our culture, the very stuff of which Canadian history was made and through which it can be studied and understood.

I am pleased to have been given the opportunity through this publication and exhibition to illuminate one aspect of our Canadian culture: traditional decorative folk art of Nova Scotia from 1780 to 1930.

A project of this magnitude is never brought to fruition solely through the efforts of one individual. My sincere appreciation goes first to Bernard Riordon, Curator/Director of the Art Gallery of Nova Scotia for his support of the exhibition concept, for putting the necessary funding in place, and for his guidance, assistance and direction over the past four years.

I acknowledge with gratitude, the significant contribution made by Janet Conover of Arts and Communications Counselors. Through the generosity of the sponsor, Mobil Oil Canada, Ltd. and the Museum Assistance Programmes, National Museums of Canada and the Art Gallery of Nova Scotia the publication and exhibition and its tour were made possible.

Gerald Ferguson, Chris Huntington and Murray E. Stewart, individuals recognized in the collection and study of Nova Scotian and Canadian folk art and furnishings, were instrumental in the development of my curatorial perspective and the exhibition. For their combined instincts, insights, knowledge of the subject and willingness to participate in the exhibition through loans, shared documentation and endless consultations, I extend my deepest gratitude.

The substance of this text is enhanced by the contributions made by Terry Kobayashi and Michael Bird, Scott Robson, Eric Ruff, Bernard Riordon, Susan M. Foshay and Murray E. Stewart whom I thank for so generously sharing their knowledge and experience and for producing essays in the various exhibition categories. To Michael S. Cross special regards for writing an historical introduction which focuses on the events which shaped Nova Scotia during the 150 year period covered.

Without the cooperation and assistance of many public institutions and their staff an exhibition of this scope could never have been realized. To the following my continued regard and appreciation for allowing me to examine and photograph objects or for making documentation available: Bill Plaskett, Lunenburg Heritage Society; Mern O'Brien, Dalhousie Art Gallery; Miles Russell, Ross Farm Museum; Mrs. Muriel Wentzell, Parkdale-Maplewood Museum; Dr. Charles Armour, Dalhousie University Archives; Marina Hamilton, Lawrence House; Wesley Mattie, National Museum of Man, Canadian Centre for Folk Culture Studies; Scott Robson, Nova Scotia Museum; Eric Ruff and Dr. Henry Ross, Yarmouth County Museum; Gary Hartlen, Queens County Museum and the Simeon Perkins House; Gary Selig, DesBrisay Museum; Elizabeth Adamson and James Davison, Randall House Museum and Wolfville Historical Society; James D. How, Fort Anne National

Lenders to the Exhibition

Dr and Mrs Charles Armour
Art Gallery of Nova Scotia
David Beck
Carl Boswick
Canadian Centre for Folk Culture Studies, National Museum of Man
Cape Sable Historical Society
George Christie
Carole Collins
Chris Cooper
Mr and Mrs Francis Coutellier
Pauline and Jowe Creighton
Dartmouth Heritage Museum/ The Quaker House
DesBrisay Museum
Pascal and Angela Dinaut
Barbara Doiron
Maurice Edwards
Gerald Ferguson
Richard Henning Field and Deborah Field
Fort Anne National Historic Park
James Denison How
Chris Huntington
Joseph Schneider House Museum
Blair and Pearl Kaiser
Paul Killawee and Judy Aymar
Terry Kobayashi and Michael Bird
Tom and Patricia Lackey
Leslie Langille
Gladys and Barry Lewis-Jennings
Maritime Museum of the Atlantic
John Marshall
June Miller
Nova Scotia Museum
Queens County Museum
Scott Robson
Earle and Judy Rhodenizer
Shelburne County Museum
Jim and Susan Snowden
Jamie Stalker
Murray Stewart
Jerry and Deborah Vidito
Wolfville Historical Society/ Randall House Museum
Yarmouth County Museum

Historic Park; Mr. G. S. Gosley, The Quaker House and Dartmouth Heritage Museum; David Fleming, Maritime Museum of the Atlantic; Mary E. Snow, Barrington Woolen Mill/Cape Sable Historical Society Centre; Mrs. Finnola Bower, Ross-Thompson House and Shelburne County Museum; and Susan Burke, The Joseph Schneider House Museum. My respects also to the galleries and museums across Canada who will host the exhibition.

I wish to express my deepest gratitude to the lenders who are identified separately. Their loan of works for as long as two years cannot be underestimated and is greatly appreciated.

George Georgakakos, the project photographer deserves special recognition for his tireless efforts in the photo documentation of the works in this exhibition. I thank him for his excellent photography and welcome companionship on study trips.

Graphic Design Associates were instrumental in establishing an exciting visual identity for the exhibition and in designing this elegant catalogue. To Jim Lotz for editorial assistance, my thanks.

Also my thanks to volunteers Wayne Strickland and Dianne O'Neill for administrative and technical assistance respectively.

I am also indebted to the staff at the Art Gallery of Nova Scotia who faced the immensity of the task at hand with humour and professionalism among them: Judy Dietz, Registrar; Laurie Hamilton and Keith Bantock, Fine Art Conservators; Deborah Young, Exhibitions Curator; Patt Beauchamp, Preparator; Sean McQuay, Gallery Assistant; Kimberley Dunn, Gallery Assistant; and Fran Fowler, Secretary.

Finally I would like to thank my wife Deborah, for her patience and understanding over the past four years, for being a good listener, and for her continued encouragement through the late nights, early mornings and lost weekends.

Minister's Foreword

Billy Joe MacLean
Minister of Culture,
Recreation and Fitness
Province of Nova Scotia

The colourful traditions of decorative art in Nova Scotia are centuries old and in many ways reflect the heritage, and the creativity of generations of Nova Scotians.

To many of us the objects are as familiar as old friends and surround us with memories as warm as winter quilts. They have graced our family homesteads and workplaces and served as sources of entertainment, enjoyment and the seed of many a fine story.

For most others, this exhibition will offer a glimpse into Nova Scotia's past. Each item was lovingly worked with an indiginous talent which mirrored the customs, priorities and values of its time and maker.

Spirit of Nova Scotia: Traditional Decorative Folk Art, 1780-1930, speaks of the joy, the beauty and the challenge of living in early Nova Scotia. I am proud that we have the opportunity to share it with you.

Corporate Sponsor's Foreword

Doyle G. Marrs
President and General Manager
Mobil Oil Canada, Ltd.

Mobil Oil Canada has long enjoyed a special relationship with Nova Scotia — with her land, the sea and her people. Through our operations in Halifax, we have, over the years developed a keen and natural interest in supporting the unique artistic expressions of the people in this province. For this reason, Mobil Oil is especially proud to sponsor the exhibition and the national tour of *Spirit of Nova Scotia: Traditional Decorative Folk Art, 1780-1930.*

Spirit of Nova Scotia, the most comprehensive survey of Nova Scotian folk art ever assembled, is an exhibition which ventures beyond the warmth and charm of its artifacts. Guest Curator Richard Henning Field has organized an exhibition that spans 150 years and examines the cultural origins and development of Nova Scotia's folk traditions. These traditions, developed by the men and women of the Atlantic region, open up a rich dialogue between past and present, and tell us of the life experiences, the homes and the communities of these artisans.

We would like to express our appreciation to Richard Henning Field and the Art Gallery of Nova Scotia for giving Mobil Oil this opportunity to share with Canadians across the country an exciting new vision of Nova Scotia, her artifacts and her people.

Contents

Spirit of Nova Scotia

Minister's Foreword VI
Corporate Sponsor's Foreword VI
Director's Foreword VII
Acknowledgements IX
Introduction
Richard Henning Field 1
Historical Perspective
Dr. Michael S. Cross 5
Colour Plates 11

Catalogue

Textiles
Introduction 28
Textiles in Nova Scotia
Scott Robson 30

Sculpture
Introduction 60
Traditional Nova Scotia Folk Sculpture
Bernard Riordon 62

Paintings, Watercolours and Drawings
Introduction 92
Aspects of Nova Scotia Folk Portraiture
Susan M. Foshay 94
Aspects of Nova Scotia Ship Portraiture
Eric Ruff 100

Decorated Utilitarian Objects
Introduction 124
The Traditional Folk Arts of Lunenburg County
Terry Kobayashi and Michael Bird 126
Background, Interpretation and Function of Decorated Utilitarian Objects in Early Nova Scotia Households
Murray E. Stewart 128

Map of Nova Scotia 209

Selected Bibliography 210

Director's Foreword

Bernard Riordon
Curator/Director
Art Gallery of Nova Scotia

This exhibition and publication celebrate the triumphs and lively spirit of many untrained Nova Scotian artists who have created works of art with charm, simplicity and honesty. The art works included in the exhibition provide a sampling of what was being done in Nova Scotia from 1780-1930 in the area of traditional decorative folk art. The exhibition demonstrates the vitality and imagination of Nova Scotia's folk artists and also indicates how important they were to the cultural development of the province. Their work is related to the heritage of the ordinary person, work that for years after its' making was relegated to the attic or basement and today is acknowledged in an appropriate manner.

The exhibition concept and proposal was presented to the Gallery by Richard Henning Field in 1981. *Spirit of Nova Scotia: Traditional Decorative Folk Art, 1780-1930* is the result of years of work by the curator of the exhibition and the support and cooperation of many individuals.

I would like to express my congratulations and thanks to the curator of the exhibition, Richard Henning Field, for his commitment to this project. Its realization has involved many years of work and dedication.

The exhibition has been made possible by Mobil Oil Canada, Ltd. the corporate sponsor for the project. Our sincere thanks are extended to Mr. Doyle Marrs, President and General Manager. We owe a debt of gratitude to Arts and Communications Counselors Ltd. for securing the generous corporate patron. Specifically, to Janet Conover and Nina Wright of this firm, I want to express our sincere appreciation. Throughout our association, they have represented the project and the corporation with the greatest efficiency and effectiveness.

We express our thanks to the Museum Assistance Programmes, National Museums of Canada for its support of the project. We are fortunate, also, to have the assistance and cooperation of Dundurn Press, Kirk Howard, President, who have taken on the co-publishing of this book. The ongoing support of the Nova Scotia Department of Culture, Recreation and Fitness is duly recognized and greatly appreciated. Our sincere thanks are expressed to the Honourable Billy Joe MacLean, Minister. We are appreciative of the excellent cooperation of the lenders to the exhibition, the contributing writers and all individuals who have offered advice and assistance. My personal thanks are extended to the staff of the Art Gallery of Nova Scotia for their excellent work in assuring the success of this important project.

Since the initial *Folk Art of Nova Scotia* exhibition organized by the Art Gallery of Nova Scotia in 1976, the Gallery has given special consideration to the exhibition and collection of folk art from the Province. This exhibition provided the beginning of a collection which is now recognized internationally and which will provide enjoyment for future generations.

We are confident that *Spirit of Nova Scotia: Traditional Decorative Folk Art, 1780-1930* will further an appreciation of folk art and will provide Canadians with a better understanding of this area of Nova Scotia's cultural heritage. We invite you to enjoy this exhibition and publication and share in the accomplishments of our folk artists.

Traditional Decorative Folk Art 1780♡1930

Richard Henning Field

Contributing Writers:
Michael S. Cross
Scott Robson
Bernard Riordon
Susan M. Foshay
Eric Ruff
Terry Kobayashi and Michael Bird
Murray E. Stewart

Organized and circulated by the
Art Gallery of Nova Scotia
Made possible by a grant from
Mobil Oil Canada, Ltd.
Supported by the
Museum Assistance Programmes, National Museums of Canada.

Art Gallery of Nova Scotia, Halifax

Dundurn Press, Toronto and London
1985

Published by

Art Gallery of Nova Scotia
6152 Coburg Road
P.O. Box 2262
Halifax, Nova Scotia
B3J 3C8

Dundurn Press Limited
1558 Queen Street East
Toronto, Ontario
M4L 1E8

Cataloguing in Publication Data

Field, Richard Henning, 1944-
Spirit of Nova Scotia

Catalogue for an exhibition organized by the Art Gallery of Nova Scotia, opening at the Mendel Art Gallery, Saskatoon, Saskatchewan Jan. 18-Mar. 9, 1986, and travelling to other galleries.
Bibliography: p.
ISBN 1-55002-006-4 (bound). - ISBN 1-55002-004-8 (pbk.)

1. Folk art - Nova Scotia - Exhibitions. 2. Decorative arts - Nova Scotia - Exhibitions. I. Art Gallery of Nova Scotia. II. Mendel Art Gallery. III. Title.

NK842.N68F53 1986 745'.09716'0740116 C86-093215-X

Editor/Guest Curator
Richard Henning Field
Photography
George Georgakakos
Editorial Services
Jim Lotz Associates
Design
Graphic Design Associates, Halifax
Typesetting
McCurdy Printing & Typesetting Ltd., Halifax
Production Co-ordination
Ron and Ron Design Photography, Toronto
Printing and Binding
Hignell Printing Company Limited, Winnipeg

The publication of this book was made possible by support from several sources. The publishers wish to acknowledge the ongoing support of the Canada Council and the Ontario Arts Council.

J. Kirk Howard, *Publisher*

Exhibition Itinerary

Mendel Art Gallery
Saskatoon, Saskatchewan
17 January - 9 March 1986

Art Gallery of Windsor
Windsor, Ontario
3 April - 25 May 1986

The Winnipeg Art Gallery
Winnipeg, Manitoba
27 June - 31 August 1986

The Nickle Arts Museum
Calgary, Alberta
10 October - 23 November 1986

Art Gallery of Greater Victoria
Victoria, British Columbia
4 December - 1 February 1987

The Art Gallery at Harbourfront
Toronto, Ontario
3 April - 10 May 1987

Confederation Centre Art Gallery and Museum
Charlottetown, Prince Edward Island
16 June - 16 August 1987

Art Gallery of Nova Scotia
Halifax, Nova Scotia
24 September - 6 December 1987

Introduction

Richard Henning Field

What intellect restores to us under the name of the past is not the past. In reality as soon as each hour of one's life has died, it embodies itself in some material object, as do the souls of the dead in certain folk stories, and hides there. There it remains captive, captive forever, unless we should happen upon the object, recognize what lies within, call it by its name and so set it free.

Marcel Proust,
Remembrance of Things Past

pirit of Nova Scotia begins with its people. It is embodied in the mind and senses, and shared by Nova Scotia's settlers and native inhabitants. It is manifested in the richly decorated objects in this exhibition which reflect these common patterns and experiences, and can be seen in carvings, decorative motifs, textiles, sculptures, painting and domestic effects. All these objects embody complex mental abstractions capturing specific native, European and American ethnic and cultural traditions, comprehensible to the original makers and owners and to their communities, and to the present-day viewer who searches diligently for meaning in this varied gathering of materials from Nova Scotia dating between the years 1780 to 1930.

The diverse array of settlers to Nova Scotia were not trapped in a crude frontier environment, they were not drab or deprived of artistic delights. Over the 150 year period represented by the objects in this exhibition, the French, English, Irish and Scottish, German, Black and American immigrants coped with disruptions in deeply rooted patterns of daily life, and created a new sense of place and identity. The decorative and material traditions brought by these groups, although not resistant to change in this new environment, retained the spirit of their cultures and survived.

Although it is always difficult to establish temporal parameters for a show of this nature, the year 1780 was selected as the starting point because of certain known objects dating from the last quarter of the eighteenth century, and because 1780 seemed a pivotal year in the history of Nova Scotia. Thirty-one years after the founding of Halifax in 1749, 27 years after the establishment of Lunenburg in 1753, 25 years after the expulsion of the Acadians in 1755, 20 years after the fall of Louisbourg and the end of the French regime in 1760, 17 years after the arrival of the Planters from New England in 1763, and five years after the American Revolution, the year 1780 sat astride the Loyalist migration between 1775 and 1785, and was to face the rise of Henry Alline and the religious revival in Nova Scotia in 1783, and the separation of New Brunswick one year later. It was a year that had already witnessed great changes in the political structure of western society, and sweeping reformations in the monarchies of Europe were still to come with the outbreak of the French Revolution in 1789. The year 1780 would see the end of the enlightened century and the beginning of the next hundred years beating to the sound of a new kind of revolution brought by the machine.

As the end point the year 1930 was chosen for very similar reasons. Only 12 years after the war to end all wars, and nine years before the war that changed all war, 1930 saw the beginning of the decline and loss of many of the decorative folk traditions represented in this exhibition. The political, social, and economic turmoil that followed the decade after 1930, and the beginning of the Second World War in Europe in 1939, effectively sounded the death knell of folk traditions even in rural Nova Scotia. The war would draw away many of the young men who could carry on these traditions, and by the time 1945 came, the technological innovations developed during the war would redirect the energies of those returning soldiers to other leisure time activities.

This is not to suggest that folk art was no longer made after World War II, simply that the traditional ethnic and cultural basis from which much of nineteenth century folk art derived, began to wane and die as the complexion of rural life changed, and more contemporary ideas and sources started to emerge in the popular imagination based on mass produced products and advertising images. At the same time the war effort resulted in the development of many new products including plastics, lighter sheet metals, and eventually the full spectrum of synthetic colours became available to the artist in both oil and water-based paints. It was no longer necessary to restrict ones imagination to traditional themes, mediums, and primary colours.

The *Spirit of Nova Scotia* is an introduction to the traditional decorative folk art of this province. It is also a historical dialogue between the past and present. The objects presented here, the majority for the first time, are statements by the various cultural groups that produced and used them. This historical dialogue examines the intricate relationship between Nova Scotia, Europe, and New England, and helps to illustrate the complexity of the transmission of culture through people, social and community practice, and material traditions.

However, it must be kept in mind that the categories and sub-categories of material folk culture represented in this exhibition — commonly called folk or decorative art today — were seldom considered art by their makers and owners, or the communities where they were made and used. "They were primarily tools to facilitate daily living and at the same time devices that helped manipulate social interaction, control the material and non-material environment of their owners, and convey meaning. These artifacts were a form of communicative expression — a 'silent' but powerful language. Material expressions actively conveyed culture, actively transmitted meaning, and were essential elements in components achieving cultural and personal goals."[1] Even the most common and plainly decorated object conveyed meaning and significance to their owners. The women who hooked the rug or made the quilt using recycled fabrics, the lumberman who carved a spruce gum box, and the sailor making a needle case were communicating shared life experiences based on traditional values, combining an understanding of the function of the object with themes and variations of decorative design.

Many of the objects in the exhibition and catalogue are masterpieces of traditional Nova Scotia decorative folk art. Except for the decoys, all the objects were made by persons no longer living. Decoy making is one of the few nineteenth century folk traditions which persisted long after World War II, even into the present day. Part of the reason for this is that duck hunting remained a necessity in the rural areas of the province, only becoming a "sport" within the last 30 years. Gradually, as the need for working decoys in wood were replaced by rubber and plastic birds, many decoy carvers turned to miniatures and non-working models where function was totally sacrificed to aesthetics and decoration.

The objects in the exhibition show that union of the functional and aesthetic that is characteristic of traditional folk art. No matter how ornate some of these objects are, they have a certain practical and recognizable function. Contemporary folk art seldom includes function as part of its inspiration. Its main drive and appeal is decorative, aimed at delighting the eye and the senses. Function, if considered at all, is usually a minor component, often involving the re-use of existing objects such as the painted tables and stands of Nova Scotia folk artist Joe Norris.

If for a moment one accepts this broad delineation between contemporary and traditional folk art, then we might approach an understanding of what is meant by *decorative folk art* as employed in the sub-title of this exhibition, and perhaps arrive at a general definition of folk art itself.

Folk art ornamentation is a form of applied art which takes in many types of material folk culture including sculpture, rooms, furniture and accessories, dress, personal adornment, domestic utensils and tools, and architectual details. Object and ornament, the article and its decoration, are closely related. Many factors influence the decoration an object is to receive. One of the most important is the nature of the material from which the object is fabricated — wood, metal, textiles, glass, clay — their very qualities effecting the technique of decoration to be employed ranging from scratching, carving, piercing, painting, appliqué, embroidery, weaving, knotting, or a combination of any of these techniques. Unusual techniques or combinations may also be employed, more so in contemporary folk art, which does not limit itself so strictly to convention and technique in applied art as traditional eighteenth and nineteenth decorative folk art did.[2]

The second factor influencing decoration is the shape and form of the article whose importance to ornamentation must be stressed, because it is the very shape of the object which provides the field for the decorative motif to develop. If we accept that decoration depends on medium and shape of object to be ornamented, it is also true that this embellishment eventually changes the object. It effects its appearance and gives decorative character and visual impact. Over time certain practical articles useful for everyday domestic or community functions may be altered by this decorative character to the point that the ornamentation decides the eventual use of the object, particularly if it has lost its original utilitarian purpose.[3] The example of how decoy carvers turned from making working birds to mantle piece models and miniatures with the introduction of mass produced rubber decoys reminds us of this process. Once an object becomes purely decorative, it may attain a higher value interest to collectors and institutions because of this aesthetic evaluation and appeal, a factor on which most assessments and definitions of folk art have been based since the late 1920's.

"The term 'American folk art' achieved currency in the late 1920's and referred to American paintings and sculpture produced by untrained or non-academic artists. Soon, decorative and mass-produced folk-like objects were included in the meaning of the term. As the expression assumed a more general character, it became difficult to arrive at a clearcut definition of folk art."[4] This beginning introduction to *Folk Art in America,* an anthology of articles from *The Magazine Antiques* published in 1979, neatly expresses the problems and frustrations faced since that time in defining folk art. Ever since the landmark public showing of American folk art at the Whitney Studio Club (now the Whitney Museum of American Art) in 1924, folk art has been considered art first, although created by untrained hands. The persistence of this "aesthetic" definition has lasted to this day on both sides of the border and in Europe.

Even Dr Russell Harper in organizing the first public showing of Canadian folk art, which opened at the National Gallery of Canada on November 30, 1973, echoed this sentiment by titling the show "People's Art: Naïve Art in Canada", an approach he later expanded in the follow up publication steming from this exhibition called *A People's Art: Primitive, Naïve, Provincial, and Folk Painting in Canada.*[5] But it took another major showing of folk art at the Brandywine River Museum in Chadds Ford, Pennsylvania, to bring new light and consideration to the definition and understanding of folk art. *Beyond Necessity: Art in the Folk Tradition* which opened on September 17, 1977, not only created controversy and debate, but was the first real attempt by Dr. Kenneth Ames, the curator of the exhibition and author of the accompanying catalogue, to challenge the long-standing concept of folk art and attempt a reassessment of its meaning.

Ames examined the objects *within their cultural context,* without separating art from artifact or removing it from its historical/cultural configuration.[6] He considered folk art as one of the most important components of the developing discipline of material history, where the past and present is studied not through the extraordinary or unique event, personality or object, but through the ordinary and typical.[7]

Ames identified and examined five myths concerning folk art: (1) the myth of individuality, (2) the myth of the poor but happy artisan, (3) the myth of handicraft, (4) the myth of a conflict-free past, and (5) the myth of national uniqueness.[8] These myths have all helped to maintain a familiar and persistent view of folk art that has permeated most definitions and explanations, and is deeply rooted in our romantic beliefs about the past, and happy and carefree craftpersons. Unfortunately this view seriously distorts the integrity of both the object and the people and communities originally associated with them.

In the *Spirit of Nova Scotia* exhibition an attempt has been made to examine and interpret these objects without losing sight of the people who made and owned them and the communities in which they were found. It is impossible to gain any artistic or historical information from an object or group of objects if one disregards the people behind them. This understanding is based on the obvious fact that objects made or altered by men, women, or children are concrete evidence of human intelligence operating at the time of fabrication, and that such objects, consciously or unconsciously, directly or indirectly, reflect the beliefs of the individuals who made, used and owned them, and by extension the larger society to which they belonged. Material folk history is the study through objects of the beliefs, values, attitudes and assumptions of a particular community at a given time.[9]

In this exhibition, an attempt has been made through the catalogue contributions and the detailed entries to present these examples of decorative art as cultural objects, and not just as works of folk *art.*[10] The quilts and hooked rugs once were used as bed and floor coverings. They took long hours of diligent and patient work to create, and kept people warm as well as adding decorative elements to the home. These objects also reflect the complex and interrelated ethnic traditions and life experiences of their makers and owners. This process is often difficult to trace because of acculturation and the slow erosion of ethnic identity.

Keeping in mind the previously discussed factors of material, and shape and form of objects in determining what is meant by decorative folk art, we can finally discuss the last consideration in this context, namely the influence and importance of the ethnic and cultural tradition of the maker. Earlier definitions of folk art seem to imply that these objects sprang from the minds and hands of their creators with no previous thought or antecedents, products of spontaneous imagination so to speak. This, of course, is simply another false conception reflecting the myths concerning folk art outlined by Ames.

Traditional decorative folk art is produced within the historical and material context of the maker, the owner and the community where both lived. Material folk culture is the expression, through objects, of ethnic traditions, life experiences, occupation, materials, skills, consumer taste and developing fashion, and the presence of similar groups of objects within the maker's domestic and communal environment. All the items in this exhibition may not embody all of these factors, but they nonetheless reflect these influences to one degree or another. It is on this basis that differences between traditional and contemporary folk art become understandable. The comtemporary folk artists have at their disposal not only a more varied set of materials, but an extraordinarily broad range of sources and influences to choose from, provided by magazines, radio, television, video, film, newspapers, to name only a few.

Traditional decorative folk art was produced within a more rigidly controlled and identifiable context where objects were made and decorated within the confines of well-defined methods and techniques of construction, and patterns of ornamentation, based on an existing set of recognized decorative motifs, which in the more elaborately embellished objects in this exhibition include the star, compass star, diamond, heart, circle and whorl.

Although traditional Nova Scotia folk art shows a remarkable variation, and on the surface a bewildering array of regional variants, there are recognizable patterns which aid classification. Although this is not the place to fully study or present these findings, a brief summary seems appropriate.

Nova Scotia can be divided into seven regions: (1) South Shore, (2) French Shore, (3) Annapolis Valley, (4) Halifax/Dartmouth, (5) Central Nova Scotia, (6) Eastern Shore, and (7) Cape Breton. (See map, page 209). Within each of these regions there are recognizable ethnic traditions, some more evident than others, depending on various historical processes of assimilation and acculturation faced by each group who migrated to the province. The ethnic traditions which can be defined are (1) Micmac, (2) French, (3) German, (4) Irish, (5) Scottish, (6) Black, (7) English, and (8) Loyalist American.[11] Although many of these ethnic groups settled in the regions described above, intermingling and overlapping with existing groups, or joined later by new arrivals, it is possible to describe each region in terms of its dominent ethnic persuasion.[12]

For example, the South Shore region is best defined on the basis of the German population in Lunenburg County, and the Loyalist American migration to Shelburne and Queens counties. The French Shore is mostly Acadian, resettled by those French who returned to the area after the Expulsion in 1755. The Annapolis Valley region is best described as English and Loyalist American, the Eastern Shore as English, Scottish and Irish, Cape Breton as mostly Irish and Scottish, Central Nova Scotia as Scottish and English, and Halifax/Dartmouth as English, Black, German, Irish and Scottish, reflecting the urban nature of this area.

Granted these relationships between geographic region and ethnic tradition are loosely defined, they are useful, when attempting to study and interpret regional variants of decorative folk ornamentation. This is based on the premise that if the provenance of an object is accurate, the decorative treatment of the piece must reflect the ethnic heritage of both the community or county where it was found, and the ethnic background of its maker. For example, if one finds a document box in Lunenburg County decorated with compass-stars, hearts, diamonds and flower-in-pot motifs, one can assume with some certainty that this piece reflects the Germanic decorative tradition of the county. In the same manner, if this piece were found in Cape Breton with hearts, diamonds, stars and the thistle or shamrock motif, one would presume its maker to have been either of Scottish or Irish background, and the community where the maker lived and worked probably settled by one of these ethnic groups.

This approach to the study of regional variations in Nova Scotia decorative folk art is still in its formative stages. To continue this work it will be necessary to record and classify motifs by establishing an index of Nova Scotia folk art ornamentation and design, based on photographic documentation of objects within each provincial region, and strict adherence to recording objects with known or positively identifiable provenance.

Many items are difficult to place once they are removed from their original setting. Identification of the county of origin is essential to aid in classification. The town and family name are even more essential if they can be determined. Unfortunately, many people who acquire these objects want to protect their sources. Through the cooperation of collectors and dealers, it has been possible to establish firm provenances for all but a few items in the *Spirit of Nova Scotia.* Objects with doubtful origins, no matter how significant, were rejected.

Four categories or types of objects are included in the exhibition to show the spirit and history of Nova Scotia over a 150-year period — textiles, paintings, sculpture and decorated utilitarian objects. Many of the finest examples of Nova Scotia decorative folk art are small objects in this last category.

Because any exhibition of this nature is limited in terms of size directly effecting the number of items that can be shown within the context of gallery space available, cost requirements for travel, crating and display, it was decided not to include certain types of objects within specific catagories. These include objects made in metal such as trivets or eel spears, objects made in clay such as ceramic vessels, and items made from glass. Another catagory excluded are baskets, and although certain native items are included such as birch bark storage containers, and some splint boxes, examples of Indian quill and bead work have been excluded, the former because of the show of Micmac Quillwork mounted by the Nova Scotia Museum in 1982. It was felt that such catagories as baskets, or glass and ceramics, were areas that warranted exhibitions all their own because of the vast number of examples available, while the types of decorative folk art selected for the *Spirit of Nova Scotia* exhibition were not as plentiful, more individual, and less oriented toward mass production or industrialization.

The study of traditional Nova Scotia folk art is still in its beginning stages. Much needs to be done to understand and preserve the material folk culture of this province. But storing the objects in museums and art galleries is not enough. We must pursue its meaning, describe and interpret its importance to Nova Scotians and Canadians. Through the past, we can appreciate the present and face the future. An exhibition such as the *Spirit of Nova Scotia* serves art scholarship by surveying our current knowledge, and shows the advances that have been made in understanding ourselves and our artistic creations.

Unfortunately, the material aspect of our common heritage is being lost every day, through neglect, misunderstanding, apathy or intentional destruction. Folk art is the tangible expression of the lives, experiences and work of ordinary people, and part of our heritage as Nova Scotians and Canadians. It is beginning to take its place as an aid in understanding our history alongside the traditional sources such as documents and correspondence. We must begin to leave behind the great man/great event/great object interpretation of history and look at the work of the common people. Folk art is the tangible extension of their lives, experiences and occupations.

This exhibition is dedicated to the people of Nova Scotia, whose spirit is embodied in the objects on display and included in this catalogue. What better way to discover this spirit than through the decorative folk art objects made by the settlers of this province? All one has to do is recognize what lies within each, call it by its name and so set it free.

1. Scott T. Swank (Ed), *Arts of the Pennsylvania Germans,* (New York: W.W. Norton and Company, 1983, p. IX.
2. Reinhard Peesch, *The Ornament in European Folk Art,* New York: Alpine Fine Arts Collection, Ltd., 1983), p. 7.
3. Reinhard Peesch, *Ibid,* p. 7.
4. Jack T. Ericson (Ed), *Folk Art in America: Painting and Sculpture,* New York: Main Street Press, 1979), p. 7.
5. Published by the University of Toronto Press, 1974.
6. Kenneth L. Ames, *Beyond Necessity: Art in the Folk Tradition,* Winterthur, Delaware: W.W. Norton and Company, 1977), p. 7-8.
7. Kenneth L. Ames, *Ibid,* p. 12.
8. Kenneth L. Ames, *Ibid,* p. 21.
9. Jules David Prown, "Mind in Matter: An Introduction to Material Culture Theory and Method" in *Winterthur Portfolio,* Spring, 1982, pp. 1-2.
10. Each contributor to the catalogue was made aware that the objects on display were being examined not only as folk art, but within their historical and cultural context. No single definition of folk art was applied to all categories and sub-categories of works within the exhibition. Each contributor was asked to write about the objects within the general framework outlined above, and to define folk art according to the needs of the subject areas they examined. This has led to a high degree of consensus about the definition and traditions of decorative folk art in the period between 1780 and 1930 in Nova Scotia.
11. This group also includes the New England "Planters" who arrived between the years 1759-1763, the Loyalists arriving between 1775-1785.
12. It must be noted at this point that although the exhibition includes objects from all regions of Nova Scotia, some counties are better represented than others. This is explained by two factors: (1) the history of settlement and population within the various regions of Nova Scotia. Areas such as Halifax/Dartmouth, the Annapolis Valley, South Shore and Central Nova Scotia had greater concentrations of settlement than regions such as Cape Breton or the Eastern Shore. This pattern directly effects the amount of material to be found in these areas. The smaller the population in a given region, county or community, the fewer the number of objects made, and even fewer the number of objects that would have survived to the twentieth century. (2) Certain areas such as Lunenburg County and the Annapolis Valley, have been more heavily visited by dealers and collectors with the result that more material has come to light which has found its way into private and public collections. In addition, certain ethnic groups had a deeper and richer decorative tradition on which to draw inspiration within the context of their ethnic identity.

The Historical Perspective 1780-1930

Dr. Michael S. Cross

Dr. Michael S. Cross is the Dean of Henson College and Professor of History at Dalhousie University in Halifax, where he resides.

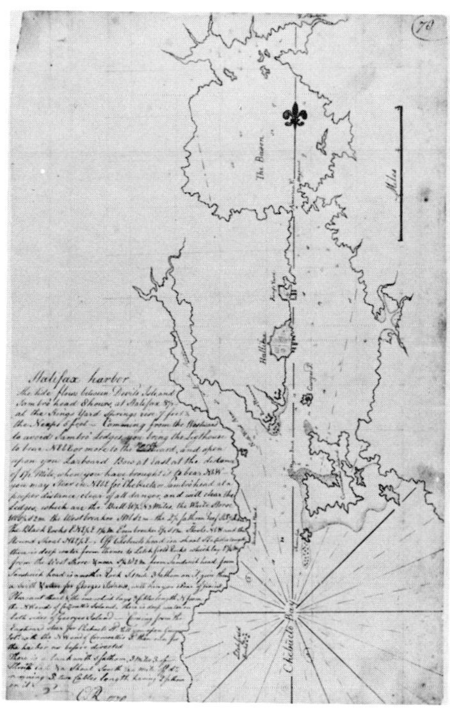

Map of Halifax
Found in New York City, New York
Watercolour and ink on paper
Drawn by Captain Charles Randle (Active 1775-1813), initialed CR in the lower left corner
Dated 1778 in the lower left corner
Dimensions: 20.0 × 31.0 cm (7⅞ × 12³⁄₁₆ inches)
Collection of Gerald Ferguson, Halifax, Nova Scotia
Refer to entry 107, page 103

Simeon Perkins was awakened in the dark of early morning by shouts from the street. It was the 13th of September, 1780, and the town was under attack. Two American schooners had put into Liverpool, Nova Scotia, and captured the fort which defended the town. Perkins, a prominent merchant and lieutenant colonel of the county militia, stumbled out into a depressing prospect. The messengers he sent to rouse the militiamen reported back that "the people were in General Disheartened & did not Incline to make any resistance, as they looked upon our Situation [as] Desperate & the Best things we could do was to be quiet".[1]

Fortunately, the townspeople mustered their courage, aided by the incompetence of the invaders. The Yankee captain, Benjamin Cole, ventured into town with a small party. They were quickly captured and, in exchange for their freedom, agreed to leave Liverpool. There was one further excitement. As the American vessels put out to sea they encountered a privateer from Halifax. The ships exchanged poorly aimed fire before the Americans made their escape.

Something more familiar to the nineteenth-century eye could be found in the Pictou area. Among the Scots farmers was a pocket of modernity, the operations of the General Mining Association at Albion Mines in Pictou County. Some of the colony's earliest steam machinery was introduced there after 1827, to lift coal from the pit, to operate a steamboat from Pictou to New Glasgow and, greatest of wonders, to drive the province's first railway locomotive which began to run from the mine to the harbour in September 1839. The other great attraction of Pictou County was its resident intellectual, Dr. Thomas McCulloch. His Pictou Academy trained generations of leaders in northern Nova Scotia and McCulloch himself went on to become the first president of Dalhousie College in Halifax in 1838. McCulloch's Academy was a highlight for any conscientious tourist such as the journalist Joseph Howe who visited Pictou in 1829. Howe was especially impressed with the ornithological museum on the second floor of the Academy which he thought "the richest treat that can be had within the Province."[10]

The area had a less enviable distinction in the virulent ethnic and religious rivalries which all too often flared into violence. The election of 1830 was a contentious one across the province. The previous session of the legislature had seen a bitter dispute over customs duties between the popularly elected Assembly and the appointed, élite-controlled Council. In Pictou, then part of Halifax County for electoral purposes, the political differences became religious ones. The Tories drew on Highland members of the Church of Scotland while the liberals were supported by lowland adherents of the "Antiburgher" movement, which had split from the Church of Scotland. The result was several days of rioting in Pictou in September, 1830, and the death of one man.[11]

Religion and ethnicity coloured most relationships. The Canso riots of 1833 illustrated how they complicated economic and territorial issues. The troubles began with clashes between local fishermen and those from Prince Edward Island over management of the fishing stations at Fox Island and Canso. When several Irish Catholics were arrested for beating an Islander, the local priest, James Grant, charged the magistrates with prejudice against Catholics. He pointed out that the magistrates had done nothing to find those who had maimed the horse belonging to another priest, John Chisholm. Before the affair was over, Catholics had burned the barn and crops of one magistrate and maimed a horse and two cows belonging to the court clerk, Mr. Cook.[12] Surveying his horse, its ears cut off, and his crippled cattle, Mr. Cook would have been conscious that the quarrels of sect and nation, and the methods of revenge they fostered, had not been left behind in migration to the new world.

As at Pictou, the traditional and the modern mixed throughout the province. The two "Great Roads" linked Pictou and Annapolis to Halifax and, after 1816, the modern traveller could enjoy the service of stage lines along them. By the 1820's those able to afford a fare of £2/10s. could board the Western Stage Company's carriage in Halifax at 8 a.m. and arrive at Annapolis Royal at 4 p.m. the next day.[13] The stages and the improved roads for horseback travel allowed one to sample the wonders of the province. One was the most modern of experimental farms, operated by Charles Ramage Prescott at Cornwallis. There improved apple stocks were developed for farmers in the Annapolis Valley. Equally impressive were the iron works established at Moose River, near Annapolis, in the late 1820's.[14] Not all examples of contemporary civilization prospered, of course. King's College at Windsor had limited success in enlightening the frontier. A perhaps biassed Methodist missionary had described the Anglican university in 1800 as being "conducted in a manner not much to the credit either of learning or piety . . ."[15] Things were not much improved four decades later when the staff had grown from one professor to three, and the student body still only numbered from 15 to 20.[16]

Some paid the price of progress. The Micmacs found few means of livelihood which did not run afoul of the advancing dominant culture. They were pushed off good agricultural land into remote, non-arable reservations. Hunting declined as white settlement increased. Their plight was expressed by their elected chief, Paussamigh Pemmeenauweet, who petitioned Queen Victoria in 1840:

> *My people are in trouble. I have seen upwards of a Thousand Moons. When I was young I had plenty: now I am old, poor and sickly too. My people all poor. No Hunting Grounds — No Beaver — No Otter — no nothing . . . All these Woods once ours. Now we cannot cut a Tree to warm our Wigwams in Winter unless the White Man please . . . We look to you the Queen . . . Pity your poor Indians in Nova Scotia.*[17]

There was to be no pity. The Micmac population was declining because of disease and crop failures such as the potato blight of 1846 to 1848. In 1847 there were only 1166 Micmacs in Nova Scotia. Some few of them were pictured in a sketch in a travel account published in 1837. The busy docks and streets of growing Halifax were depicted as viewed from a Micmac encampment on the Dartmouth shore, an encampment of rough skin wigwams and harsh poverty.[18]

The imported animosities of the Scots suggested that, in areas where particular ethnic groups settled in relative isolation, integration into a new society was slow and uneven Their experience, and that of the Micmacs, made clear this was not a society of the melting pot; it was a colonial society shot through with traces of ethnic and religious traditions. How much survived was dependent on several factors. What was functional and what was not economically disadvantageous could last. In Lunenburg the Germans prospered and maintained a rich culture of crafts, domestic architecture and household arts. Their language proved less useful and harder to retain. By the 1780's many of the younger people were disdaining German in favour of the surrounding society's English. Location was also an important factor. The Lunenburg Germans sustained their culture by living it. In English Halifax, Germans tried to remain themselves by erecting institutions. The community was centred on St. George's Church. When it was consecrated in 1761 its congregation was almost entirely German. But, despite reinforcements of German-American Loyalists and disbanded Hessian troops, the culture struggled. A "High German" society was formed to give new cultural life and in 1787 Halifax printer Anthony Henry began to publish a German almanac. By the late 1790's, however, the almanac ceased publication and the German Society was defunct. The minister at St. George's reported of his parishioners that "very few of them retain their own [language], at least they all speak English much better than they do German."[19]

The elements were in place that would produce a Nova Scotian society. At its head was an elite centred in Halifax. Until the 1840's the Tory elements of the elite controlled the government of the province. Socially and economically the elite survived the loss of political power. Indeed, politics had divided, not defined, the elite. William Young was a liberal lawyer but clearly a social and economic leader. Elite lifestyle was reflected in his journal of a family visit to England and France in 1839. Among his purchases were a suit of clothes and a frock coat bought in Bond Street, "the prices extravagant, but it is necessary that I shd. be fashionably drest . . ." A gold watch bought in London cost Young £14. For comparison, a skilled worker at the ropeworks at home in Halifax would have laboured 15 weeks to earn a sum equivalent to the price of Mr. Young's watch, another six or seven weeks for the chain Young bought to append his watch. The Youngs visited factories in Birmingham to buy household furnishings — tables worth 50 guineas, a 15 shilling card case, screens at £2, dish covers and tureens costing £35. In London they added a china dinner set, a silver coffee pot, asparagus tongs, clothes and books. The final item purchased for shipment home was a "monumental tablet for Father," — John Young, the famed "Agricola" — who had died in 1837.[20]

The impression of stability and respectability given by the élite could be misleading. Until bourgeois values gained a firm grip by the 1850's, the upper class itself was prone to brawling and duelling. Even Government House was not a pillar of respectability. Tongues wagged over the late-night female visitors during the governorship of the bachelor Sir James Kempt between 1820 and 1828, and over the street brawling of Lieutenant Governor Harvey's son Frank, who was arrested by city police in June 1848 and who was seriously hurt in a fight in the spring of 1849.[21] Collective violence was common enough. It reached into the legislature in 1829 when a mob freed a popular member of the Assembly, John Alexander Barry, who had been arrested by the sergeant-at-arms for libelling another member.[22]

The most frequent site for violence was the brothel district in the streets east of Citadel Hill. Major riots took place there in 1838, 1847, 1848 and 1850. The brawlers were usually soldiers and sailors, angry because one of their number had been robbed, injured or killed in a brothel. In August of 1848, for example, seaman Henry Lynch of H.M.S. *Wellesley* was beaten to death in a Barrack Street brothel, apparently in revenge for the death of a prostitute a few days earlier. The brothel was the target of an unsuccessful arsonist the next day. Two nights later arsonists succeeded. As the brothel burned, thousands of sailors and soldiers cheered in the street. During the excitement a citizen was injured by a stone thrown from the crowd and a soldier was crushed to death between two fire engines.[23]

The street brawling of the imperial forces was painful evidence of the continuing links of Nova Scotia with Britain. Yet within those continuing links Nova Scotians were developing an assertive self-awareness. Shifting the focus from the 1820's to the 1860's, the picture becomes one of a society with a strong sense of itself. Led by Joseph Howe, liberal Nova Scotians had won a large measure of self-government by 1848. With it came a triumph of liberal bourgeois values as the province entered its "golden age". The railway was the symbol of material progress in that "golden age", the railway that Howe called

"God's work . . ."[24] The glitter became real in 1861 with the discovery of gold at Tangier and the resultant rush along the Atlantic coast added to Nova Scotia's prosperity.

It was the flowering of the old trade of shipping which has given the "golden age" most of its aura. World demand called forth a shipbuilding boom in Nova Scotia, until the market for wooden ships collapsed in the 1890's. It was in the 1870's that the largest ships were built, such as Bennett Smith's 1966 ton *Jessore,* launched at Windsor in 1870. The biggest wooden ship built in the Maritimes was William D. Lawrence's namesake vessel, the 2459-ton giant which sailed from Maitland in 1874. The *Lawrence* cost $107,452 but in 8½ years of service it paid off the investment and made a profit of $104,848.[25]

Shipbuilding was of great value to the local economy. Shipping itself was perhaps less so. In 1890, 1065 ships with 24,000 sailors came into Halifax alone.[26] Most of those sailors were foreigners. At Yarmouth, Nova Scotians made up 12 percent of ships' crews in the 1860's, only 5 percent in the 1890's.[27] The figures are reminders that, even in the "golden age", the economy did not supply enough jobs for Nova Scotians. The province received few immigrants after the 1840's and even natural increase could not be absorbed. An outmigration to New England and Canada began and Nova Scotia's population growth fell further and further behind the Canadian average. The gap was modest in the 1870's when the provincial population increased by 13.6 percent against a Canadian average of 17.2 percent. During the national boom years of 1901 to 1911, though, Canada's population soared 34.2 percent, Nova Scotia's only 7.4. In the 1920's, Canada grew by 18.1 percent, Nova Scotia's population fell by 2.1 percent. *(See table on page 8)*

The "golden age" ended with the disappearance of markets for wooden ships in the 1890's. If the period had not assured the economic future of Nova Scotia, it had been one of development of a provincial culture and sense of identity. Politics had contributed to that sense. Most Nova Scotians opposed Confederations in the 1860's. Confederation was imposed nevertheless, but Nova Scotian opposition did not disappear. As late as 1886 the Liberals could successfully campaign on a platform of secession from Canada.

Nova Scotians bitter about their unwelcome partnership in Canada could point to the successes of their own provincial culture. There was a literary tradition extending back to the 1820's and 1830's when Oliver Goldsmith, Thomas McCulloch and Thomas Chandler Haliburton gave their reflections on Nova Scotia's Anglo-American society. That tradition flowed through writers such as Mary Jane Katzmann, editor of the short-lived but sophisticated literary magazine, the *Provincial,* or *Halifax Monthly Magazine* in 1852 and 1853. Katzmann would also publish a history of Dartmouth and environs and a posthumous collection of poetry, *Frankincense and Myrrh,* which appeared in 1893. More popular were the historical novels of Sydney newspaperman Charles M'Kinnon. His potboilers, in the style of Sir Walter Scott, were serialized in his own papers and the Boston *Waverley Magazine* in the early 1850's. In 1853, however, M'Kinnon deserted literature for religion, becoming a Methodist preacher. He was embarrassed by his frivolous fiction and, until his death in 1862, he searched out and destroyed as many copies of his novels as he could find.[28]

Two Nova Scotian authors were major international successes. James DeMille's two lives fit together in curious juxtaposition. He was a scholar and teacher at Acadia College from 1860 to 1865 and at Dalhousie College thereafter and author of an influential text, *The Elements of Rhetoric,* published in New York in 1878. But his fame was as a writer of juvenile adventure novels, especially *The Dodge Club* which first appeared in serialization in *Harper's* magazine in 1868. In all, DeMille produced 29 novels, many of them considerable successes.[29] Even DeMille, however, could not compare in popularity with Margaret Marshall Saunders. Born in Milton, Nova Scotia, in 1861 she burst on the literary scene with *Beautiful Joe,* published in Philadelphia in 1894. This impassioned novel, written on behalf of animal welfare, became the first Canadian book to sell one million copies. While none of her subsequent efforts equalled the impact of *Beautiful Joe,* she continued to publish novels in the interest of social reform; the last, *Esther de Warren,* appeared in 1927.[30]

High culture flourished in the many colleges in Nova Scotia. The plethora of colleges frequently produced political controversy and scattered educational resources. But they also produced a rich intellectual tradition. Philosophers and theologians such as John Mockett Cramp, president of Acadia from 1851 to 1853 and 1860 to 1869, and his contemporary at the Truro Theological Seminary and Dalhousie, William Lyall, were scholars of international reputation. The sciences were especially strong at Dalhousie, led by men such as physicists J. Gordon MacGregor and J.J. Mackenzie, botanist and chemist George Lawson and chemist H.H. Bayne. Dr. David Honeyman was the founder and curator of the Provincial Mu-

The National School at Halifax
Halifax, Nova Scotia
Watercolour on paper
Joseph Partridge
Circa 1817-1819
Dimensions: 39.4 × 27.3 cm (10¾ × 15½ inches)
Photograph courtesy of the Public Archives of Nova Scotia
This piece is not included in the exhibition

seum which was established in the attic of the Provincial Building — the Dominion building after 1871 — in 1868.[31]

Amherst, the industrial centre of the northern mainland, did have a show of militancy in 1919 when workers staged a general strike in sympathy with those on strike in Winnipeg. And Halifax was torn by citizen rioting in 1913 in support of striking street railway workers. Most outbursts, though, were more traditional. Imperial forces were withdrawn from Halifax in 1906, removing one source of disorder. Their Canadian successors carried on where the imperials had left off. Military violence was common enough during World War I, culminating in a major riot in May, 1918, when servicemen, angered by the arrest of one of their number, fought police in the streets and sacked Halifax city hall.[41] The weary city, still recovering from the explosion of the previous year, swept up the debris and once again contemplated the profits, and the costs, of the empire's wars.

There were few profits to count for the next 20 years. The final picture, of the 1920's, is one of economic distress. The Great Depression which began in 1929 in urban North America was by then a decade old in Nova Scotia. Most manufacturing industries had been stripped away from the province before World War I by a concentration movement which consolidated industry in the financial heartland of the continent. Slumping markets for natural products compounded the problem. The value of fish landed in the Maritimes declined steadily from the mid-1920's until, by 1933, it was little more than half that of 1926.[42] Primary industries buckled under market pressure, leading to the troubles in the coal fields and steel mills of Cape Breton and the ultimate devastation of the island's economy.

There were consolations. If the legitimate economy suffered, the illicit flourished. The iron men now carried rum in their wooden ships, to slake the thirst of prohibition-ridden America. The still-expanding economies of New England and upper Canada drew off population from the declining economy of Nova Scotia. That was especially true of the rural areas where the population declined by over five percent during the 1920's. It was a hard solution, the draining away of the young to foreign jobs, but it eased the strain on the rural economy. So did traditional activities, the crafts and handwork which had always been significant, and the rural economy's lack of specialization. Farmers and fisherfolk worked woodlots when their primary trades were slack, forest workers fished and gardened, all bartered in an important "informal" economy.[43] From scrimshaw and Micmac baskets to wooden butterflies, rural Nova Scotians also found ways to turn sparetime handicrafts into cash.

Rural Nova Scotia was forced in upon itself. The failure to establish a place in the industrial world had heavy material costs but it permitted the maintenance of traditional cultural forms. Out of American and British roots had grown crafts, entertainments, dialects, which were identifiably Nova Scotian. The continuing flow of people to other parts of North America, however, meant the rural culture was never frozen; it was always in intimate contact with influence from the modernizing continent.

Isolation was not possible, at any rate, in the age of the automobile. The first automobile had been imported to Halifax in 1899. Attempts to create a native industry failed with the closure of Amherst's Nova Scotia Carriage and Motor Car Company in 1915, but the automobile itself captured the popular imagination. Although there were only 6½ miles of paved roads in 1930, Nova Scotians struggled through the mud and dust in over 36,000 cars and trucks that year.[44] Increasing use of cars meant increasing numbers of visitors. Those who prized seclusion were already clucking over the intrusion. Peggy's Cove, for example, was no longer only an obscure haunt for artists. Dorothy Duncan, who came to Nova Scotia in 1936, complained, "In no time at all Peggy's Cove is going to be spoiled, for already the tourists have found it . . . the road to Peggy's Cove will doubtless soon be a paved highway, save the day."[45]

For a devotee of the traditional such as Duncan, Halifax had its shabby charm. The city was still a melange, "an unbelievable mixture of slums, homes of the proper, brothels, and manses."[46] A great divide had been crossed in the last 50 years in urban North America as cities took on the characteristics of industrialism — the division of workplace and living place, the division of the working class and the middle class — with the accompanying change in the outlook on society. Halifax, as with most of Nova Scotia, had remained pre-industrial and traditional, with social patterns as close to the colonial past as to the North American future.

The Great Depression of the 1930's and the world war which followed it would force North America over another divide, into a world of the welfare state, the consumer society and a truly North American culture. Nova Scotia would move, slowly perhaps but surely, across that divide. If the picture is frozen in 1930, however, it is still recognizable as the Anglo-American Nova Scotia formed out of imperial trade and war, overlaid with Yankee blood ties and New England style.

Population and Origins *Nova Scotia*

Year	Population	"African"	English	French	Irish	Scottish
1827	123,630					
1851	276,854					
1871	387,800	6,212	113,520	32,833	62,851	130,741
1901	459,574	5,984	159,753	45,161	54,710	143,382
1931	512,846	7,361	193,170	56,629	56,453	139,992

Birthplaces of Population, 1871 *percentages of total population*

	Canada	Nova Scotia	Ontario
Canada	83.2	92.5	72.9
Born in the province		90.6	69.8
England	4.2	1.0	7.7
Ireland	6.3	1.9	9.4
Scotland	3.5	3.7	5.6
United States	1.8	0.6	2.7

1. D.C. Harvey, ed., *The Diary of Simeon Perkins, 1780-1789* (Toronto, 1958), 41.
2. For accounts of Halifax in the period: Patrick M'Robert, *A Tour Through Part of the Northern Provinces of America* (Edinburgh, 1776); John Robinson and Thomas Rispin, *Journey Through Nova Scotia* (York, Eng., 1774).
3. On Alline and the "Great Awakening": Gordon T. Stewart, ed., *Documents Relating to the Great Awakening in Nova Scotia, 1760-1791* (Toronto, 1982); Stewart and G.A. Rawlyk, *A People Highly Favoured of God: The Nova Scotia Yankees and the American Revolution* (Hamden, Conn., 1972).
4. Robinson and Rispin, *Journey Through Nova-Scotia*, 21.
5. *Ibid.*, 24.
6. W.S. MacNutt, *The Atlantic Provinces: The Emergence of Colonial Society, 1712-1857* (Toronto, 1965), 156; D. Campbell and R.A. MacLean, *Beyond the Atlantic Roar: A Study of the Nova Scotia Scots* (Toronto, 1974), 43.
7. Robinson and Rispin, *Journey Through Nova-Scotia*, 19; Campbell and MacLean, *Beyond the Atlantic Roar*, 50.
8. Joshua Marsden, *The Narrative of a Mission to Nova Scotia, New Brunswick, and the Somers Islands* (Plymouth, 1816), 57.
9. On the arrest of pirates: Public Archives of Nova Scotia [PANS], Executive Council Minutes, 25 November 1826. On Cape Breton in the 1820's: John M'Gregor, *Historical and Descriptive Sketches of the Maritime Colonies of British America* (London, 1828).
10. Joseph Howe, *Western and Eastern Rambles: Travel Sketches of Nova Scotia*, ed. by M.G. Parks (Toronto, 1973), 154-5.
11. *Novascotian* (Halifax), 7 October 1830; *Acadian Recorder* (Halifax), 6 November 1830; Campbell and MacLean, *Beyond the Atlantic Roar*, 51.
12. See: PANS, Executive Council Papers, vol. 240 and *Colonial Patriot* (Pictou).
13. Howe, *Western and Eastern Rambles*, 14-23.
14. *Ibid.*, 81, 90. 105.
15. Marsden, *Narrative*, 19.
16. According to Joseph Howe in 1843: Joseph Andrew Chisholm, ed., *The Speeches and Public Letters of Joseph Howe* (Halifax, 1909), I, 424.
17. L.F.S. Upton, *Micmacs and Colonists: Indian-White Relations in the Maritimes, 1713-1867* (Vancouver, 1979), 188-92.
18. *Ibid.*, plate 14, from Lieutenant R. Petley, *Sketches in Nova Scotia and New Brunswick* (1837).
19. Winthrop Pickard Bell, *The "Foreign Protestants" and the Settlement of Nova Scotia* (Toronto, 1961), 623-6.
20. "Journal of William Young, 1839," Public Archives of Nova Scotia *Report* (1973), 28-9, 46, 53, 59-61; David Sutherland, ed., "The Stanyan Ropeworks of Halifax, Nova Scotia: Glimpses of a pre-Industrial Manufactory," *Labour/Le Travailleur*, 6 (1980), 157.
21. George Patterson, *More Studies in Nova Scotian History* (Halifax, 1941), 72-88; J. Murray Beck, *Joseph Howe* (Kingston and Montreal, 1982-1983), I, 20-1; II, 23.
22. Duncan Campbell, Nova Scotia in its Historical, Mercantile and Industrial Relations (Montreal, 1873), 261-5; *Novascotian*, 2-23 April 1829.
23. *Acadian Recorder*, 26 August, 2 September 1848. On other riots: PANS, Halifax County Quarter Sessions, 22 September 1838; *Acadian Recorder*, 8 May 1847, 6 July 1850.
24. Chisholm, *Speeches and Public Letters*, II, 170-81.
25. Gwendolyn Vaughan Shand, "Windsor, a Centre of Shipbuilding," Nova Scotia Historical Society *Collections*, XXXVII (1970), 53; Charles A. Armour, "Lawrence, William Davidson," *Dictionary of Canadian Biography* (Toronto, 1982), XI, 502.
26. Judith Fingard, *Jack in Port: Sailortowns in Eastern Canada* (Toronto, 1982), 27.
27. David Alexander, "Literacy Among Canadian and Foreign Seamen, 1863-1899," in Rosemary Ommer and Gerald Panting, eds., *Working Men Who Got Wet* (St. John's, 1980), 3-33.
28. Lois Kernaghan, "Katzmann, Mary Jane (Lawson)," *Dictionary of Canadian Biography*, IX, 462-3; G. Davis, "William Charles M'Kinnon: Cape Breton's Sir Walter Scott," Royal Nova Scotia Historical Society *Collections*, XLI (1982), 21-46.
29. Patterson, *More Studies*, 121-43.
30. Karen E. Sanders, *Margaret Marshall Saunders: Children's Literature as an Expression of Early Twentieth Century Century Social Reform* ((unpublished M.A. thesis, Dalhousie University, 1978).
31. Barry Moody, "Cramp, John Mockett," *Dictionary of Canadian Biography*, IX, 209-10; Janet Vey Guildford, *Technical Education in Nova Scotia, 1880-1930* (unpublished M.A. thesis, Dalhousie University, 1983), 16 f.f.; Phyllis Blakeley, *Glimpses of Halifax, 1867-1900*, Public Archives of Nova Scotia publication no. 9 (Halifax, 1949), 65.
32. Blakeley, *Glimpses*, 10, 30.
33. Gwendolyn V. Shand, "The Industries of Windsor, Nova Scotia," Nova Scotia Historical Society *Collections*, XXXIV (1963), 147-50.
34. Blakeley, *Glimpses*, 65-6; Ruth Kedzie Wood, *The Tourist's Maritime Provinces* (New York, 1915), 84.
35. Ruth Holmes Whitehead, "Christina Morris: Micmac Artist and Artist's Model," *Material History Bulletin*, III (1977), 1-14.
36. Father Anselm Chiasson, "Traditions and Oral Literature in Acadia," in Jean Daigle, ed., *The Acadians of the Maritimes: Thematic Studies* (Moncton, 1982), 485-9.
37. Wood, *Tourist's Maritime Provinces*, 54-7.
38. Charles Haight Farnham, "Cape Breton Folk (1886)," in James Doyle, ed., *Yankees in Canada: A Collection of Nineteenth-Century Travel Narratives* (Toronto, 1980), 175-96.
39. The Marchioness of Dufferin, wife of the governor general, described the *Hibernia* in Sydney harbour in *My Canadian Journal, 1872-8* (London, 1891), 95.
40. Dawn Fraser, *Echoes from Labor's War: Industrial Cape Breton in the 1920's*, introduction by David Frank and Donald Macgillivray (Toronto, 1976), 51.
41. Thomas H. Raddall, *Halifax, Warden of the North* (Toronto, 1971), 257-8.
42. Canada, Royal Commission on Price Spreads Report (Ottawa, 1937), cited in Michiel Horn, ed., *The Dirty Thirties: Canadians in the Great Depression* (Toronto, 1972), 102.
43. The informal economy of more recent times has been studied at Dalhousie University's Institute of Public Affairs: D.H. Clairmont and F. Wien, "The Marginal Work World Research Program at Dalhousie University," *The Social Sciences in Canada* (September 1978).
44. George MacLaren, "Early Automobiles in Nova Scotia," *Nova Scotia Historical Quarterly*, IV, 1 (1974), 37-48.
45. Dorothy Duncan, *Bluenose: A Portrait of Nova Scotia* (New York, 1942), 131.
46. *Ibid.*, 118.

Colour Plates

Colour plate I: **Crazy Quilt** (Refer to entry 34, page 50)

Colour plate II: **Hooked Rug** (Refer to entry 5, page 36)

Colour plate III: **Sail-Cloth Mat** (Refer to entry 28, page 47)

Colour plate IV: **Hooked Mat with Diamond Motifs**
(Refer to entry 14, page 40)

Colour plate V: **Yarn Sewn and Hooked Mat with House** (Refer to entry 2, page 35)

Colour plate VI: **Yarn Sewn and Hooked Mat of Horse** (Refer to entry 3, page 35)

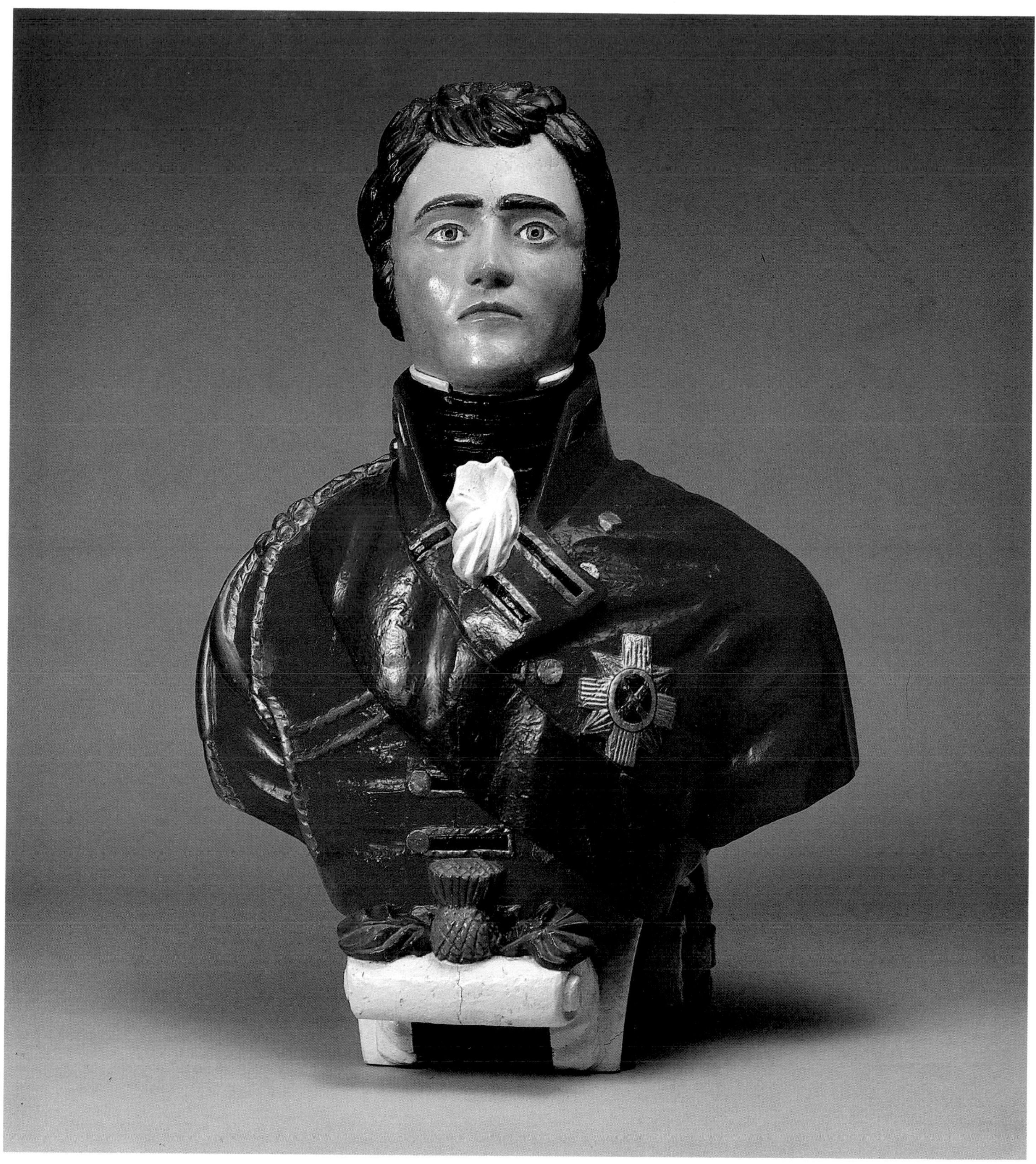

Colour plate VII: **Figurehead of the Earl of Dalhousie** (Refer to entry 86, page 81)

Colour plate VIII: **Billethead** (Refer to entry 103, page 90)

Colour plate IX: **Merganser Drake and Hen** (Refer to entry 66, page 71)

Colour plate X: **Rocking Horse** (Refer to entry 76, page 75)

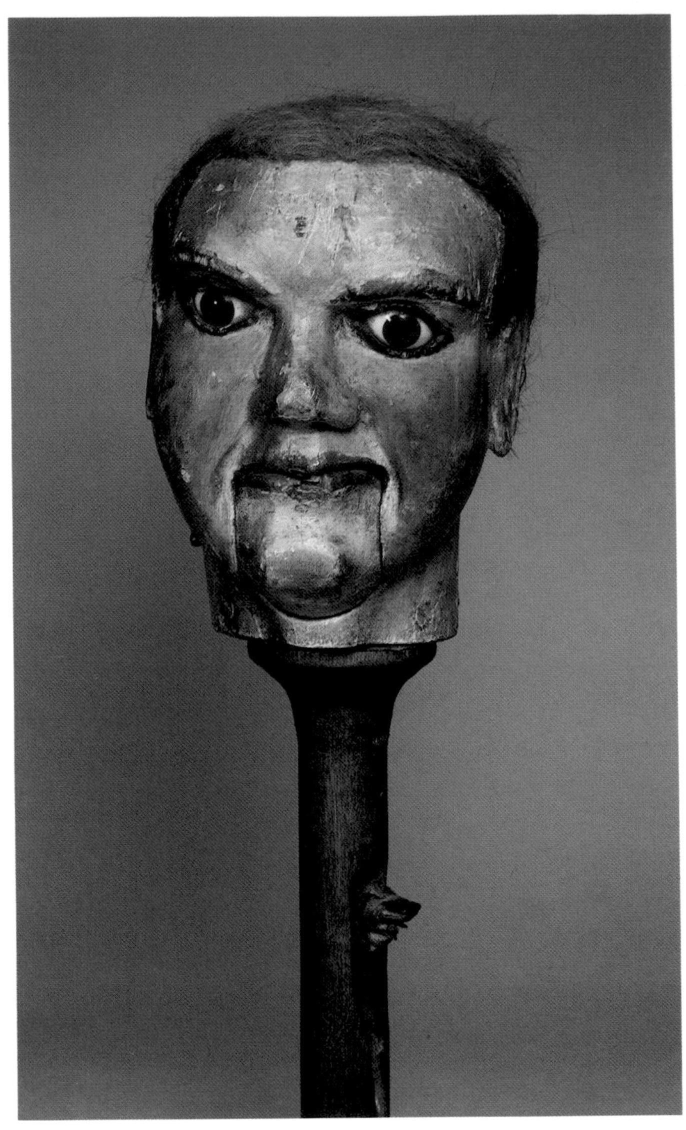

Colour plate XI: **Ventriloquist's Dummy Head** (Refer to entry 84, page 80)

Colour plate XII: **Weathervane** (Refer to entry 71, page 73)

Colour plate XIII: **Portrait of John Payzant** (Refer to entry 111, page 105)

Colour plate XIV: **Ship Portrait of the** "Kurramanny of Calcutta" (Refer to entry 118, page 108)

Colour plate XV: **Five-Masted Ship Portrait** (Refer to entry 125, page 112)

Colour plate XVI: **Girl in Red Dress** (Refer to entry 114, page 106)

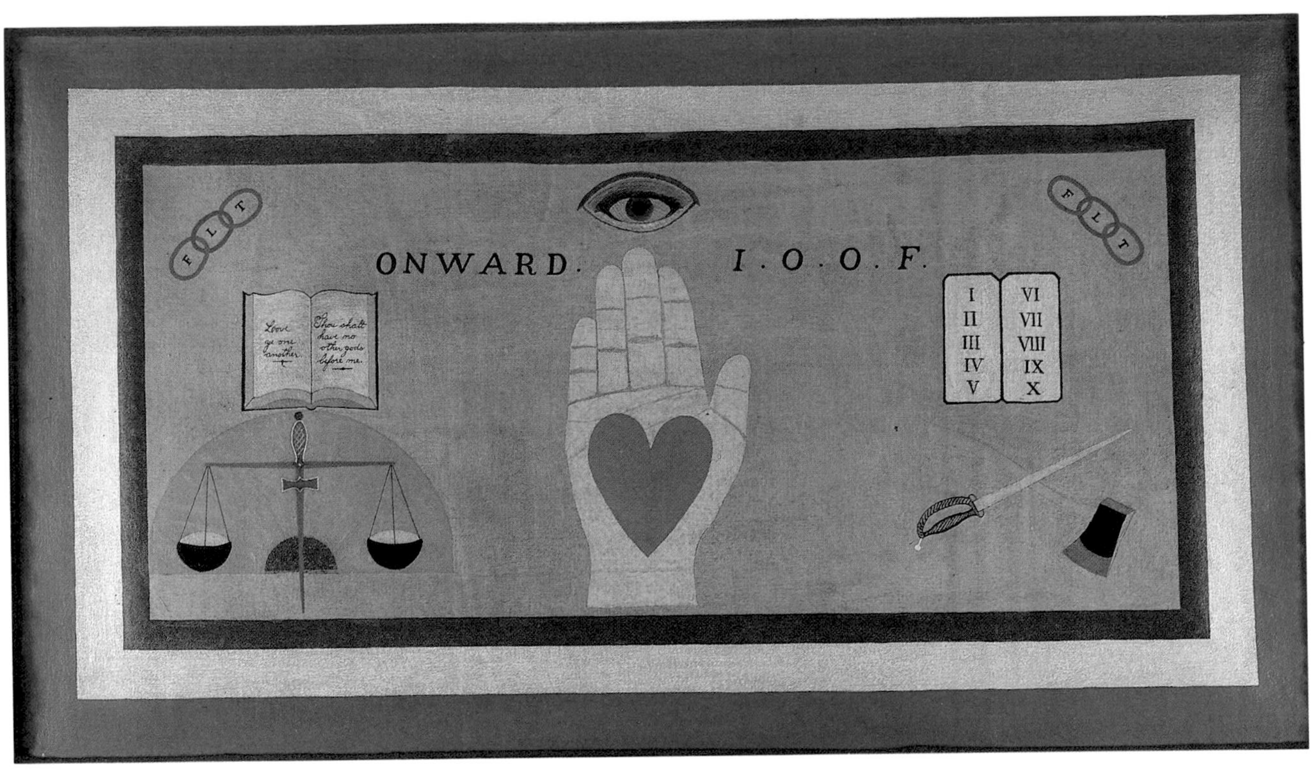

Colour plate XVII: **Lodge Painting,** "Onward I00F" (Refer to entry 147, page 123)

Colour plate XVIII: **Birth and Baptismal Record** (Refer to entry 145, page 122)

Colour plate XIX: **Gameboard** (Refer to entry 259, page 188)

Colour plate XX: **Document Box** (Refer to entry 184, page 147)

Colour plate XXI: **Sailor's Valentine** (Refer to entry 222, page 169)

Colour plate XXII: **Sail-Cloth Wall Hanging** (Refer to entry 183, page 147)

Colour plate XXIII: **Splint Box** (Refer to entry 160, page 136)

Colour plate XXIV: **Spruce Gum Boxes** (Refer to entry 199, page 156)

Catalogue

Notes

Dimensions are in centimetres, followed by conversion to the nearest sixteenth of an inch in parenthesis; the horizontal measure precedes the vertical measure followed by depth.

The history notations apply only to institutional collections and deal with the acquisition history where provided by individual institutions.

Notations made on the medium, condition and conservation of the works, as outlined under the structure category, are those of the Editor/Guest Curator.

INTRODUCTION

Textiles

Richard Henning Field

Textiles played a very important part in the lives of all Nova Scotians between the years 1780 and 1930. They were used for clothing, floor, bed and table coverings, bed and window curtains, and were a visible means of not only indicating the social station of a person through his or her dress, but helped to differentiate the houses of the rich, such as merchants, from the working class farmer or fisherman. They also helped to decorate the domestic interior with pattern and colour.

Estate inventories from the late eighteenth through the nineteenth century indicate how highly prized various textile possessions were, particularly bedding and bed curtains, floor coverings and clothing. For example, in the estate inventory for John Philip Heyson (PANS RG 48, Reel 842) taken on January 9, 1813 in Lunenburg, entries 7 and 8 list a bed and bedstead[1] valued at £6 and £4 respectively. This is more than the value assigned by the appraisers to the farm animals including 3 cows at £3 each and 9 sheep at £5/12. Only the pair of oxen were valued more at £16 making these important farm animals the most valued property followed by the beds.

The estate inventories of merchants are also indicators of just how important textiles were to the inhabitants of a particular town or community. One such inventory is that of Casper Wollenhaupt of the Town of Lunenburg. Taken between the 18th and 20th of July 1809, the inventory was not completed until January 10, 1810 (PANS RG 48, Reel 842). In his will Wollenhaupt refers to himself as a merchant. At the time of his death his estate was valued £1008/12/7¼ which did not include his vast real estate holdings.

His shop inventory which was valued at £499/11/2¼ included a selection of textiles, printed cottons and silks suggesting that almost every type of clothing for men, women, children and infants, household linen for tables, toweling, ticking and other bedding, as well as textiles suitable for bed and window curtains, upholstery, slipcovers, table and chest covers, and floor coverings were available for purchase.[2]

Other entries in the Wollenhaupt inventory illustrate that textiles were available for all uses within the domestic interior. For example, there are listings for red, blue and yellow furniture cotton (entries 94-100), rugs (entry 142), blankets (entry 142) and muslin drapes (entry 207).

However, it is important to differentiate between these textiles and those that are on view in the *Spirit of Nova Scotia* exhibition. These were not purchased but were made at home of either recycled materials (as in the case of quilts and hooked mats), or spun and woven from the raw cotton and flax and sheep wool. It is quite possible that the local weavers and rug and quilt makers were influenced by the colour and pattern of textiles that were available for purchase in a shop such as Wollenhaupt's, but their manufacture was still accomplished at home.

The textiles included in the *Spirit of Nova Scotia* exhibition fall into four sub-categories: *floor coverings* which includes hooked mats, sail-cloth mats and woven carpets; *bed coverings* including quilts, and coverlets; *table coverings* which includes penny mats and other appliquéd table rugs, and *embroidered samplers*. Textiles are very fragile cultural artifacts. They are often made from recycled fabrics, and because of constant use within the household seldom survive except in fragments. Very few textiles (except samplers) found in Nova Scotia can be dated with certainty before 1850. Those that have survived from the mid nineteenth century are usually mats, quilts and coverlets. Probably the three most important floor mats ever found in Nova Scotia are included in this exhibition. Entry numbers 1 to 3 are the earliest floor coverings dating from the 1850-1860 period. Not only is the yarn sewn technique on linen an early method of construction, but the free-hand patterns are probably the work of the same maker or family. Certainly the mat of the horse is one of the most enduring decorative folk images found in this show representing the best of the *Spirit of Nova Scotia*.

Antique textiles are too valuable as historical documents to be discarded. Even fragments can be important sources of information on the domestic interiors of the nineteenth century.

1. The bed and bedstead often referred to the bedding, bed curtains, pillows, sheets etc.
2. Florence Montgomery, *Textiles in America, 1650-1870* (New York: W.W. Norton and Company, 1984), p. xi.

Textiles in Nova Scotia

Scott Robson

Scott Robson is the Curator of Historic Buildings and Furnishings with the Nova Scotia Museum in Halifax. Robson, a native Haligonian, has lectured often on the subject of antique furnishings and quilts.

Today, the production of textiles by early settlers is too often perceived with a romantic notion, as craft and as "folk art", but most textiles were of great necessity, even more than furniture. The people who came to settle our towns, villages and rural areas brought certain possessions with them; of particular importance were clothing and bedding, as well as other textiles such as tablecloths, towels, and perhaps curtains, rugs and carpets. Initial efforts were to construct temporary shelters or more permanent homes, and to clear the land and plant food and enclose livestock. Some settlements were encouraged by supplies from the colonial government, but life was still harder than would have been anticipated. Winter was colder and longer than in the homelands of Great Britain, France, Germany or the New England colonies, and warm clothing and bedding were even more important here. As a result, cloth was valued and used carefully. Small pieces of fabric from worn clothing were saved for re-use.

Since wool is the warmest of the three textile fibres used in Nova Scotia (wool, linen and cotton), some farmers tried to establish flocks of sheep. Their effort was not always rewarded — attacks from wild animals and disease could quickly eliminate these supplies of wool and meat.

In spring, the sheep were sheared to remove the matted wool which was then sorted, washed, picked free of debris and carded to prepare it for spinning into yarn for knitting or weaving.

Linen was also produced locally, but as with other crops planted in the newly-cleared land, growing flax was an uncertain business. Poor soil, erosion, dampness, dryness and disease could cause an entire crop to fail. But if the crop succeeded, the plants would be pulled by hand to preserve as much as possible of the long fibres. The unusable portions of the plant had to be separated; first the seeds were taken off, then the coarse shive was "retted" (rotted) and removed with a flax brake and a scutching knife. The flax fibre was then combed with a hackle into several grades, ready for spinning.

The craft of spinning was not universal. But among rural people, it was common for most women of a household to contribute to spinning wool or linen yarns for knitted goods or woven fabrics.

The third fibre, cotton, could not be grown locally, but yarn and thread were imported for sale in local stores. By 1860, cotton had almost entirely replaced linen as a warp yarn in woven goods; linen was then only used for towels, where its durability and absorption were required, or for tablecloths and napkins, where in addition to these qualities the subtle shine of the long fibres was desired for its elegant appearance.

For most early settlers in Nova Scotia, imported cloth was a part of everyday life, but so was locally-produced cloth. Wealthier families could purchase imported damask-weave linen tablecloths, and fine woolen or luxurious silk fabrics for clothing. As the 1800s progressed, these materials were available to a larger portion of the population, and production of hand-spun, hand-woven wool or linen cloth diminished, except in a few small or isolated places.

Weaving

Settlers in Nova Scotia brought with them many skills and trades: some were carpenters, masons, farmers or blacksmiths; others had no particular skills at all, and were not well prepared for the New World. A few were weavers who had made cloth in their own homes or in the factories of Britain. They were usually men, but increasingly the craft in North America included women. By 1870, there are few weavers listed, probably because handwoven fabric was already being replaced by blankets and woolen suiting made in small local factories, or by imported fabric.

When weaving was widespread, it was carried on at two levels — production for home use, and production for sale or trade. Household weaving was often simple, on a loom with just two or four harnesses, to produce blankets, sheets, sacking and clothing material. Endless yards of plain, basic fabric were produced, used and discarded. If the weaver were professional, production would have been on a four-harness loom (more complex looms have not been recorded in this province), using pattern weaves such as overshot, and M's & O's. It is these fancier weaves which more often have been saved.

The simplest fabric and simplest to produce was of plain ("tabby") weave. Sometimes a twill weave was employed to make a fabric which would drape more softly than with plain weave. Blankets, sheets, clothing materials and everyday linens were produced with these weaves. Often the natural colour of wool was used. Especially desirable was wool of "black" sheep, actually various shades of brown and grey; with that, the effort of dyeing was not necessary to obtain a dark fabric which would not show dirt as readily as would white wool. For certain projects, some yarns would be dyed various colours, producing simple stripes or checks.

Other weaves were used to produce patterns for fancier things: M's & O's weave for tablecloths and linens, and overshot weave for bed coverlets as well as tablecloths and carpets. Judging from surviving examples of overshot, motifs of circles ("chariot wheels") and squares ("tables") are far commoner than the optical designs (such as "olive leaf" and "sunrise") found elsewhere.

With these designs made on two- or four-harness looms, the limitations of patterning appear rather rigid and restrictive, especially to a non-weaver. However, within restraints there is often room for personal or regional variation. Some coverlets have no borders, others have beautiful wide ones, and in Digby County the borders are occasionally separated by a narrow band of twill weave.

Colour also provided opportunity for variation. In coverlets, the most common colour is indigo blue on a white cotton ground; this blue, from imported dyestuff, was relatively colourfast and bright. (This colour is still very popular today for making blue jeans.)

The second common colour seems to have been red, from imported logwood or possibly cochineal (an insect). Some weavers combined several colours in one coverlet. Some dyed the ground threads which are usually left white. In at least one recorded example, the wool pattern weft has been left undyed (cream-coloured) on a dyed blue ground; this example is further atypical for its use of a woolen ground in place of the usual cotton.

The hand of a professional or accomplished weaver can be seen in the evenness of the selvage and in the matching of the two strips seamed at the centre of a coverlet. Work by a lesser weaver is not as even, showing slight irregularity of pattern or perhaps even a section of incorrect treadling.

As mentioned, production of linen required hard work. Therefore, when cotton warp thread became commercially available about 1850, it soon took the place of linen on the loom. It is sometimes maintained by family tradition that certain coverlets are "made of wool from sheep on the farm and from flax grown in the fields", but only one example from Nova Scotia of a coverlet with a linen warp has yet been confirmed (Nova Scotia Museum, see Burnham, *The Comfortable Arts,* item #110). Few early textiles have survived decades of daily use; but this rarity may also indicate how complete was the change-over to cotton warp yarn.

The new length of fabric was finished by milling, which shrinks the yarn and produces a tighter, more durable cloth. The action of pounding the wet cloth against a board table causes the wool to "fuzz" a bit, producing a napped surface, and a softer, warmer fabric for blankets, clothing, etc. Milling was often a community social event which in parts of Cape Breton has survived to this day. However, newly-woven cloth is now rarely used; as the event is purely social, the traditional songs are repeated with surrogate lengths of old blankets to beat in rhythm.

Throughout Nova Scotia in the mid-1800s, water-powered mills were constructed to take over the routine tasks of carding and spinning wool into yarn, plying yarn, weaving fabric for blankets and suiting, and napping and finishing the material. Gradually through the late 1800s, the mechanical assistance of mills replaced textile handcrafts, except in remote or independent communities.

Quilt-making

The quilts included in this exhibition all date after the mid-1800s. Quilts were made in Nova Scotia long before then, but the oldest example known to survive, dates only from about 1810 (Nova Scotia Museum collection). That quilt is notable for its utilitarian appearance. While most quilts here are rather decorative, the older quilt is a simple four-patch block made of re-used scraps of old clothing, hand-woven wool material.

With the effort required to raise sheep and to produce woolen yarn and finished fabric, even small pieces of warm material were valued. In quilts, those fragments were assembled to produce a warm bedcovering. Wool fabric was preferred for top and back, and the filler was often carded wool batting. As leisure time permitted, and as fabric became more easily available (or affordable as settlements prospered), the patterns probably became more decorative.

Imported cotton fabric had been available in the mid-1700s, but as quilts from that period do not survive, we do not know how widely cotton might have been used. Though less warm than wool, cotton cloth was very popular and available in a wide range of colours and prints. However, it is reasonable to assume that in the earlier period, woolen quilts were preferred in rural areas because of practicality. In the mid-1800s, woolen quilts would still have been made for warmth, but more decorative examples were made of cotton, and for the better quilts new fabric was preferred. Today some quiltmakers extend this preference for new fabric to include careful "colour-coordination", but some of the most appealing old pieced quilts derive their interest from a less restricted use of colours and prints.

When quilts are made from mixed prints and colours, the maker must sort the fabrics to be used. The pattern block is usually of very simple geometry, but a variety of fabrics contributes subtlety to the finished quilt. In general, to maintain the pattern block, colours and prints are selected according to tone — dark, medium and light — for use in matched parts of the design, so that where dark is required to produce a pin-wheel for example, the fabrics may be of different shades or even of different colours, but the pattern is still apparent at a glance.

At a time when quilts were made containing 20 or 30 fabrics, some quilts were made of only two: one colour or print, and white. When this was done with new, brightly-coloured fabric, it would demonstrate that the maker could afford to purchase all-new cloth. In the period around 1850, "Turkey" red was especially popular, in combination with white.

Most quilts made in Nova Scotia are of pieced construction, that is, small pieces assembled to produce pattern blocks, which are in turn assembled with other blocks to produce the quilt top. Much less common are appliqué quilts, that is, those in which the small pieces are applied ("appliqué" in French) onto a large background piece already the size of the final block or quilt top.

Pieced quilts are geometric in conception, almost always with straight seams, but occasionally with simple curved seams. Appliqué technique does not require seams; the stitching of one fabric on top of another allows curves and angles of nearly any shape. But in Nova Scotia, appliqué quilts remained symmetrical over all, and in the older quilts, motifs are rarely more pictorial than conventionalized flowers.

The simple geometric designs of pieced quilts were easily remembered and passed on to friends and relatives. Similar basic quilt patterns appear all across eastern North America. A letter to Yarmouth from cousins in New England might have included a sketch of a quilt block being made there. Or a trip by sailing ship along the coast or to the "Boston States" gave opportunity to see the quilts of other makers. Sometimes a sample block would be sewn as a sort of note made in fabric; the quilter could then vary colours and prints to suit taste or available materials. Patterns were also published in women's magazines and newspapers of the late 1800s, but many of these diagrams were for silk patchwork projects, such as pincushions and parlour decorations.

Strong, simple block patterns were popular in Nova Scotia; some used only squares (Irish Chain, Double Irish Chain, Four-Patch and Nine-Patch). Other blocks present a wide range of designs using squares with right-angle triangles; usually these are variations drawn on a nine-patch grid. Common among these are several forms of eight-pointed star (known in the U.S. as Variable Star, Ohio Star, etc.).

Quilt patterns today are usually identified by the names recorded in American quilting books published from about 1930, but we cannot be sure what names were used by our own ancestral quiltmakers; the quilts may remain, but regional names rarely do. No doubt for many of them the same name applied as in New England, but a suggestion of the Nova Scotian interpretation of well-known designs remains in a name such as "Fisherman's Reel" for a pattern known in the U.S. as "Flying X" or "Fox and Geese".

Local variations also occur in the setting together of pattern blocks. In some designs the blocks look best assembled one against another, producing a larger over-all pattern. In the most intriguing of these, the juxtaposition of blocks creates pattern between the patterns, negative and positive motifs, and diagonal movement; the resulting quilt top is far more powerful than the sum of its parts.

A quiltmaker sees the pattern block as a basic unit. In some quilts, the pattern blocks are set together alternating with plain blocks, checker-board fashion. In others, the units are set with stripes or a window-sash set, or with a secondary pattern block. The effect would also be varied by turning the blocks "on the diagonal". Therefore, one pattern could be made into several quite different quilts, especially with the additional variables of print or plain fabric, light or dark tone, or a wide range of colour and shade.

Crazy quilts were made as part of a mid-Victorian fashion, to be displayed and admired in the parlour. Although called quilts, they were rarely quilted or constructed with a filler (batting). Silk and velvet fabric saved from dressmaking, or purchased through newspaper advertisements for patchwork scraps, were assembled using erratic shapes arranged randomly.*

More formalized versions can include regular shapes of triangles or trapezoids, or can be assembled in blocks or with a large centre and borders. In almost all cases, edges of the patches are ornamented with decorative embroidery stitches, complexity reflecting the maker's ability. As well, the patches provided space for further decoration; often this was embroidered motifs of flowers, animals and initials, and since painting pictures on velvet was a genteel pursuit, that technique is also sometimes seen on crazy quilts. The use of these more representational motifs could be construed today as "folk art" but in reality most of them originate in patterns published in the newspapers or needlework books common in the 1880s and 1890s, during the height of the crazy quilt craze.

Log cabin quilts are constructed in blocks, but each block does not contain the pattern. Fabrics are arranged to make one portion light, another dark. Then when the blocks are assembled, light in one block against light (or dark) in another, the pattern progressively becomes evident. The three most popular arrangements produce large graphic patterns: diagonal lines, concentric diamonds, or repeating diamonds of light and dark. The usual technique of making each block by sewing the "logs" onto a ground fabric causes several thicknesses of cloth; therefore this type of quilt is not often quilted.

Of all these types, appliqué quilts provide the most freedom of design; almost any shape is possible. However, the constraints of pieced quilts provide an amazing range of possibilities; it is this very containment which generates the most vital and personal quilts. That vitality is more essential to our modern appreciation of quilts as "folk art" than is the freer expression possible in appliqué work. Perhaps Nova Scotian quiltmakers have felt more comfortable working with the bolder, more angular designs of piecing. For whatever reasons, few appliqué quilts seem to have been made here until the early 1900s, and pieced quilts continue to be more popular, even today.

*The adjective "crazy" describes the erratic directions of the lines, much like the "crazed" or crackled glaze of some ceramics; it was not intended to refer to any form of dementia caused by doing all of that embroidery, nor to the state of mind required to embark on such a project.

Mat-hooking

Carpets and other floor-coverings have not always been stylish. It was not until the mid-1700s that their use was adopted by wealthy families, and probably not until after 1800 that the practice became familiar in Nova Scotia. Among those people less able to afford imported carpeting but able to make their own cloth, fabrication of rugs and carpets was still limited. Valuable wool and cotton yarns were more needed for warm clothing and bedding. In many Nova Scotian homes, it would have been extravagant to put fabric on the floor.

But through the early 1800s, the fashion increased, encouraged by growing prosperity. Handwoven carpets, in striped designs or (less often) patterned in the overshot technique, could be produced by weavers throughout the province. The introduction of factory-spun cotton warp at mid-century gave a boost to the production of all sorts of handwoven material, but the concurrent influx of factory-woven cloth likely discounted the effect.

It was probably in the second quarter of the 1800s that hooked rugs began to appear in our region. Documented examples from this period are not known to survive, so that evidence of the origin and transmission of the technique in Nova Scotia is unavailable.

Several researchers have considered these questions. William Winthrop Kent proposed in the 1930s that hooked rugs were of British origin, but his view has been challenged due to a lack of early examples or references there. To be sure, there is a British tradition for hooked rugs, but it is not as old as in eastern Canada and the United States. There is another tradition for a type of rag rug with a pile, but these were "pegged" or "prodded" (also "brodded"), that is, made with short lengths of rag poked with a sharpened stick through the canvas, from *behind.*

Others have seen connections with rugs made in Scandinavia, but the actual technique varies. The main feature of hooking is that the maker works from the top of the backing fabric using a blunt hook; with one hand underneath holding the yarn or rag, the top hand pushes the hook through the fabric to pull some of the material above the surface, forming a looped pile. In some ways this is related to tambour embroidery, which also employs a hook, but the loops are chained together; this style of embroidery was widely known in Asia, India and Europe in the 1700s.

Among the rugs displayed here are two rare examples of yarn-sewn technique. This type is often grouped with hooked rugs because of the similar appearance of the pile, but these rugs were made with a large needle instead of a hook; therefore, they are related to bed rugs, known in the American colonies from at least as early as the 1720s, but unknown in Nova Scotia. Yarn-sewn rugs which survive in the eastern United States date from about 1800-1840. Perhaps this established form of rug, made with a needle-produced yarn pile, was altered by the later introduction of the hooking technique.

Some writers suggest that hooking might even have originated in the Atlantic provinces, Maine and New Hampshire, spreading to the rest of New England and the Atlantic seaboard by the 1860s. But whatever the origin, hooked mats have a long and strong association with Nova Scotia. Possibly they were made here before 1840, but the craft did not burgeon until after mid-century. Before this, linen was used as a ground fabric, but in the 1850s, burlap made of jute fibres from India was introduced. The coarse, inexpensive material was intended for use as sacking, but was soon recognized as being suitable as the ground fabric for hooked mats, and was then widely used for that purpose.

Perhaps there was a larger quantity of mats produced in the early period, if so, the survival rate has been very poor. Hooked mats, like other floor coverings, were not kept once they had been worn too much. How many mats would have been replaced by new ones, and demoted to use as doormats before being discarded?

Rugs serve a function of making the floor of a home more warm underfoot and less drafty. Simple, plain material would have served as well, but decoration was also a function for which mats were intended. A certain pleasure derives from seeing patterned textiles in a room. Designs sketched on burlap, hooked with left-over materials, gave satisfaction in using what was useless to make something useful once more.

The designs chosen varied according to the intended room. Parlours and more formal rooms were provided with floral patterns; occasionally these were imitations of factory carpets, but most often they were more simple with a central group of flowers on a plain ground, edged with scrolls and a dark border. (Hooked mats were often used on top of carpets, so imitation was not a purpose of the maker.) These patterns for "good" rooms were planned with care, perhaps copied from illustrations in books or magazines, or from other hooked mats.

In kitchens the patterns would be geometric, simple and bold, and a little easier to draw and make. Some hookers balked at rendering a floral motif on burlap, too self conscious of their lack of formal artistic skill. But drawing squares, following the warp and weft threads of the backing fabric, seemed manageable.

In addition to this floral/geometric "hierarchy", there was another set of preferences according to materials. Because of the greater value of woolen yarn and of woolen fabric, these materials were only used for better hooked mats. They were floral in design, and the best used only woolen yarn. Sometimes they were given a clipped pile, in imitation of the imported luxury of factory-woven carpet. Wool and woolen rag were also favoured because of the vibrant colours possible with dyes.

For lesser mats, the rags could be of cotton, or mixed wool and cotton. There are of course exceptions to this approach, but few cotton rag florals are seen.

When rags are used in mats, they are almost always of wide variety; these mixed fabrics can be dyed to make them of similar colour, but each type of cloth receives the dye differently, producing slightly uneven tones. These colours fade unevenly too, becoming softer and more mottled than when originally worked. Therefore, for the best mats, a hooker would have preferred to use similar materials of similar colour. In the twentieth century, some mat hookers have saved worn-out Stanfield's woolen underwear to use for cream-coloured backgrounds, or to be dyed for important sections of the design.

Among the mats most highly-prized today are those which were hand-drawn scenes or motifs of flowers, animals and birds. These can demonstrate the vitality of conception and the innocence of execution seen in drawings by children. More sophisticated people, perhaps educated formally, are made self-conscious of such expression, aware of what is seen as artistic shortcoming. For them, there is comfortable security in the copying of designs drawn by others, copying other mats, or borrowing from pictures printed in books. But even the more original mat-makers seem to have been aware of the formal requirements of the "idea" of a hooked mat — flowers or other designs at centre, scrolls at corners, and a dark border.

Although pattern mats are not included in this exhibition, their introduction had a great effect. In the United States after the Civil War in the 1860s, backs for rugs were available with drawn or stamped designs, to be worked at home with fabric scraps or wool. In the 1870s, Edward Sands Frost in Maine produced some of the best-known in the eastern United States, but patterns were also produced in Nova Scotia. In Yarmouth for instance, Perry & Grantham formed a partnership in 1879 to stamp mat patterns. Unfortunately, examples of their work have not been identified.

The biggest manufacturer of patterns in Nova Scotia was Garrett's in New Glasgow. In 1892, John E. Garrett established his mat printing business; ten years later, the company could supply nearly one hundred designs. A considerable amount of business was done by mail, sending patterns to places in Nova Scotia, Prince Edward Island and New Brunswick. The Garrett line was also sold through Eaton's, the Hudson's Bay Company, Holman's (P.E.I.), Dupuis Frères (Montreal) and by agents in Great Britain and elsewhere. There was also a branch of the business in Malden, Massachusetts, to supply requests in New England.

Along with patterns, Garrett's also sold woolen yarn in a range of colours suitable for their designs. In 1926, Mr. Garrett patented the "Bluenose rug hooker", a hand-held device using yarn, and worked from the back of the rug.

Wells & Richardson, Montreal, also sold stamped patterns in Nova Scotia. Their famous Diamond Dyes came in over one hundred colours for dyeing wool or cotton, rendering scrap fabrics bright and colourful. To promote use of their dyes, the company published stamped patterns and catalogues; editions from at least two years (1899 and 1900) have been found in Nova Scotia.

These commercial patterns all had an effect on home-drawn designs. Makers would copy a catalogue picture, or a printed burlap back, or a mat worked by someone else. Certain mats made on these patterns are today sometimes mistaken for original designs.

Since at least the 1920s, considerable quantities of our oldest and best hooked mats have been sold to the United States. There are numerous stories of dealers buying every mat in the house, perhaps offering to exchange for a nice new piece of linoleum. The Nova Scotia origin of many of these mats is now likely forgotten; after so many years in the U.S. they are probably referred to as being of New England origin.

Although the makers rarely received much money for their efforts when they traded, the revival of interest indicates that mats had become fashionable; this permitted development of a craft industry.

In the 1920s, Lilian Burke came from the United States to visit Mrs. Alexander Graham Bell at her summer home near Baddeck, Cape Breton. By 1927, Miss Burke had organized a home-craft industry in Chéticamp to produce finely-hooked wool rugs for sale to New York decorators and others, and thereby helped create employment and income for the families in the community.

The designs and colourings were carefully planned by her to appeal to the American market. Those designs have since become so firmly established that they are sometimes considered to be traditional, although they were created by an artist less than sixty years ago. Occasionally among these rugs are a few which demonstrate the maker's personal contribution in design or colour, but the conventionalized flower shapes, with leaves and petals shaded in soft colours as advocated by Lilian Burke, continue to dominate this very successful rug production.

1 Yarn Sewn and Hooked Mat with Basket of Flowers

Merigomish, Pictou County

Handspun yarn and home-dyed wool with small amount of cotton rag on handspun and woven linen ground

Artist unknown (probably by member of MacKay family)

Circa 1850

Dimensions: 155.0 × 90.5 cm (61 × 35⅝ inches)

Collection of Nova Scotia Museum, Halifax, Nova Scotia

This could be the earliest mat known from Nova Scotia predating, by a few years, the mat with the house, and the mat with the horse. All three of these mats were donated by the same family and found in the same house in Pictou.

Structure: Unclipped pile. Small amount of cotton rag, handspun yarn and home-dyed wool rag on handspun and woven linen ground. Selvedge shows top and bottom, hand drawn design — blue lattice basket in the center holding long green stems with red buds. Branches of 3 flowers each in a row across the bottom and upside down across the top, alternate indigo blue, gold and red with green leaves. Top and bottom have a hill-like form in yellow, pale blue and pink. Background is off-white. Bluebird on each side of basket four yellow and gold hearts at each end, with spaced filled in with indigo blue.

Of the 3 rugs received from the donor this one is said to be the oldest — made by member of Mrs Mackay's family who lived in donor's present house since it was build in 1852.

2 Yarn Sewn and Hooked Mat with House

Merigomish, Pictou County

Wool on linen base

Artist unknown (probably by member of MacKay family)

Circa 1855-1865

Dimensions: 163.0 × 82.0 cm (64³⁄₁₆ × 32⁵⁄₁₆ inches)

Collection of the Nova Scotia Museum, Halifax, Nova Scotia

This is one of the earliest mats known from Nova Scotia which is both hooked and yarn-sewn with home dyed and homespun wool. The house which is depicted was built in 1852, and may be the home of the donor in which the mat was found, but which has been greatly altered through the years.

Structure: Hooked rug all home-dyed, homespun wool yarn — some parts hooked, others "yarn-sewn" with a needle. Clipped pile, very thick in the center, thinning towards the edges. Handwoven linen backing with top and bottom selvedges. Hole lower right corner — patched hole upper center edge — pile on lower edge worn away.

Refer to colour plate V, page 14

3 Yarn-Sewn and Hooked Mat of Horse

Merigomish, Pictou County

Multi-ply wool yarn with small amount of rag on handwoven linen ground

Artist unknown (probably by member of MacKay family)

Circa 1850-1860

Dimensions: 151.0 × 70.5 cm (59½ × 27¾ inches)

Collection of the Nova Scotia Museum, Halifax, Nova Scotia

This is a truly fine example of an early textile floor covering dating from the mid-nineteenth century. The decorative quality of this mat makes it one of the great examples of traditional Nova Scotia folk art.

Structure: Yarn sewn rug with a very small amount of hooking. Almost entirely multi-ply wool yarn with small amount of rag on handwoven linen ground. Design — horse (dark green wool) standing on yellow background. On either side of the horse a "tree" with blue trunk, green leaves and red and blue circular flowers. At each end, 2 star-shaped flowers in gold with blue outline. Border (approx. 9cm) of dark green wool. Backing made of 2 pieces. Clipped pile.

Refer to colour plate VI, page 14

4 Hooked Place Mat "Lour"

Blandford, Lunenburg County
Cotton and wool on burlap backing
Artist unknown
Circa 1870-1890
Dimensions: 41.0 × 33.0 cm (16⅛ × 13 inches)
Collection of Paul Killowee and Judy Aymar, Queensland, Nova Scotia

A great hooked place mat showing a buffalo next to a tree, with red blossoms or perhaps apples. The word "Lour", which means buffalo in French, is hooked along the bottom of the mat.

Structure: The mat is hooked with remnants of cotton and wool fabric on a commercial burlap backing.

5 Hooked Rug

Hamms Hill, Lunenburg County
Cotton and wool hooked on burlap
Made by Mrs George Hughes
Dated 1888
Dimensions: 172.7 × 86.3 cm (68 × 34 inches)
Private collection

This particular rug was found by Chris Huntington in his circa 1800 Cape Cod style house. It is one of the few rugs known from Nova Scotia that has hooked into the design the names of the maker and owner and the date when it was made. The inscription around the border of the rug reads, "Mrs George Aulenbach's mat hooked by Mrs George Hughes in 1888". In the centre of the rug are a series of decorative motifs, including two opposing pots of flowers (tulips ?), and a central design of tulip-like flowers growing from a single bloom with four birds sitting in the branches.

The tulip motif is most closely associated with Pennsylvania-German folk art[1] and is considered a rare exception in the decorative arts of the Lunenburg-Germans[2], that is until recently. Over the past few years more objects have come to light from Lunenburg County which include tulip motifs. The tulip and tulip and leaf motif are perhaps Persian in origin[3] and are interpreted as a symbol of fertility, strength, success and plenty, and in general suggest the same meaning as the tree of life motif[4]. Tulip motifs are not only found on Germanic decorative arts, but are common to pottery from many areas of Europe[5], and were incorporated into the intricate designs of the seventeenth and early eighteenth century Hadley chests found in the Connecticut River valley.[6]

The paired birds (whether in twos or fours) and tulip design in a combined motif, as found in the central decoration of this rug, is common to Pennsylvania and Ontario-German fraktur[7], and is only beginning to be found more often in Lunenburg decorative arts. The flower-in-pot seems to be the most preferred Lunenburg-German form and probably can be best interpreted as a tree of life symbol standing for richness and prosperity.

Structure: Cotton and wool hooked on burlap. When found the rug had several holes through the burlap backing and was frayed and damaged along the edges. Since then the rug has been repaired.

Exhibited: Decorated Nova Scotia Furnishings, Dalhousie University Art Gallery, Halifax, Nova Scotia, July 5-August 6, 1978.

Published: Tom Lackey. *Decorated Nova Scotia Furnishings* (Halifax: Dalhousie University Art Gallery, 1978), p. 23, 34. The rug is illustrated in as found condition.

1. Arlene Palmer Schwind, "Pennsylvania German Earthenware", In Catherine E. Hutchins (Ed), *Arts of the Pennsylvania Germans*, (New York: W.W. Norton & Company, Inc., 1983), p. 195.
2. Michael Bird and Terry Kobayashi, *A Splendid Harvest: Germanic Folk and Decorative Arts in Canada*, (Toronto: Van Nostrand Reinhold Ltd., 1981), p. 51, illustration 37. Bird states in the caption that, "The tulip, a popular motif in the decorative arts of the Pennsylvania Germans, is virtually unknown in Lunenburg Germanic folk art." He illustrates the Eisenhauer gravestone with its tulip motif as a rare exception. Since this statement, several objects unknown to Bird have been found in Lunenburg County with tulip motifs indicating that the tulip is perhaps more common as a decorative embellishment on Lunenburg German folk art than previously thought.
3. Arlene Palmer Schwind, *Ibid*, p. 195.
4. Richard Lawrence Greene, "Fertility Symbols on the Hadley Chests", In *The Magazine Antiques*, Volume CXII, No. 2 (August 1977), pp. 250-257.
5. Arlene Palmer Schwind, *Ibid*, p. 195.
6. Richard Lawrence Greene, *Ibid*, p. 250. According to Greene who refers to Clair Franklin Luther (*The Hadley Chest*, Hartford, 1935) as a source, genealogical studies by Luther suggested that the Hadley chests were generally given as hope chests to girls about twelve years old who were beginning to accumulate personal possessions in anticipation of marriage. In this context, the tulip motif which was included in the decorative embellishment of many of these chests, remains a strong symbol of fertility, strength and abundance.
7. Michael Bird, *Ontario Fraktur: A Pennsylvania German Folk Tradition in Early Canada*, (Toronto: M.F. Feheley Publishers Limited, 1977), See illustrations on pages 36, 46, 60, 62, and 78-79.

• *Refer to colour plate II, page 12*

6 Geometric Mat with Circle Motifs

Lunenburg County
Wool rag and yarn on burlap
Artist unknown
Circa 1880-1900
Dimensions: 58.5 × 122.0 cm (23 × 48 inches)
Collection of the Nova Scotia Museum, Halifax, Nova Scotia

This mat is an example of an early free-hand geometric pattern with a combination of circles forming a central motif, flanked by two *fleur de lis* motifs.

Structure: Wool rag and yarn with burlap backing. The hooking is loose, and the mat has seen years of use.

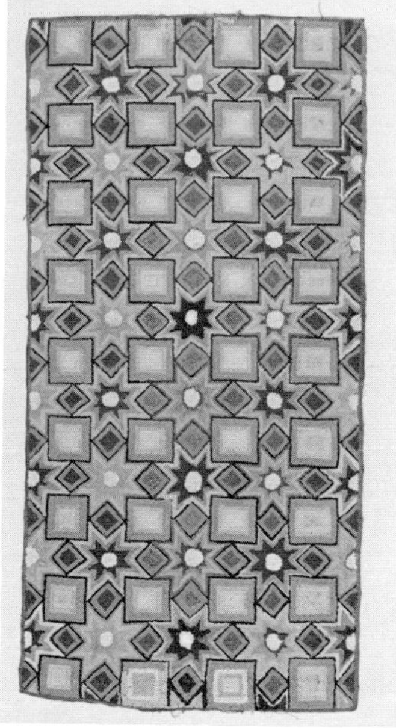

7 Hooked Mats with Star and Block Patterns

Antigonish, Antigonish County
Cotton and wool on burlap
Made by Zena Cameron of Antigonish
Circa 1880-1900
Dimensions: left — 136.0 × 67.5 cm (53$\frac{9}{16}$ × 26$\frac{9}{16}$ inches)
right — 120.0 × 71.0 cm (47$\frac{1}{4}$ × 27$\frac{15}{16}$ inches)
Collection of George Christie, Bear River, Nova Scotia

These mats were made by Mrs Zena Cameron of Antigonish and exhibit an intricate and lively pattern, combining star and block motifs. The colour range, including various reds, greens and blues, adds significantly to the visual impact of this pair of hooked floor coverings.

Structure: Both mats are hooked using cotton and wool on burlap backing. Both rugs have undergone some previous repair and rehooking.

8 Hooked Mat

Colchester or Cumberland County
Mixed rag on burlap
Artist unknown
Circa 1890-1910
Dimensions: 89.5 × 97.5 cm (35¼ × 38⅜ inches)
Collection of the Nova Scotia Museum, Halifax, Nova Scotia

A very lively patterned hooked mat with a central motif of diamonds and an outer border of abstract shells. The four corners are decorated with floral designs.

Structure: Mixed cotton and wool rag on burlap

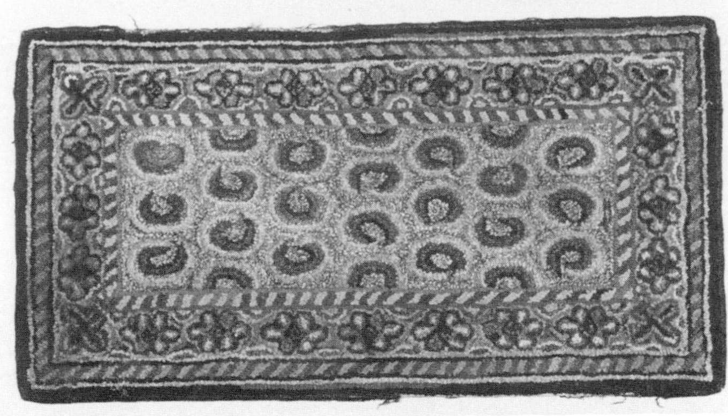

9 Hooked Mat with Floral Border

Annapolis Valley
Cotton and wool on burlap
Artist unknown
Circa 1890-1910
Dimensions: 86.3 × 47.0 cm (34 × 18½ inches)
Collection of George Christie, Bear River, Nova Scotia

This small rug has a lively oriental pattern, particularly in the centre section. The design is very effective, using a combination of brown, black, beige, dark blue and deep orange fabrics, and is finely hooked.

Structure: Cotton and wool on burlap backing. The mat is in good condition retaining good fabric colour.

10 Hooked Mat *Blandford Type*
Lunenburg County
Cotton and wool on burlap backing
Artist unknown
Circa 1900-1920
Dimensions: 158.8 × 74.5 cm (62½ × 30$^{5}/_{16}$ inches)
Collection of Carole Collins, Hamilton, Ontario

Mats of this type are often called *Blandford*[1] referring to the area where they were supposedly first found, and to the fact that these types of patterns, and their many similar variations, are believed to be based on late nineteenth and early twentieth century linoleum designs. It is well known that dealers from the United States door-knocked Nova Scotia during the early twentieth century, trading linoleum for hooked mats, and in some cases room-sized hooked rugs.[2] It is therefore easy to understand how patterns on linoleum could work their way into the repertory of hooked rug designs during this time. Although many of the women may have traded their hooked floor coverings for more modern products, this did not mean they stopped making or creating hooked rug patterns.

Structure: Cotton and wool on burlap backing. The mat is in 'as found' condition.

1. Blandford is in Lunenburg County, about 20 miles from Halifax.
2. For information on finding hooked rugs in Canada, see William Winthrop Kent, *The Hooked Rug*, (New York: Tudor Publishing Company), 1930, p. 144. See particularly the chapter "A Hunt for Rugs in Canada".

11 Hooked Mat *Blandford Type*
Chester, Lunenburg County
Cotton and wool on burlap backing
Artist unknown
Circa 1900-1920
Dimensions: 183.0 × 90.0 cm (72 × 29$^{7}/_{16}$ inches)
Collection of Judy and Earle Rhodenizer, Pleasantville, Nova Scotia

This is a fine example of a *Blandford* type mat with excellent colour.

Structure: The mat is made with cotton and wool fabric hooked through a burlap backing.

12 Hooked Runner *Blandford Variation*
Lunenburg County
Cotton and wool on burlap backing
Artist unknown
Circa 1900-1920
Dimensions: 161.0 × 51.2 cm (63⅜ × 20$^{3}/_{16}$ inches)
Collection of Carole Collins, Hamilton, Ontario

An example of a mat with a variation on the *Blandford* pattern. As a runner, it was probably used in the hall or beside a bed.

Structure: Cotton and wool on burlap backing, the fabric has retained good colour.

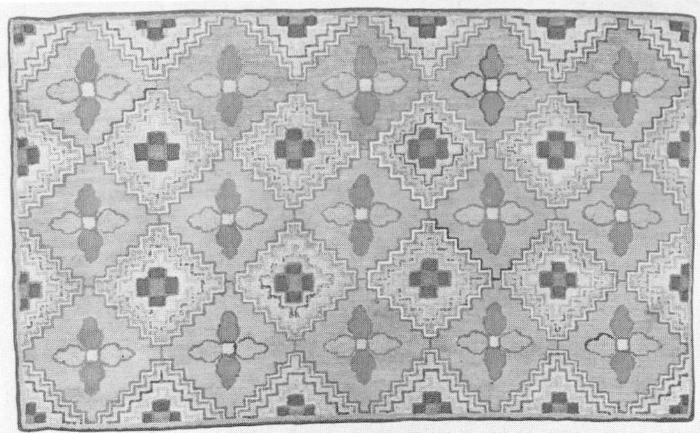

13 Hooked Mat with Diamond Block Pattern and Flowers *Blandford Variation*

East Chester, Lunenburg County
Cotton and wool rag on burlap
Artist unknown
Circa 1910-1930
Dimensions: 130.8 × 80.0 cm (51½ × 31½ inches)
Collection of the Nova Scotia Museum, Halifax, Nova Scotia

This particular mat has a geometric block pattern with alternate stylized single flowers in red, blue, green and yellow on a light purple ground. The mat is designed so that there are horizontal rows of block diamonds, the edges of which form the diamond, with central four-petal flower.

Structure: Cotton and wool rag on burlap bound with brown cotton edging.

14 Hooked Mat with Diamond Motifs

Lunenburg County
Wool and cotton on burlap backing
Made by Augusta Vogler
Circa 1900-1920
Dimensions: 150.5 × 79.1 cm (59¼ × 31⅛ inches)
Collection of Carole Collins, Hamilton, Ontario

This is one of the most dramatic geometric rugs known, combining strong design and colour. The maker used diamond and triangle motifs to create a bold and energetic mat, reflecting the best in folk art textiles.

Structure: The mat is hooked with cotton and wool fabrics on a burlap backing.

Refer to colour plate IV, page 13

15 Hooked Mat

Smith's Cove, Digby County
Largely wool rag with some cotton rag on burlap ground
Artist unknown
Circa 1900-1920
Dimensions: 96.0 × 60.0 cm (37¹³⁄₁₆ × 23⅝ inches)
Collection of the Nova Scotia Museum, Halifax, Nova Scotia

This very colourful and dynamic rug with an exterior border of red diamonds, was used at the "Out of the Way Inn", at Smith's Cove in Digby County.

Structure: The wool rag (with some cotton rag) is looped through the burlap ground forming a thick pile.

16 Hooked Place Mat

Kings County
Cotton and wool on burlap backing
Artist unknown
Circa 1900-1920
Dimensions: 54.0 × 29.5 cm (21¼ × 11⅝ inches)
Collection of June E. Miller and Murray E. Stewart, Berwick, Nova Scotia

A small hooked mat used for the top of a chest or table with a modified central star motif.

Structure: Remnants of cotton and wool fabric hooked through a burlap backing. The edges of the mat have been sewn with a metallic gold thread to deter unraveling.

17 Hooked Mat with Rocking Horse

River John, Pictou County
Wool and cotton on burlap backing
Artist unknown, although the name Maud appears on one end of the rug
Dated 1912
Dimensions: 100.0 × 66.0 cm (39⅜ × 26 inches)
Collection of Pascal and Angela Dinaut, Great Village, Nova Scotia

An excellent example of a free-hand patterned mat with a rocking horse motif. The name Maud appears opposite the date 1912. This name probably refers to the maker, owner, or the nickname of the rocking horse.

Structure: The fabric used for hooking is a combination of wool and cotton. The border is in red, the background in a combination of black and grey-brown, and the horse hooked mostly with yellow-orange remnants.

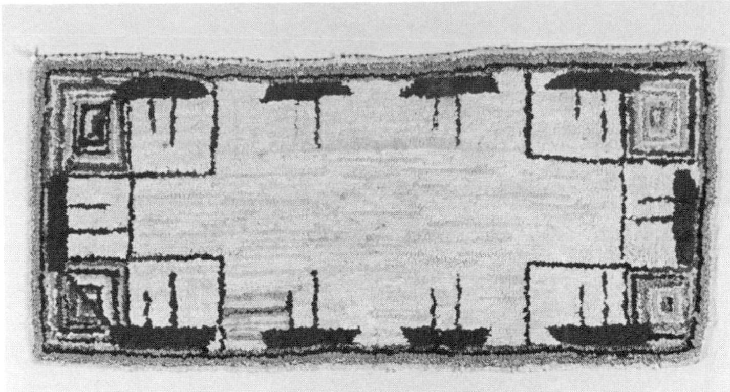

18 Hooked Mat with Two Masted Vessels

Probably Halifax, Halifax County
Cotton rag with some wool rag on burlap sacking
Artist unknown
Circa 1920-1940
Dimensions: 89.0 × 42.0 cm (35 × 16½ inches)
Collection of the Nova Scotia Museum, Halifax, Nova Scotia

This particular mat has a very "folky" appeal in the way the ships are hooked around the outside border. Again it is an example of decorative folk art reflecting the environment of the maker and the seafaring and shipbuilding traditions of Nova Scotia.

Structure: Cotton rag with some wool rag on burlap sacking; looped pile; repeat pattern (around border) of 2-masted vessels (4 each side, 1 across each end); boats are green wool on faded pale blue ground; square in each corner; edge hemmed under after hooking completed.

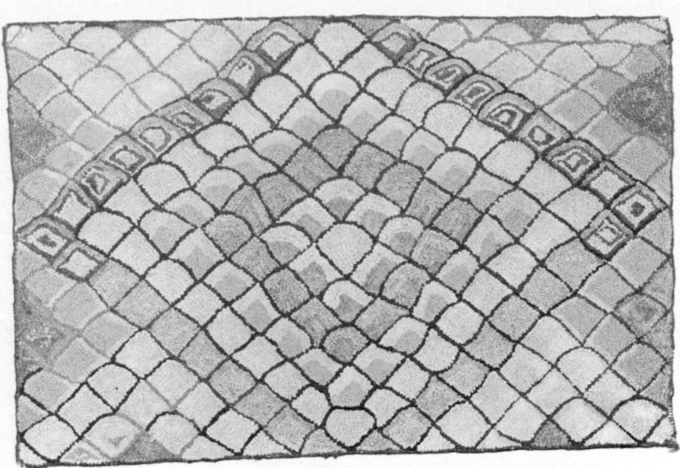

19 Hooked Mat with Multicoloured Geometric Shell Pattern

Halifax, Halifax County
Mostly wool rag on burlap backing
Artist unknown
Circa 1920-1930
Dimensions: 98.5 × 66.0 cm (38¹³⁄₁₆ × 26 inches)
Collection of the Nova Scotia Museum, Halifax, Nova Scotia

There are two examples of this same shell pattern, both by the same maker. Only one has been included in the exhibition. The design has been hooked in such a way as to create an interesting three dimensional tunnel effect.

Structure: Multicoloured geometric design outlined in black. Shell pattern with yellow centre and red diamond; mostly wool rag on burlap; looped pile; bound with brown crochet.

20 Hooked Mat "Home Sweet Home"

Pictou, Pictou County
Wool rag with some cotton rag on a burlap base
Artist unknown
Circa 1920-1930
Dimensions: 134.5 × 91.5 cm (52 15/16 × 36 1/16 inches)
Collection of the Nova Scotia Museum, Halifax, Nova Scotia

An example of a mat with the image of a house and the motto "Home Sweet Home", which reflects the sentiments often found expressed on hooked mats and textiles dating from the first quarter of the twentieth century.

Structure: Black, green and brown border next to a ring of flowers; light beige centre filled in with a brown roofed house and green fence and trees, motto: "Home Sweet Home" hooked in yellow script directly below the house.

21 Hooked Mat

Mahone Bay, Lunenburg County
Wool on burlap backing
Made by Florence Lantz
Dated 1924
Dimensions: 160.0 × 82.0 cm (63 × 32 1/4 inches)
Collection of Murray E. Stewart, Berwick, Nova Scotia

This mat has the letter M and the date 1924 hooked into the border designs, which include a wide variety of lodge symbols representing the Masons and Oddfellows, along with other objects drawn from everyday experience, including a duck, flag, anchor, umbrella, lighthouse and steamship. It is quite possible that this work falls into the category of "autobiographical rug", so called because the maker filled the rug with objects, symbols and numbers that have a special personal meaning.[1] It is uncertain why the 'M' is hooked into the design, unless this was the initial of the owner for whom the mat was made, or the maiden initial of the artist, or perhaps it stands for 'Mason'.

Structure: The mat appears never to have been used in a high traffic area, or perhaps was made and simply put in storage. The wool is very tightly hooked with 80 "knots" per square inch. The edge of the burlap backing is bordered with unbleached cotton sewn to the burlap.

1. For other examples of contemporary "autobiographical rugs" see, Joel and Kate Kopp, *American Hooked and Sewn Rugs: Folk Art Underfoot,* (New York: E.P. Dutton & Co., Inc., 1975), pp. 120-121.

22 Hooked Mat with Diamond Pattern

Mahone Bay, Lunenburg County
Wool rag with small amount of cotton rag on burlap
Artist unknown
Circa 1930-1940
Dimensions: 92.7 × 94.0 cm (36½ × 37 inches)
Collection of the Nova Scotia Museum, Halifax, Nova Scotia

A very colourful mat using zig-zag lines crossing diagonally to form diamonds.

Structure: Wool and small amount of cotton rag on burlap. The mat is in good condition.

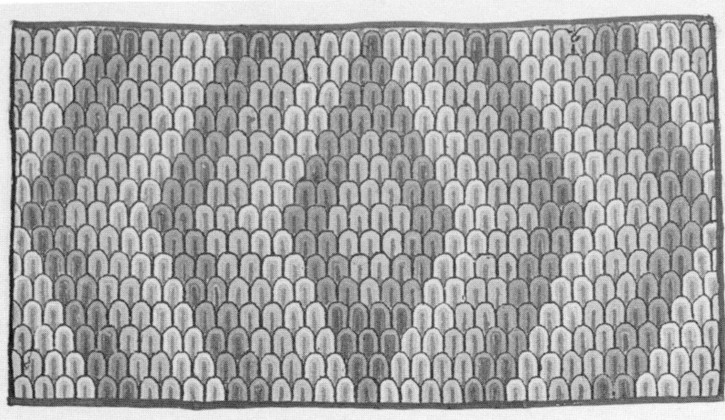

23 Hooked Mat with Fish-Scale Motif

East Chester, Lunenburg County
Wool yarn on burlap
Artist unknown
Circa 1930-1940
Dimensions: 135.0 × 74.0 cm (53³⁄₁₆ × 29⅛ inches)
Collection of the Nova Scotia Museum, Halifax, Nova Scotia

This particular pattern is also known as clam-shell and is commonly found throughout Nova Scotia. Although this particular mat is late, earlier examples dating from the turn of the century are known, particularly from the South Shore of the Province.

Structure: Looped pile; green, red and beige fish scales outlined in black; set in a radiating diamond pattern; black cotton binding.

24 Hooked Mat with Flower Basket

New Glasgow, Pictou County
Cotton and wool rag on burlap
Artist unknown
Circa 1930-1940
Dimensions: 86.0 × 136.0 cm (31⅞ × 53½ inches)
Collection of the Nova Scotia Museum, Halifax, Nova Scotia

Although one of the latest examples of hooked mats in this show, dating from the beginning of the second quarter of the twentieth century, this mat nonetheless retains the dynamic design and decorative spirit of earlier hooked mats.

Structure: Cotton and wool rag on burlap. The hooking is coarse and typical of examples dating from circa 1930.

25 Shaking-Hands Sail-Cloth Mat

Lunenburg County
Painted and decorated sail-cloth
Artist unknown
Circa 1860-1880
Dimensions: 148.0 × 55.0 cm (58¼ × 21⅝ inches)
Collection of Chris Huntington, Hamm's Hill, Nova Scotia

This sail-cloth mat is probably one of the best examples known of this decorative folk art form. The central compass star motif and painted multi-coloured scalloped border are complemented by two shaking-hand motifs, probably reflecting a hands-across-the-border or hands-across-the-ocean theme between American, Canadian and British sailors during the last quarter of the nineteenth century.

Sail-cloth mats were traditionally used on board the Grand Banks fishing schooners as floor mats next to the sleeping bunks or hammocks. Although they are mostly found along the South Shore of Nova Scotia, examples are known from New Brunswick as well. Their origins probably lie in the painted domestic floor coverings, and painted sea-chest coverings of the nineteenth century. Decorated examples of sail-cloth mats are still found in use as floor coverings in Lunenburg County homes.

Structure: The mat is in excellent condition, decorated with oil paint on sail-cloth.

26 Sail-Cloth Mat "Home Again"
Blockhouse, Lunenburg County
Painted cotton sail-cloth
Artist unknown
Circa 1880-1890
Dimensions: 122.0 × 56.0 cm (48 × 22 inches)
Collection of the Nova Scotia Museum, Halifax, Nova Scotia

An example of a sail-cloth mat expressing the sentiment of sailors at sea. The "Home Again" slogan is one often found on nautical folk art and is incorporated into sailors' valentines brought back from voyages to the Caribbean Islands.

Structure: Painted sail-cloth which is made from heavy sail-cloth canvas.

27 Sail-Cloth Mat with Flower Pot
Lunenburg, Lunenburg County
Painted sail-cloth
Artist unknown
Circa 1890-1910
Dimensions: 127.0 × 56.0 cm (50 × 22 inches)
Collection of the National Museum of Man, Canadian Centre for Folk Culture Studies (Gerald Ferguson Collection), Ottawa, Ontario

A good example of a painted sail-cloth with floral motifs in blue and grey with red, yellow and green border frame.

Structure: There is some fading along the edges and corners.

28 Sail-Cloth Mat

Lunenburg County
Painted sailcloth with knotted ends
Artist unknown
Circa 1890-1920
Dimensions: 138.0 × 56.0 cm ($54\frac{5}{16}$ × $22\frac{1}{16}$ inches)
Collection of Joseph Schneider House, Kitchener, Ontario

This is one of the most important examples of a sail-cloth mat known. The central motif of a compass rose painted in red and yellow is surrounded by four "flying" swastikas in the corners, and an over-all border of intersecting half-circles forming a scallop-type pattern. The ends of the mat are knotted and stained with red madder. The overall background is a putty green colour.

Structure: A single piece of sail-cloth painted in various shades of red, yellow, green, and blue. The ends are knotted and tied into groups of fringes with nine strands per grouping.

Published: Michael Bird and Terry Kobayashi, *A Splendid Harvest: Germanic Folk and Decorative Arts in Canada,* (Toronto: Van Nostrand Reinhold, Ltd., 1981), p. 46.

Refer to colour plate III, page 12

29 Sail-Cloth Mat of Schooner

Lunenburg, Lunenburg County
Painted sail-cloth with knotted and painted border
Artist unknown
Circa 1900-1930
Dimensions: 50.0 × 94.0 cm ($19\frac{11}{16}$ × 37 inches)
Collection of Carl Boswick, Halifax, Nova Scotia

An example of a pictorial sail-cloth mat found in the town of Lunenburg.

Structure: A single piece of sail-cloth painted in various oil colours including black, orange and yellow. The border is knotted and painted white.

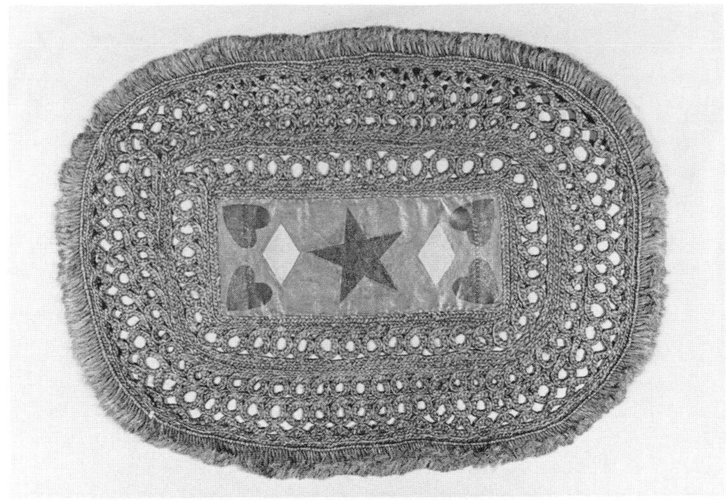

30 Sail-Cloth Mat

Lunenburg, Lunenburg County

Painted sail-cloth with knotted hemp border

Made by Johnson Conrad

1920

Dimensions: 120.0 × 84.0 cm (47¼ × 33$^{1}/_{16}$ inches)

Collection of Chris Huntington, Hamm's Hill, Nova Scotia

This particular mat was made by Johnson Conrad in 1920 on a trip from St. Georges, Bermuda, while serving on board the Bernie Zinck,[1] which sailed out of Lunenburg. According to family tradition he made twenty of these mats while on the return voyage, with this the only surviving example known. This mat combines the art of painted sail-cloth, which according to custom was used as a floor covering by seamen beside their bunks while on board ship, with the typical sailor's art of knotting. It is difficult to determine whether this group of mats was made as a token of friendship and love to be given as gifts once in port, or were meant to be used in the home by friends and family of Johnson Conrad. It is obvious from the condition of this example that it was not used on the floor, or if it was, in an area of low traffic.

The painted decorations are typical of the motifs found on other sail-cloth mats from Lunenburg County, and in general on the decorative arts of the Lunenburg-Germans. It is also an example of just how persistant the decorative traditions of this ethnic group were, this mat dating from 1920, with other examples being made as late as the second quarter of the twentieth century also incorporating similar geometric designs. Sail-cloth mats are rarely found outside of Nova Scotia, with New Brunswick providing some examples, and seems to be mostly a Lunenburg-South Shore tradition in their function as floor coverings on board ship and in the home. Sail-cloth was commonly used as a covering on the lids of sea-chests, and these were often painted with various decorations and names, but this custom is more wide-spread, being found not only in the Atlantic provinces but Maine and New England as well.[2]

Structure: The mat was probably never used as a floor covering. The sail-cloth is sewn to the hemp border which is in turn composed of various decorative sections also sewn together. The decorations are executed in an oil-base paint using red, green and yellow colours on a grey ground. The underside of the sail-cloth is also painted grey.

1. Probably the Bernice Zinck listed in the 1918 *Department of Marine and Fisheries List for Canada* (Ottawa: Government of Canada, 1918) on page 117 as sailing out of Lunenburg. *Lloyd's Registry of Shipping* for 1927-1928 lists the Bernice Zinck as a wood schooner of 100 tons built and owned by Smith and Rhuland of Lunenburg and Captained by J. Lohnes.
2. There are exceptions to this general statement about sail-cloth mats. For an example from Maine see Robert Bishop, *Folk Painters of America,* (New York: E.P. Dutton, 1979), p. 50 (figure 61). It is difficult to determine from the information given if the provenance for this mat is based on sound data. This particular mat could certainly have easily been found in Lunenburg County, and Captain Rumill who is said to have made it for his young wife shortly after marriage, certainly has a Germanic name, which could be a variation or bastardization of Rahmig or Rhuland which are common Lunenburg surnames.

31 White Cotton Quilt with Floral Wreaths

Torbrook, Annapolis County

White cotton

Made by either Mrs Ezekial Foster (married 1821) or her daughter (in law ?), Mrs Andrew Foster

Circa 1870-1890

Dimensions: 213.4 × 203.2 cm (84 × 80 inches)

Collection of the Nova Scotia Museum, Halifax, Nova Scotia

This white quilt, dating from the mid-nineteenth century, has a central four-sided figure of diamonds with a background of "stipple" quilting. At the sides and corners are pineapple motifs outlined with a line cable and a border motif of scrolled plumes.

Structure: White cotton. The quilting lines are spaced about one-half inch apart. The original binding has been replaced.

32 Bisquit Quilt

Mahone Bay, Lunenburg County
Cotton and silk on cotton backing
Made by Anna Victoria Strum
Prior to 1877
Dimensions: 158.0 × 135.5 cm ($62\frac{3}{16} \times 53\frac{3}{8}$ inches)
Collection of the DesBrisay Museum, Bridgewater, Nova Scotia

Referred to as a "bisquit" quilt, because it is made of alternating dark and light squares of plain and printed silk stuffed with "puffs" of cotton, this example was probably used as a child's bed covering.

It was made by Anna Victoria Strum of Mahone Bay, who was born in 1853, prior to her marriage to Daniel Ritcey in 1877. After her marriage she relocated with her husband to Winchester, Massachusetts.

History: The quilt was donated by Mildred Feindel of Bridgewater, Nova Scotia in 1976.

Structure: Cotton and silk on cotton backing. As might be expected with a textile of this delicacy, it is damaged in areas, particular the silk, which has simply worn out through the years of obvious use. No restoration has been attempted except to protect the quilt with a permanent display structure.

33 Signature Quilt

Yarmouth County
Patchwork cotton on cotton backing
Made by the Women's Institute of the Holy Trinity Anglican Church of Yarmouth
Dated 1881-1882
Dimensions: 198.0 × 165.0 cm (78 × 65 inches)
Collection of the Yarmouth County Museum, Yarmouth, Nova Scotia

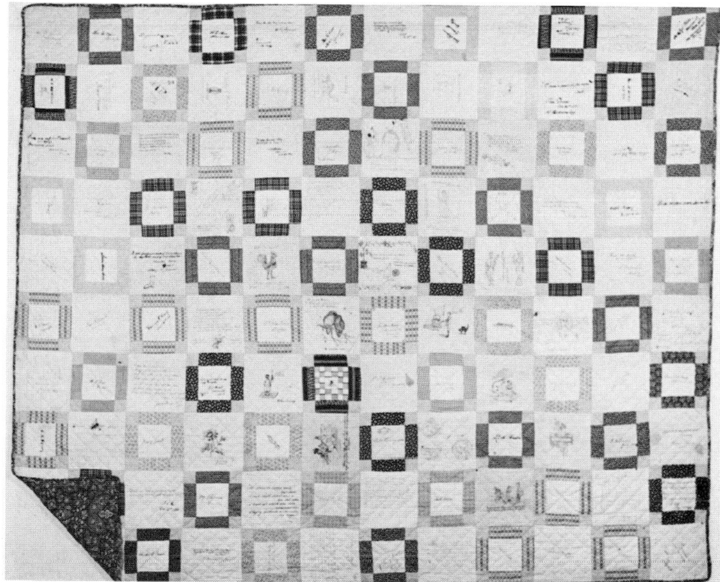

This quilt is made of 120 squares of patchwork, each square autographed by a prominent man or woman, sometimes with drawings depicting their occupation or with proverbial sayings of Yarmouth between 1881 and 1882. It was made by the Women's Institute of the Holy Trinity Church to raise money for the missions.

History: This quilt was donated by Mrs Anna Spicer in 1972 to the Yarmouth County Musuem.

Structure: The autographs and drawings are written in ink directly on the cotton squares. The quilt is made from a combination of multi-patterned cotton fabrics on a solid white cotton backing.

Exhibited: Early Nova Scotia Quilts and Coverlets, Dalhousie Art Gallery, Halifax, Nova Scotia, November 26, 1981 to January 3, 1982.

Published: Mern O'Brien, *Early Nova Scotia Quilts and Coverlets,* (Halifax: Dalhousie Art Gallery, 1981), p. 16.

34 Crazy Quilt

Wolfville, Kings County
Cotton on cotton backing with lace border
Initialed H.L.T.
Dated 1885
Dimensions: 154.0 × 156.0 cm ($60\frac{5}{8} \times 61\frac{7}{16}$ inches)
Collection of the Nova Scotia Museum, Halifax, Nova Scotia

Crazy quilts are one of the most abstract types of textiles and decorative folk art produced during the ninteenth century. Recognized as a specific pattern, crazy quilts were often made from odd pieces of cloth not suitable for making other quilt patterns due to size, shape, or fabric colour. This particular example is initialed H.L.T. and dated 1885.

Structure: Odd pieces of solid and multi-coloured fabric appliquéd to a red cotton (satin) backing. The lace border appears handmade.

Refer to colour plate I, page 11

35 Star of Bethlehem Quilt

Chester, Lunenburg County
Multi-patterned cottons on cotton backing
Made by Rebecca Crandall Irvine
Circa 1880-1900
Dimensions: 244.0 × 240.0 cm ($96 \times 94\frac{1}{2}$ inches)
Collection of the DesBrisay Museum, Bridgewater, Nova Scotia

The Star of Bethlehem quilt pattern is one of the more popular designs of the late nineteenth and early twentieth century quiltmakers.[1]

History: Donated by Ianthe Irving to the DesBrisay Museum in 1967.

Structure: Multi-patterned cottons on cotton backing.

1. For a similar quilt from Lunenburg County see Mern O'Brien, *Early Nova Scotia Quilts and Coverlets,* (Halifax: Dalhousie Art Gallery, 1981), p. 8 (figure 3). This is an exhibition catalogue of a show of Nova Scotia quilts mounted at the Dalhousie Art Gallery from November 26, 1981 to January 3, 1982.

   For other examples of Star of Bethlehem quilts see, Carleton L. Safford and Robert Bishop, *America's Quilts and Coverlets,* (New York: E.P. Dutton, 1980), pp. 100-101, 103-105, 113, 117, 119, 121, 128.

   Ruth McKendry, *Quilts and Other Bed Coverings in the Canadian Tradition,* (Toronto: Van Nostrand Reinhold Ltd., 1979), pp. 136, 138-139.

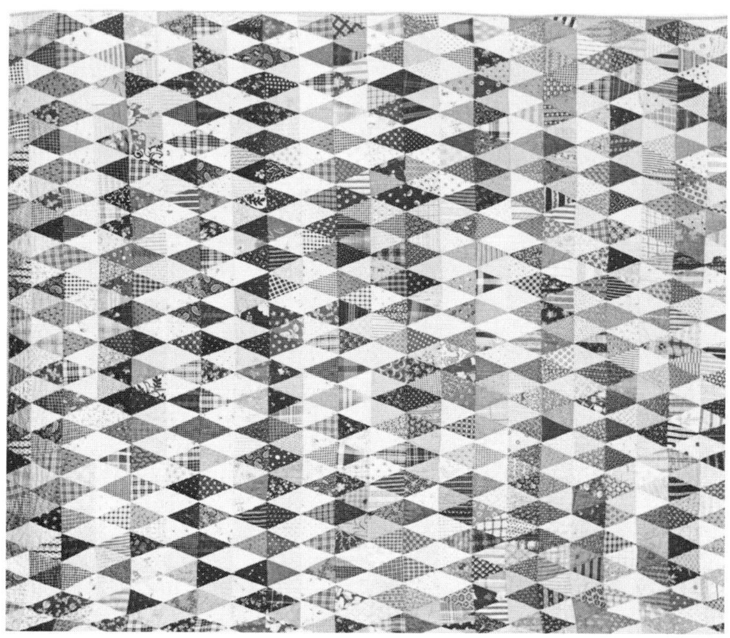

36 Charm Quilt *Diamond Quilt*

Darling Lake, Yarmouth County

Multi-patterned cotton on plain cotton backing

Made by Lillian W. Ellis (b. March 27, 1877/ d. June 23, 1939)

Circa 1900-1910

Dimensions: 230.0 × 192.0 cm (90½ × 75⅝ inches)

Collection of Yarmouth County Museum, Yarmouth, Nova Scotia

A very intricate and detailed quilt made of multi-coloured fabrics in red, brown, beige and blue.

History: This quilt was donated by Miss Josephine Ellis of Brooklin, Massachusetts to the Yarmouth County Museum.

Structure: The multi-patterned and coloured cotton fabrics of the quilt top are backed with a plain cotton.

Exhibited: Early Nova Scotia Quilts and Coverlets, Dalhousie Art Gallery, Halifax, Nova Scotia, November 26, 1981 to January 3, 1982.

Published: Mern O'Brien, *Early Nova Scotia Quilts and Coverlets,* (Halifax: Dalhousie Art Gallery, 1981), p. 14.

37 Quilt *Tulip*[1] *and Leaf**

Maplewood, Lunenburg County

Red and green polished cotton appliqué on white cotton top and backing

Maker unknown

Circa 1900-1920

Dimensions: 186.0 × 191.0 cm (73¼ × 75³⁄₁₆ inches)

Collection of Richard Henning Field and Deborah Field, Halifax, Nova Scotia

This quilt is made entirely of red and green cotton fabrics which are appliquéd to individual white cotton squares that are sewn together along the edges and quilted. The absence of filling between the quilt top and backing suggests that this was a "summer" bed covering. The overall tulip and leaf design is bold and dramatic creating a powerful textile design.

Structure and Condition: The quilt is slightly faded along one edge where it was obviously exposed to strong sunlight which affected the dyed colours of the fabrics. There is as well some small brown circular stains scattered throughout the quilt.

1. This design has also been called rose and leaf. For similar quilt motifs see Carlton L. Safford and Robert Bishop, *America's Quilts and Coverlets,* (New York: E.P. Dutton, 1980). pp. 192 (figure 282), 196 (figure 293).

*This piece will be on view in Halifax only.

38 Red and White Quilt *Fisherman's Reel*

Shelburne County
Cotton on cotton backing
Artist unknown
Circa 1930
Dimensions: 183.0 × 178.0 cm (72 × 70⅛ inches)
Collection of Scott Robson, Halifax, Nova Scotia

An example of a red and white quilt pattern. This is an "everyday" quilt typical of many of the quilted bed coverings made as simple and very useful utilitarian objects lending warmth, pattern and colour to a bedroom.

Structure: Cotton on white cotton backing. The quilt is in good condition.

39 Overshot Curtain or Coverlet *Sunrise Variation*

Lunenburg County
Wool weft and natural cotton warp
Artist unknown
Circa 1865-1885
Dimensions: 254.0 × 107.0 cm (100 × 42⅛ inches)
Collection of the Nova Scotia Museum, Halifax, Nova Scotia

According to Burnham and Burnham (p. 195) this is one of two similar pieces, wider and longer than normal, that may have been woven as curtains, a use for overshot that is known from the Maritime Provinces in the late nineteenth century. This pattern is often called "Sunburst or Horse Blanket" suggesting that these vibrating designs were popular for the wool storm blankets used in sleighs.

Structure: Overshot coverlet (in two pieces); dark blue wool weft, natural cotton harp. Lineal border along both sides and a 17.8 cm border of bars and "V's" along one end; ends hemmed.

Published: Harold B. Burnham and Dorothy K. Burnham, *"Keep Me Warm One Night": Early Handweaving in Eastern Canada,* (Toronto: University of Toronto Press, 1972), p. 195.

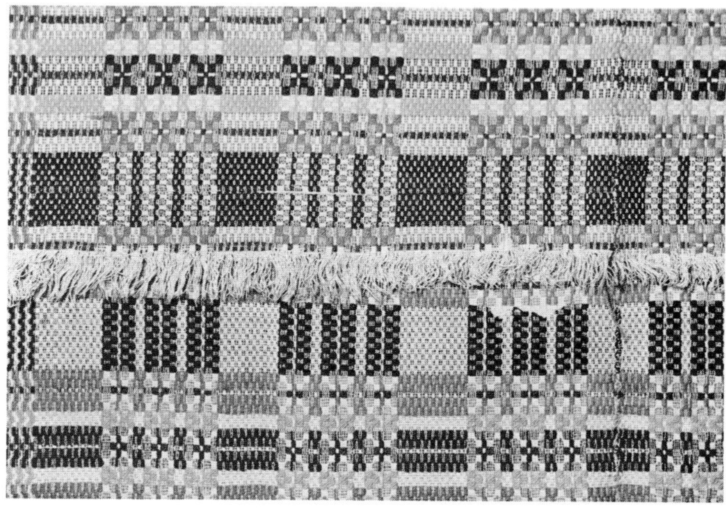

40 Overshot Coverlet

Windsor, Hants County
Natural cotton warp with wool weft
Artist unknown
Circa 1880-1910
Dimensions: 182.9 × 152.4 cm (72 × 60 inches)
Collection of the Nova Scotia Museum, Halifax, Nova Scotia

As usual with coverlets of this type, it is made from two woven sections and joined in the centre. In this case, however, one section was cut short to match the other so an extra 7.6 cm was added on the horizontal seam. This is often referred to as an overshot coverlet because the technique employed in making these coverlets uses a plain ground (usually cotton) over which shoots an extra pattern of wool.

Structure: Natural cotton warp with an overshot pattern of wool. Each section measures 72.6 cm wide. One end is bound, the other is unravelling.

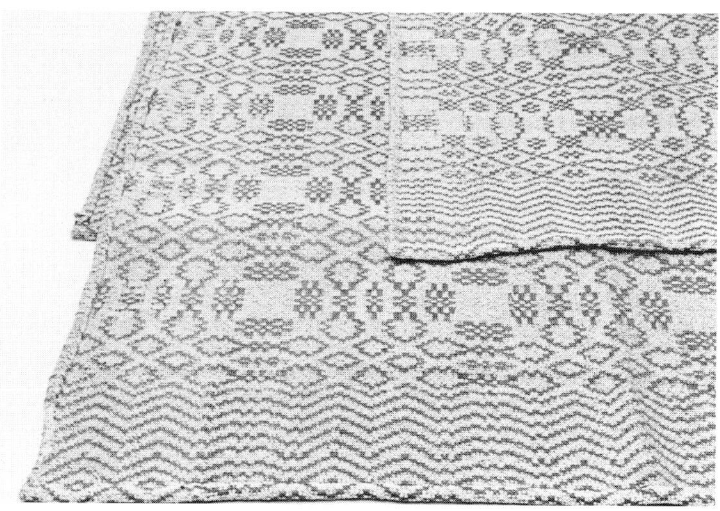

41 Overshot Coverlet

Pictou County
All wool warp and weft
Artist unknown
Circa 1860-1880
Dimensions: 210.0 × 154.0 cm ($82^{13}/_{16}$ × $60^{5}/_{8}$ inches)
Collection of the Nova Scotia Museum, Halifax, Nova Scotia

It is unusual to find wool warp in overshot coverlets.

Structure: Indigo blue on dull nondescript colour (probably natural dye from bark and leaves); centre seam; hemmed 4 sides.

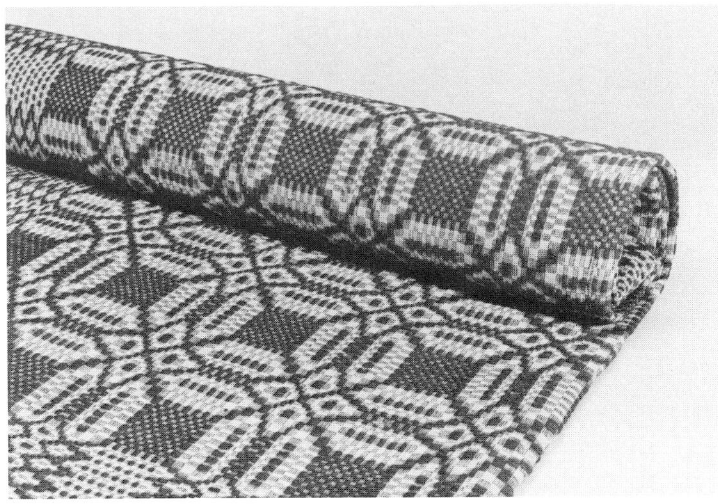

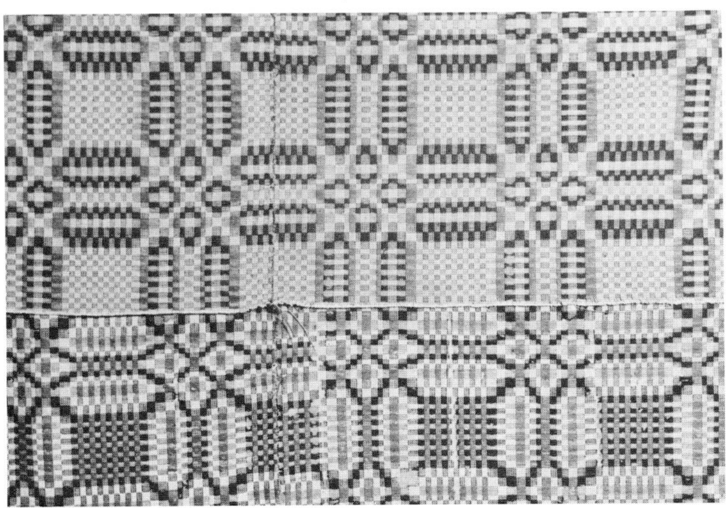

42 Overshot Coverlet *Monmouth Pattern*

Cookville, Lunenburg County
Hand woven overshot coverlet of wool and cotton
Attributed to Mrs Simeon Cook
Circa 1880-1890
Dimensions: 200.0 × 178.0 cm (78¾ × 70$^{1}/_{16}$ inches)
Collection of the DesBrisay Museum, Bridgewater, Nova Scotia

The pattern of this coverlet has been found in Cape Breton and Lunenburg County, and is also common to New Brunswick, Chateauguay County in Quebec, and Ontario. It is possible that this pattern is named after the Duke of Monmouth, son of Charles II, who was beheaded following his unsuccessful Rebellion against his uncle, James II, in 1685. He married the Countess of Buccleuch and was long remembered in Scotland even after his fate.[1]

History: The coverlet was donated to the DesBisay Museum in 1978 by Miss Lydia Langille of Lunenburg County.

Structure: The coverlet is woven with a red wool pattern weft and natural cotton warp and weft. The ends are hemmed.

1. Harold B. Burnham and Dorothy K. Burnham, *"Keep Me Warm One Night": Early Handweaving in Eastern Canada,* (Toronto: University of Toronto Press, 1972), p. 200.

43 Handwoven Floor Carpet *Chariot Wheels*

Queens County
Natural cotton warp and weft with handspun wool pattern weft (2 ply)
Artist unknown
Circa 1860-1880
Dimensions: 190.0 × 158.0 cm (74$^{13}/_{16}$ × 62$^{3}/_{16}$ inches)
Collection of the Nova Scotia Museum, Halifax, Nova Scotia

This section of a woven floor covering is dyed in red and dark brown-green and woven in two strips joined in the centre. One end is bound with homespun material while the other end has been cut and is frayed.

Structure: Heavy natural cotton warp and weft with 2 ply handspun wool pattern weft.

The Talcott Family
Probably Hamilton, New York area
Watercolour and pencil on wove paper
Deborah Goldsmith, (1808-1836)
Circa 1832
Dimensions: 36.2 × 45.1 cm (14¼ × 17¾ inches)
Photograph courtesy of Colonial Williamsburg, Abby Aldrich Rockefeller Folk Art Centre, Williamsburg, Virginia.

This portrait is considered Deborah Goldsmith's most ambitious and important work, and is valued for its documentation of costume and furnishings. Note the pattern of the floor covering, showing how these woven carpets were used within the domestic interior.

This piece is not included in the exhibition.

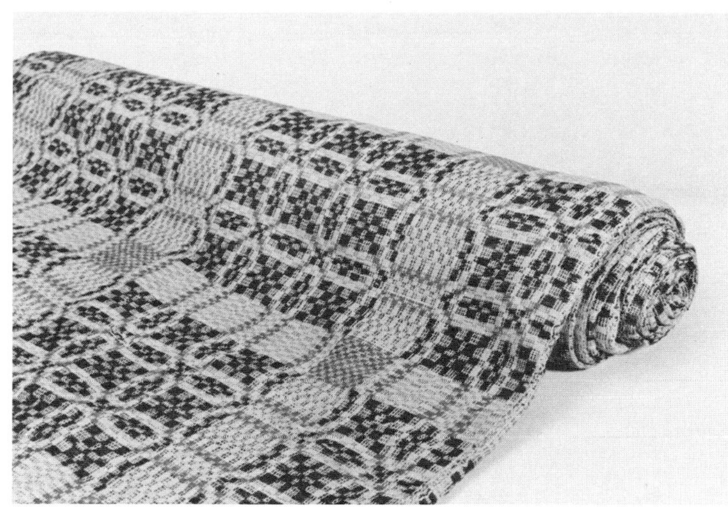

44 Woven Floor Covering

Hopewell, Pictou County
Handspun wool and cotton ground
Artist unknown
Circa 1870-1890
Dimensions: 396.0 × 259.0 cm (155⅞ × 102 inches)
Collection of the Nova Scotia Museum, Halifax, Nova Scotia

This overshot carpet is woven in three strips and is typical of the textile floor coverings found throughout the Maritime Provinces from the mid to late nineteenth century.

Structure: Handwoven overshot carpet woven in 3 strips; handspun blue wool and red wool forming a pattern of 9-star blocks on orange cotton ground; 9-star sections, blue; table sections, red; pattern thread, single ply wool; warp threads, 2-ply cotton; weft tabby threads; double 1-ply cotton.

45 Sampler *Sophia Cogszell*

Halifax, Halifax County
Silk and wool on linen
Made by Sophia Cogszell
Circa 1800-1820
Dimensions: 50.0 × 44.5 cm (19¹¹⁄₁₆ × 15½ inches)
Collection of the Nova Scotia Museum, Halifax, Nova Scotia

A very colourful sampler embellished with baskets of flowers, trees, and crowns combined with hearts. The verse is an adaptation of an epigram on providence, which appeared as early as 1731 on a Philadelphia sampler.[1]

Structure: Silk and wool on linen. The sampler is damaged along the borders at various places and in three of the corners.

1. Ethel Stanwood Bolton and Eva Johnson Coe, *American Samplers,* (Boston: The Massachusetts of Colonial Dames of America, 1921), pp. 53, 297.

46 Sampler *Susan Caroline Randall*

Halifax (?), Halifax County
Silk on linen
Made by Susan Caroline Randall
Circa 1838
Dimensions: 43.0 × 43.7 cm ($17\frac{15}{16} \times 17\frac{1}{4}$ inches)
Collection of the Nova Scotia Museum, Halifax, Nova Scotia

The verse reads; *"The judge of all will soon come down*
Bright on His everlasting throne
Summon the nations to his bar
And I shall take my trial there"

As with many samplers the verse is spiritual in nature, usually reflecting the folly of life and the inevitable Last Judgement which is sure to follow.

Structure: Silk on linen. There are some small tears in the upper left hand corner.

47 Sampler *Mary Clark Harris*

Clements, Annapolis County
Silk on linen
Made by Mary Clark Harris
Dated March 2, 1836
Dimensions: 41.0 × 43.1 cm ($16\frac{1}{8} \times 17$ inches)
Private collection

The inscription reads, "Sampler work by Mary Clark Harris in the 20th year of her age in Clements Bear River County of Annapolis 3 March 1836 under the tuition of Miss Sarah Cridley". It is unusual to have a sampler made by a woman of age 20. Most samplers were accomplished by young ladies who had not reached this 'mature' age, such as that of her sister Henrietta who made the sampler that follows in her 14th year. This suggests that at age 20 Mary remained unmarried.

Structure: Silk on linen. The sampler is in excellent condition.

48 Sampler *Henrietta Harris*
Clements, Annapolis County
Silk on linen
Made by Henrietta Harris
Dated March 14, 1836
Dimensions: 40.9 × 42.3 cm (16⅛ × 16⅝ inches)
Private collection

The inscription reads, "Sampler work by Henrietta Harris in the 14 year of her age born Sept' the 14 1822 in Clements Bear River County of Annapolis 14 March AD 1836 under the tuition of Miss Sarah Cridley". As with the preceding example, also made under the instruction of Miss Cridley, the most important element in this sampler is the building. One of these could represent the school house where Miss Cridley taught, a local meeting house or other structure important to the local community.

Since both samplers are dated only 14 days apart, one can assume that sisters, Mary Harris and Henrietta Harris,[1] were in the same class although perhaps in a different age group. A check of records has not led to any identification of who Miss Cridley was, other than the fact that she taught needlepoint to young ladies in the Clements/Bear River area in the year 1836.

Structure: Silk on linen. The sampler is in excellent condition.

1. Their grandfather Henry Harris was born in 1757. In 1783 he married Elizabeth Hall. Their second child was Joseph (b. 1785) who married Elizabeth Clark. The third child born was Mary Clark who married Isacc Beals (b. 1815). The fourth child born was Henrietta who married William H. Dunn. (W. A. Calnek and A.W. Savary, *History of the County of Annapolis,* (Toronto: Briggs, 1897), p. 522. Reprinted by Mika (in 1973.)

49 Sampler *Anges Elizabeth Blytner*
Probably Lunenburg County
Cotton on cotton
Made by Anges Elizabeth Blytner
Dated 1856
Dimensions: 30.0 × 32.5 cm (11$^{13}/_{16}$ × 12¾ inches)
Collection of the DesBrisay Museum, Bridgewater, Nova Scotia

The earliest samplers were made as ready reference works on the types of stitches a women could employ. Some of the earliest New England samplers, dating from the late seventeenth century, incorporate a vast array of stitches.[1] By the end of the seventeenth century, samplers assumed a larger role in the life of a young lady, acting both as examples of her accomplishment in needlework, and as an indication that she was ready for marriage. According to Toni Flores Fratto, it was for this very reason that samplers were never fully explored as an art form on the part of their makers. Because they were such an important part of the socialization process of young women prior to marriage, they were judged on their conformity, restraint and sentimentality.[2]

This particular example is one of the simplest forms of samplers, comprised of numbers and alphabets in upper and lower case, rendered in various types of stitches. Dated 1856, it is a late example, and was probably executed on commercially available sampler linen, judging by the faint verticle blue lines. These lines could be used to plan the location of the letters and numbers, and therefore avoid space problems often found on "free-hand" samplers.

Structure: Cotton on cotton. The sampler is slightly faded probably due to exposure to strong sunlight.

1. For an example of an early sampler with a vast array of stitches dated 1678, see C. Kurt Dewhurst, Betty MacDowell and Marsha MacDowell, *Artists in Aprons: Folk Art by American Women,* (New York: E.P. Dutton, 1979), p. 2 (figure 2).
2. Toni Flores Fratto, "Samplers: One of the Lesser American Arts," In *The Feminist Art Journal,* Volume 5, No. 4 (Winter 1973), p. 12.
See also C. Kurt Dewhurst, Betty MacDowell and Marsha MacDowell, *Ibid,* p. 14.

50 Appliquéd Tablecover *Penny Mat*

Yarmouth or Annapolis County

Cotton circles appliquéd to white cotton with light brown tabby weave backing

Artist unknown

Circa 1880-1900

Dimensions: 76.0 × 64.0 cm ($29^{15}/_{16}$ × $25^{3}/_{16}$ inches)

Collection of the Nova Scotia Museum, Halifax, Nova Scotia

This tablecover is a remnant from a much larger piece, and is one of the best examples of this textile form.

Structure: Nineteen groups of 3 appliquéd circles superimposed with buttonhole stitch and applied to a hexagonal piece of white cotton; rows of hexagons alternate with rows of diamonds; 9 applied groups in a variety of dull colours (reds, browns, blues). It is backed with light brown tabby weave with narrow strips of darker brown; blue binding.

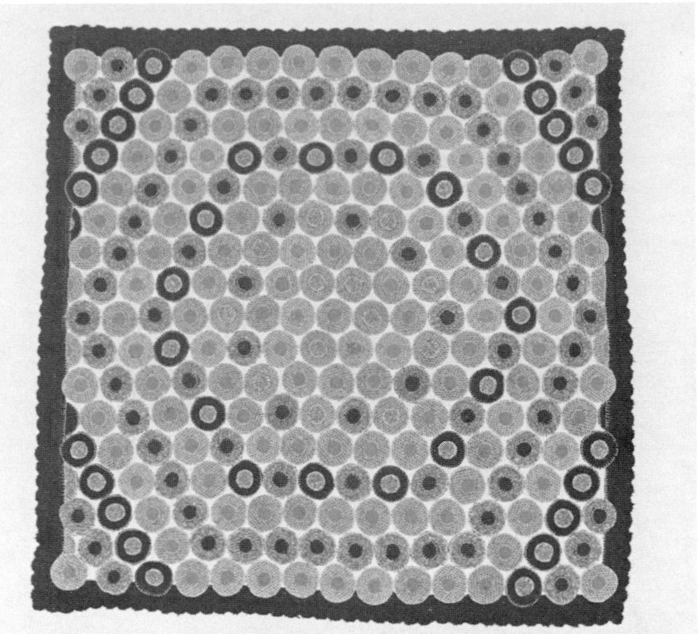

51 Table Mat

Probably Annapolis County

Sewn and appliquéd cotton and wool on cotton backing

Artist unknown

Circa 1890-1910

Dimensions: 77.0 × 76.0 cm ($30^{5}/_{16}$ × $29^{7}/_{8}$ inches)

Collection of Jerry and Debbie Vidito, Kentville, Nova Scotia

Another fine example of a table mat with a subtle decorative pattern.

Structure: The circles of fabric are applied to the cotton backing which is lined with another cotton cloth, perhaps to stop the mat from "running" on the table.

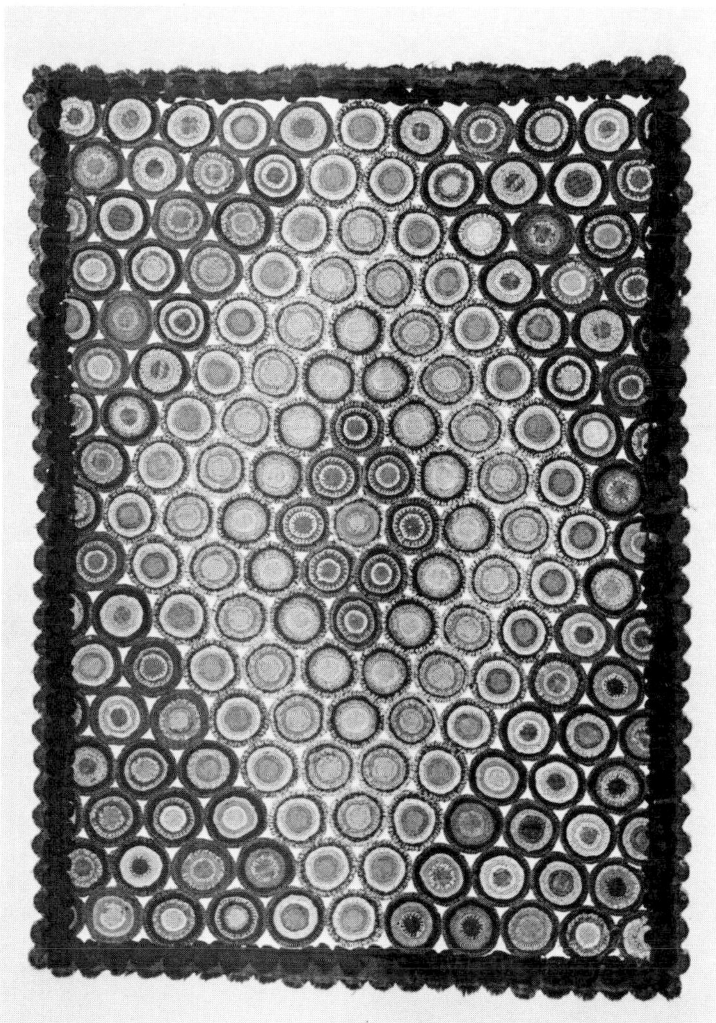

52 Table Mat

Probably Annapolis County
Sewn and appliquéd cotton and wool on cotton backing
Artist unknown
Circa 1900-1920
Dimensions: 110.0 × 78.0 cm ($43\frac{5}{16}$ × $31\frac{11}{16}$ inches)
Collection of Jerry and Debbie Vidito, Kentville, Nova Scotia

A very intricately designed example of a table or penny mat. The design is created using three layers of cotton circles sewn with coarse coloured thread. The double scalloped border adds to the visual complexity of this piece.

Structure: The white cotton backing shows through between the "pennies".

53 Appliquéd Table Mat*

Ohio, Yarmouth County
Appliquéd cotton on wool and cotton with white cotton backing
Artist unknown
Circa 1920
Dimensions: 143.5 × 72.0 cm ($56\frac{1}{2}$ × $28\frac{3}{8}$ inches)
Collection of Richard Henning Field and Deborah Field, Halifax, Nova Scotia

A very interesting table mat with appliquéd tulip and cloverleaf motifs. The alternating dark blue and grey squares add to the richness of this textile.

Structure: Cotton and wool squares sewn together and applied to a white cotton backing. The cloverleaf and tulip designs are in turn sewn onto the grey and blue squares.

*This piece will be on view in Halifax only.

INTRODUCTION

Sculpture

Richard Henning Field

The desire to pick up a piece of wood and whittle or carve it into an object is probably one of the oldest impulses of man. The tradition of carving is one of the most enduring in the field of American and Canadian folk art. Its flowering occurred during the nineteenth century, but was not completely forgotten with the advent of the twentieth century and hand-powered tools. As is evident in this exhibition, decoy carving is still a strong Nova Scotia tradition with roots in the latter half of the nineteenth century, and although the birds carved today no longer attract their wild counterparts for hunting, many fine examples of mergansers, black ducks and whistlers still grace mantlepieces in some homes as examples of contemporary folk art.

Folk sculpture seems to show no common approach within its many diverse forms, and although certain subjects and themes were favorites, most were created for a distinct purpose — to lure the wildfowl from the sky, to mark a grave, indicate wind direction, identify a shop, or grace the bow of a ship. The materials at hand often determined the form and decoration, such as with root head decoys which use the natural bend in a branch to create the illusion of neck and head.

As with decorated utilitarian objects, there is more individualism to be found in folk sculpture than in folk painting or textiles which generally observe unities of pattern, form and style. Although there were specific traditions of carving found in figureheads and shop figures, these tended to be centered in the urban areas. It was in the rural districts where strong individual folk carving flourished.

The sub-categories of sculpture included in the exhibition range from decoys to ship models, dioramas, whirligigs, weathervanes, animal carvings, rocking horses and sailor's valentines. Throughout this material there exists a strong flavor of Nova Scotia captured in the whirligig of a sailor or the diaramas of various sailing vessels. It is in this assessment that the viewer can find a unifying force behind this array of folk carvings. The seafaring and farming traditions of the province are both well represented here in various forms. Although some are more universal in appeal, such as the rooster weathervane, the renditions in this exhibition have firm Nova Scotia provenance and long histories of ownership.

On the other hand items such as the carving of "Blackie" illustrate a more individual interpretation of the all important farm horse, while creating a toy which was in keeping with the occupation of the family, and educational in suggesting to the children that played with it that they too would probably follow in their parents' footsteps.

Folk sculpture is one of the most enduring and popular forms of folk art for two reasons: (1) because of the individuality and eccentricities often expressed in the carving no matter how functional or marginally functional the object may be, and (2) because the human figure is often the subject of the sculpture. There is little doubt that most people have a certain fascination with the carved human form, and that this appeal often increases with the level of eccentricity associated with the piece.

Probably this is one reason that ventriloquists were so popular as forms of entertainment. In the hands of a master, the wooden dummy with a happy or evil face comes alive. The promise of the carved life-like features actually living and talking is fulfilled and the fantasy completed.

The folk sculpture in this exhibition represents a substantial cross-section of the types of objects which could be found in the nineteenth century communities of Nova Scotia. Shop and trade signs were carved with fancy decorative embellishment, usually reflecting the nature of the business it named, weathervanes adorned barns and outbuildings telling both the direction of the wind and the relative velocity, and wooden decoys were carried off in the autumn and spring to take advantage of the migration. A reflection of the common purpose and problems faced by all Nova Scotians which helped to bind them together as a society is exemplified in these folk carvings.

Traditional Nova Scotia Folk Sculpture

Bernard Riordon

Bernard Riordon has been the Curator/ Director with the Art Gallery of Nova Scotia in Halifax since 1973 and is responsible for the development of the Gallery's significant folk art collection.

The folk art of the Province of Nova Scotia reflects the rich diversity of ethnic traditions and the resourcefulness and vivid imagination of its people. The majority of folk sculpture included in the Spirit of Nova Scotia exhibition was created out of necessity whereby a particular object was made for a particular use — a physical and mental activity with form often following function. It was when the work was embellished with special features that the doors to creativity were opened resulting in a true and honest expression of the spirit of our people. Folk sculpture in many cases functioned and evolved from craft traditions with the application of art techniques. Many utilitarian objects were made into a thing of beauty by the vivid imagination and careful execution by our folk artists.

The folk sculptor takes a direct and honest approach to the creation of his art resulting in works of conceptual richness, practical application and astonishing variety. The work of the folk artist has the flavour of an independent spirit expressed through the resourceful use of materials introducing integrity and honesty to the direct solution of technical or aesthetic problems. Technical problems are solved intuitively and in a simplistic manner which becomes part of the appeal of the work. Its vitality and freshness of approach give it a universal appeal. The hallmark of folk art is its individuality which produces a pure art form, unpretentious and natural, created with energy and conviction. In many cases the interpretation is "child-like" but in all cases the end result is a work that contains inherent joy. The folk artists of Nova Scotia commented on the human condition of our people, and by doing this they enriched their own lives and the lives of their family and friends and contributed to the cultural life and heritage of the Province.

Folk sculpture in Nova Scotia grew out of the utilitarian needs and the individual situations in which the settlers to a new land found themselves at any particular time. Immigration patterns in Nova Scotia provided specific craft traditions and skills in particular areas. The diversity added to the richness of our folk art. In the 18th and 19th centuries the influences of British and American society were very great and combined with the many other ethnic groups — integration into a new homogeneous society was slow. The levelling process normally associated with a new frontier environment did not take place quickly and ethnic and religious differences remained for some time. By 1850 a Nova Scotia society began to emerge and an expressive self awareness was prevalent. This was fostered by a prosperous period in Nova Scotia's history and with prosperity, a golden age resulted throughout the Province. It was a time whereby a Nova Scotian spirit was apparent in society and the self-taught or trained carver was in an important and prominent position. Generally, it can be said that no common approach in folk sculpture prevailed in Nova Scotia during the period covered by this exhibition (1780-1930), and the diversity in style and approach added to the richness and appeal of our folk art. Only in the area of ship construction did carving take on a formal and recognizable role and establish a tradition. Examples of figureheads, billetheads, and other vessel ornamentation, such as nameboards, attest to the activity of trained and apprenticeship sculptors in the ship building ports of Nova Scotia.

In early Nova Scotia wood carving was important in helping to shape the everyday lives of the early settlers. Our early inhabitants built their own houses and barns and carving skills were necessary for survival.

Wood was in abundance in Nova Scotia and it did not take long for it to be transformed into sculpture by both self-taught and trained artists. Although early life was crude and humble it did not take long for artistic expression to be introduced into the making of decorative objects for everyday living. The folk sculpture produced in the Province was as varied as the circumstances of the maker. Many individual items were carved and decorated beyond the practical level of what was required in daily living. By embellishing the object with paint or other materials, it was transformed into an item with personality, character and charm.

This creative spirit brought about a whole range of sculpture completed in Nova Scotia in the period from 1780 to 1930 including ship ornamentation, decoys, weathervanes and whirligigs, ship models, toys and a variety of human and animal carvings. Carving was an individual activity often based on the occupation and everyday activity of the maker, and had an additional character when it was made for pleasure and relaxation. As Marie Elwood pointed out in the Nova Scotia folk art exhibition produced by the Art Gallery of Nova Scotia in 1976, (*Folk Art of Nova Scotia* featured works by contemporary twentieth century Nova Scotia folk artists and helped to give due recognition to the art of the ordinary person):

> *"The folk artist tends to work by himself for himself. Into the silent world come people who find an answering pleasure in looking at these works and see pleasure in them. The folk artist approaches the task of carving without an academic knowledge of the craft of sculpture. He solves his many technical problems intuitively and with a simplicity and directness that is part of the approach of his work."*[1]

Much of the inspiration for the folk artist came from the immediate environment and objects were produced from materials which were readily at hand.

Since Nova Scotia and its people have always had an important relationship with the sea, it is very fitting that much early carving was nearly always confined to ship decoration. Shipbuilding was a major industry in Nova Scotia in the 18th and 19th centuries and together with the trade to the American colonies, Great Britain and the West Indies, Nova Scotia prospered. It was in this time of prosperity that the need for woodcarvers was very great. Economic conditions had an important bearing on the development of carving skills in the Province.

Figureheads had a special significance for the ship and its crew, symbolizing the living spirit of the ship and the romance of the sea. So important were these objects to the ship that many captains would refuse to sail without them. They were generally carved out of a single block of wood with the arms and other projecting parts fastened on separately. They were painted in many colours and often had gold leaf and other ornamental detail. The carvers worked with the grain of the wood to make it look natural and to achieve the likeness of the figure. Figureheads were round and massive with an emphasis on anatomy and forceful characterization. They were treated with reverance and respect and oftentimes featured the ship's owner or his wife or the wife of the shipbuilder. Other common figures included noblemen, naval heroes, statesmen and beautiful maidens. In the choice of figures a strong influence of British and American traditions and subjects was evident. One important carver was George Crouse who worked in Queens County. Crouse was born in Milton in 1835 and supplied figureheads and other ship ornaments that were built in Liverpool on the Mersey River. He is responsible for the bust carving of Samuel Kempton. While this is the only existing example of his work, it is an excellent piece of folk sculpture that demonstrates a simplistic and honest approach. The result is the transformation of a piece of wood into a human form that provided joy to his peers and to viewers ever since it was carved in 1853.

Many figurehead carvers also did nameboards and billetheads as well as other ships' ornaments. Nameboards were normally carved in relief and contained the name of the ship and sometimes a pictoral representation of the owner or a member of his family. The nameboard of the *SS Edna R* with Masonic symbol is an example of this type of ship ornamentation.

By 1880 the shipbuildinng industry was in decline thereby initiating the decline of the art of making figureheads. George MacLaren, noted Nova Scotia historian and curator stated in his book on the woodcarvers of Nova Scotia:

> *"As the twentieth century approached more of the native craftsmen who had produced our finest woodcarving had passed on and the figurehead carving by Alfred Nichols for the three-masted schooner Irma Bently and launched at Port Greville, Cumberland County in 1908 appears to be the last created for a local ship."*[2]

Waterfowl hunting played an important role in the everyday lives of many of the settlers to Nova Scotia. The art of how to fool the bird manifested itself in a form of folk art that saw the functional transformed into the aesthetic as decoys were carved for hunters to attract their prey. The decoy-makers concerned themselves with sculptural form and painting qualities.

Decoys in Nova Scotia were often carved out of a block of wood with a drawknife and a jackknife. Normally, the head was carved separately from the body. The most common birds carved in Nova Scotia were waterfowl such as the blackduck, scoter, merganzer and eider. Shorebirds mounted on sticks and put into the sand were less common in the Province. The style and range of birds varied with the particular skill of each individual carver. Some of the decoy carvers whose work is included in the exhibition and who mastered the art are William Rowlings from the Eastern Shore, and Captain Bachman from Lunenburg County. The decoy makers included in the exhibition satisfy the state of the craft on a functional and aesthetic level. Noted Canadian folk art collector Gerald Ferguson described the art of decoy making in the following manner:

> *"Decoys are to ducks as portraits are to people. They vary in style considerably. This is the most elementary observation anyone can make when viewing decoys for just one sub species. They range from the most rudimentary to the finest most detailed carving and paint work. While the decoy-maker is primarily concerned with attracting ducks, the making activity is inevitably transformed into a pleasure generating one. Specific characteristics of style in painting and sculptural form, and varying degrees of versimilitude emerge."*[3]

With the change of duck hunting in the twentieth century from a necessity to a sport, decoy-making became a dying art. Fortunately a few individuals continued the tradition and passed it on to others. These masterpieces are excellent examples of traditional decorative folk art in Nova Scotia.

A very useful form of sculpture is the weathervane. Weathervanes were essential for our ancestors to predict the weather in order to organize activities such as the planning of a voyage by sail and were executed on a large scale. Weathervanes were very popular in Nova Scotia during the period covered by the exhibition. Many subjects were used and in many ways were inspired by the special and local interest of the people in a particular area or region of the Province. Subjects included arrows, Indians, horses and other domestic animals and fish of various kinds. The techniques for carving were as varied as the subjects. They were made with chisels or cut from plans, and most often painted or gilded for protection and decoration. Metal vanes were cut from a flat sheet of metal such as copper or zinc. The Rooster weathervane included in the exhibition and attributed to John Oliver is a good example showing the skilled hand of the folk artist at work. Weathervanes in Nova Scotia were placed on barns, houses, churches and other buildings, and in some cases were used as trade signs. The effect which exposure to the elements had on weathervanes added to the character, creating interesting colouration and providing a special effect which adds to the appreciation of the object as a piece of folk art. By the 1880's mass produced factory weathervanes were replacing original hand crafted works.

While weathervanes were made for indicating wind direction, whirligigs were made for enjoyment and amusement. They were and still are a common area of individual expression. The lively movement of these windtoys showed innovation by the folk artist, and the subject depicted a story taken from the everyday life of the common person. They vary from single figure whirligigs with rotating arms to multifigure pieces that have a maze of rods and gears. Those objects are a true form of folk art expression combining marginal functional use provided by windpower with decorative embellishment. Subjects in the exhibition include a tin man, a soldier and a sailor which span the period from 1850 to 1930.

Other works in the exhibition which show the versatility of Nova Scotia folk artists are toys such as 'Blackie', a good example of a child's toy made between 1860 and 1880. This and other toys in the exhibition demonstrate the folk artists' abilities to create recreational items which provide enjoyment and lasting beauty.

The 'Sculptured Hand' by an anonymous artist, from the collection of the Art Gallery of Nova Scotia, was probably used as a sign for a store, a directional marker, or possibly used on a church. It displays interesting painting qualities with the effect of weathering very apparent.

Other small figure and animal carvings were very common during the period covered by the exhibition showing us a world of fantasy and reality with subjects such as birds, horses and circus men. In the case of small sculpture, many of the objects were dictated by the natural form of the wood. There is a noticeable absence of religious influences in the folk sculpture of the Province.

Folk art sculpture in Nova Scotia is a true form of expression that mirrors the many joys and triumphs of the ordinary person — a fullness of artistic and aesthetic expression which begins in most cases with functional interests. The sculpture in the 'Spirit of Nova Scotia' exhibition demonstrates the lively spirit of our people of many origins who have come together and developed a sense of place and identity. The end result is a group of art objects that lift our spirit and are close to the heart. While folk art has long been neglected as an important aspect of Canadian art history, it is now recognized as having played an important role in the cultural heritage of the Province of Nova Scotia and is a major factor of Canadian culture from the beginning of our nation to the present time. Although outside the mainstream of art, folk sculpture in Nova Scotia has made a significant contribution.

1. *Folk Art of Nova Scotia,* (Halifax, 1976) Art Gallery of Nova Scotia, p. 10
2. George E. G. MacLaren, (Halifax, 1972) *The Woodcarvers of Nova Scotia,* Nova Scotia Museum, Historical Series #3, p. 17
3. *Decoys of Nova Scotia,* (Halifax, 1984) Art Gallery of Nova Scotia, p. 6

54 Merganser Drake

Mahone Bay, Lunenburg County

Original carved and painted softwood

Attributed to Captain Edwin Bachman (1872-1914)

Circa 1890-1900

Dimensions: 43.2 × 17.8 × 16.5 cm (17 × 7 × 6½ inches)

Collection of Judy and Earle Rhodenizer, Pleasantville, Nova Scotia

This is a very early merganser drake attributed to Captain Edwin Bachman. Although the tail design is different, the sleekness of the head and wooden comb are similar to Bachman's work. According to the Guyettes "(Bachman's) mergansers have long delicate bills which protrude cone-like from the head. The crests are wooden and thin and start somewhat far forward on the head. The drake mergansers have particularly intricate paint".[1] The paint on the decoy is not original. Considering the fact that Guyette states he carved very few birds, ". . . fourteen mergansers and perhaps twenty-five whistlers and scoters,"[2] this particular decoy is either an unrecorded and/or earlier Bachman form, or was carved by an unknown maker imitating Bachman.

Structure: The body is carved from a single block of softwood. The head is turned slightly and nailed into the body and the comb is carved out of the solid. The paint is not original, and the bill has been repaired or completely replaced.

1. Dale and Gary Guyette, *Decoys of Maritime Canada,* (Exton, Pennsylvania: Schiffer Publishing Ltd., 1983), p. 18. (See illustrations on pp. 41, 69, 78.)
2. Dale and Gary Guyette, *Ibid,* p. 18.

55 Whistler Hen

Lunenburg, Lunenburg County

Carved and painted softwood

Made by Captain Edwin Bachman (1872-1914)

Circa 1900

Dimensions: 33.0 × 15.2 × 15.2 cm (13 × 6 × 6 inches)

Collection of Jamie Stalker, Montreal, Quebec

An example of a very stylish whistler hen carved by Captain Bachman. According to Guyette,[1] he carved perhaps 25 whistlers and no more than 14 mergansers. This particular bird has tremendous style and folk appeal, typical of the strong flowing lines and carving style of Bachman.

Bachman worked as an offshore fisherman and captain of a cargo schooner which he sailed out of Lunenburg. In his work he travelled to the West Indies, Europe and Newfoundland. At the outbreak of the First World War he set sail in his three-masted schooner the "William Cortada" for the West Indies, but was never heard from again.

Structure: The body and head are carved from solid blocks of softwood. The head is "inletted" into the body and nailed. The paint is original, and there is still buckshot in the sides of the body and head.

1. Dale and Gary Guyette, *Decoys of Maritime Canada,* (Exton, Pennsylvania: Schiffer Publishing Ltd., 1983), p. 18.

56 Merganser Drake and Hen

Tancook Island, Lunenburg County
Carved and painted softwood
Made by Manson Young (1883-1953)
Circa 1910
Dimensions: Drake — 49.0 × 17.2 × 15.8 cm ($19\frac{5}{16} \times 6\frac{7}{8} \times 6\frac{1}{4}$ inches)
Hen — 50.0 × 17.8 × 15.2 cm ($19\frac{11}{16} \times 7 \times 6$ inches)
Private collection

Manson Young lived on Big Tancook Island where he worked as a fisherman and farmer. These two decoys were made in his late thirties. He also made an assortment of other decoys including seaducks, oldsquaw, whistlers, and several loons. Manson spent a lot of time on Ironbound Island where many of his decoys have been found.[1]

Structure: Both birds are in their original painted decoration. The bodies and heads are carved from blocks of softwood. The heads are pegged onto the body.

Published: Dale and Gary Guyette, *Decoys of Maritime Canada,* (Exton, Pennsylvania: Schiffer Publishing Ltd, 1983), p. 19, the decoys are illustrated on page 49.

1. Dale and Gary Guyette, *Decoys of Maritime Canada,* (Exton, Pennsylvania: Schiffer Publishing Ltd., 1983), p. 19.

57 Yellowlegs Decoys*

Musquodoboit Harbour, Halifax County
Original painted and carved softwood
Made by William Rowlings (1891-1962)
Circa 1910-1920
Dimensions: left — 31.0 × 44.0 × 9.5 cm ($12 \times 17\frac{5}{16} \times 3\frac{3}{4}$ inches)
right — 29.0 × 51.0 × 10.5 cm ($11\frac{7}{16} \times 20\frac{1}{16} \times 4\frac{1}{8}$ inches)
Collection of Gerald Ferguson, Halifax, Nova Scotia

William Rowlings was the postmaster of Musquodoboit Harbour and a decorated World War One veteran. He was well known in the region as a decoy carver and an avid hunter. He made decoys for his own personal use and to sell. These yellowlegs are some of the few examples of shorebirds known from the Atlantic coast of Nova Scotia. Rowlings seems to be the only individual known to date to carve these types of birds, including rock plovers and stick-up geese.[1] These two decoys are called rootheads because the necks, heads and bills are carved from a single L-shaped twig or branch. Obviously this is a very simple but effective technique for creating the illusion of a realistic shorebird.

Structure: The birds have some cracking due to the drying of the solid blocks of softwood used to carve the bodies. The necks, heads and bills are carved from a single L-shaped branch and pegged into the bodies. The paint is original and the decoys are in good condition.

Published: See information in footnote.

1. Dale and Gary Guyette, *Decoys of Maritime Canada,* (Exton, Pennsylvania : Schiffer Publishing Ltd., 1983), p. 23, illustrated on p. 92.)

* These pieces will be on view in Halifax only.

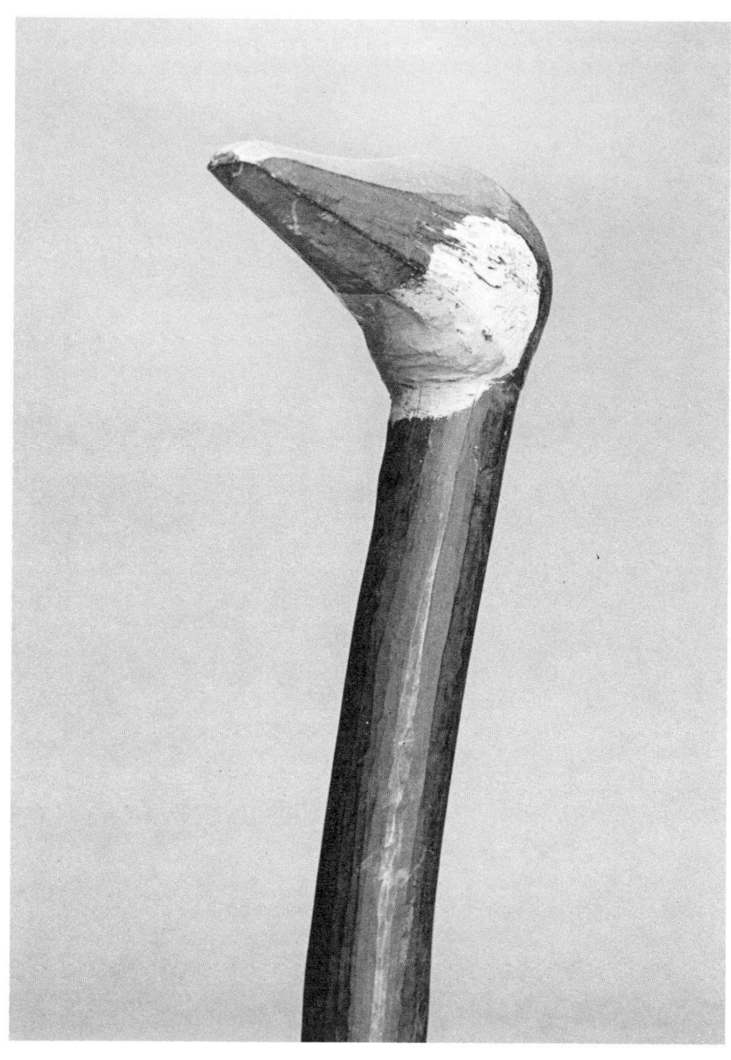

58 Stick-Up Canada Goose Decoy

Ostrea Lake, Halifax County
Original carved and painted softwood
Made by Captain Leonard Williams (1883-1967)
Circa 1925-1950
Dimensions: 68.5 × 16.5 (at head) cm (26$^{15}/_{16}$ × 6½ (at head) inches)
Collection of Gerald Ferguson, Halifax, Nova Scotia

Leonard Williams from Ostrea Lake worked out of Halifax as the Captain of a schooner, hawling coal and lumber to New York City. Williams carved a number of these stick-up decoys of Canada geese and is also known to have carved a large rig of seaduck decoys. He served in the Canadian Navy in both the first and second World War.[1]

Structure: This is an excellent example of this type of stick-up decoy, simply pushed into the ground, usually in a grouping to attract migrating geese and other water fowl. The hole in the elongated neck was used to carry a string of these decoys into the field.

1. Dale and Gary Guyette, *Decoys of Maritime Canada,* (Exton, Pennsylvania: Schiffer Publishing Ltd., 1983), p. 23.

59 Blackduck Decoy

Lunenburg County
Original painted softwood, hollow body
Made by Dennis White (b. 1899)
Circa 1925-1950
Dimensions: 33.5 × 19.0 × 14.0 cm (13$^{3}/_{16}$ × 7½ × 5½ inches)
Collection of Gerald Ferguson, Halifax, Nova Scotia

Dennis White after living most of his life in Stonehurst, moved to Lunenburg in the 1950's. His life as a lobsterman and fisherman led him easily to hunting, and so in the 1920's he began carving whistler decoys both for his own use and for selling. He is also known to have carved miniatures that are exact models of his working decoys.[1] This is a very stylish decoy with tucked head and raised, crossed tail feathers carved from the solid wood.

Structure: This decoy is in excellent condition with a hollow body carved out of softwood. The plank bottom base is nailed into place with round nails. The carved head is also nailed into the body. The paint is original although it has been waxed.

1. Dale and Gary Guyette, *Decoys of Maritime Canada,* (Exton, Pennsylvania: Schiffer Publishing Ltd., 1983), p. 19.

60 Whistler Drake and Hen

Lunenburg County
Original painted and carved softwood
Made by Orran Hiltz (1901-1950)
Circa 1930-1950
Dimensions: Drake — 40.0 × 15.0 × 13.0 cm ($15\frac{3}{4} \times 5\frac{7}{8} \times 5\frac{1}{8}$ inches)
Hen — 37.5 × 13.3 × 12.5 cm ($14\frac{3}{4} \times 5\frac{1}{4} \times 4\frac{15}{16}$ inches)
Collection of Chris Cooper, Dartmouth, Nova Scotia

Born in Indian Point, Lunenburg County, Orran Hiltz is one of the best known Nova Scotia decoy makers, probably because of his early discovery and distinct Lunenburg styling.[1] Hiltz carved more than 500 decoys in his lifetime turning eventually to miniature decoys. These birds date from his later period when he simplified the lines of his decoys by eliminating the raised wings of his earlier carvings, and lowering the tail.[2]

Structure: Both of these birds are worked from blocks of softwood, the heads individually carved and pegged into the bodies. The works are in excellent condition including the paint, although there is a repair to the bill of the drake.

1. Dale and Gary Guyette, *Decoys of Maritime Canada,* (Exton, Pennsylvania: Schiffer Publishing Ltd., 1983), p. 21.
2. Dale and Gary Guyette, *Ibid,* p. 22.

61 Common Merganser Drake Decoy

Indian Point, Lunenburg County
Carved and painted softwood
Made by Orran Hiltz (1901-1978)
Circa 1925-1950
Dimensions: 42.0 × 15.5 × 18.0 cm ($16\frac{9}{16} \times 6\frac{1}{8} \times 7\frac{1}{16}$ inches)
Collection of Gerald Ferguson, Halifax, Nova Scotia

A prolific carver of seaduck, whistler and merganser decoys, Orran Hiltz is one of the best known Nova Scotia decoy makers. The raised wings is one of the characteristics of Hiltz's decoy carving.

Structure: The body of the decoy is carved from a solid block of softwood including the raised wings. The head is pegged and nailed into the body.

62 Hen Merganzer

Indian Point, Lunenburg County
Original carved and painted softwood
Made by Orran Hiltz (1901-1978)
Circa 1930-1940
Dimensions: 48.2 × 14.6 × 15.2 cm (19 × 5¾ × 6 inches)
Collection of the National Museum of Man, Canadian Centre for Folk Culture Studies, Ottawa, Ontario

Orran Hiltz is one of Nova Scotia's better known decoy carvers, probably because of his early discovery (one of his merganser decoys is pictured in Starr, *Decoys of the Atlantic Flyway,* (New York: Winchester Press, 1974, p. 209), and because of his very distinctive styling, which includes a wooden serrated-edged crest, and raised wings and tails. This particular merganser is one of the finer examples of his middle phase style carving.[1]

Structure: The body is carved from a solid block of softwood. The head is both pegged and nailed into the body and carved from the solid.

Published: Dale and Gary Guyette, *Decoys of Maritime Canada,* (Exton, Pennsylvania: Schiffer Publishing Ltd., 1983), p. 67.

1. Dale and Gary Guyette, *Decoys of Maritime Canada,* (Exton, Pennsylvania: Schiffer Publishing Ltd., 1983), pp. 21-22.

63 Drake Surf Scoter

Villagedale, Shelburne County
Carved and painted softwood
Made by Fred Nickerson (1902-1980)
Circa 1930
Dimensions: 44.5 × 14.0 × 17.0 cm (17½ × 5½ × 6$^{11}/_{16}$ inches)
Collection of Jamie Stalker, Montreal, Quebec

Fred Nickerson carved decoys in both Nova Scotia and Massachusetts, where he worked as a boat-builder and inspector for the U.S. Navy. Although he carved many decorative birds during the 1970's, while living in Florida, his working decoys of the 1930's are some of his finest.[1]

Structure: This decoy is hollow-bodied and made of three laminated sections of softwood. The head is attached to the body with nails. The eyes are glass, and there is still buckshot in the neck and body, a helpful sign that this bird was used for hunting.

1. Dale and Gary Guyette, *Decoys of Maritime Canada,* (Exton, Pennsylvania: Schiffer Publishing Ltd., 1983), p. 16.

64 Drake Merganser

Shelburne County
Original carved and painted softwood
Made by Fred Nickerson (1902-1980)
Circa 1930-1935
Dimensions: 50.0 × 14.0 × 14.0 cm ($19^{11}/_{16}$ × $5^{1}/_{2}$ × $5^{1}/_{2}$ inches)
Collection of the National Museum of Man, Canadian Centre for Folk Culture Studies, Ottawa, Ontario

Fred Nickerson was born in Villagedale, Nova Scotia. He carved his decoys in Nova Scotia and while living in Massachusetts where he worked periodically for nearly 31 years. Although he carved bluebills, whistlers, scoters and eiders, his finest carving was reserved for his merganzer decoys. The crests are usually of horse hair, and the paint is simply but carefully done.[1] This particular merganser is an example of his finer work.

Structure: The body is carved from a solid block of softwood. The head is pegged to the body. The crest is missing from this example.

1. Dale and Gary Guyette, *Decoys of Maritime Canada,* (Exton, Pennsylvania: Schiffer Publishing Ltd., 1983), p. 16.

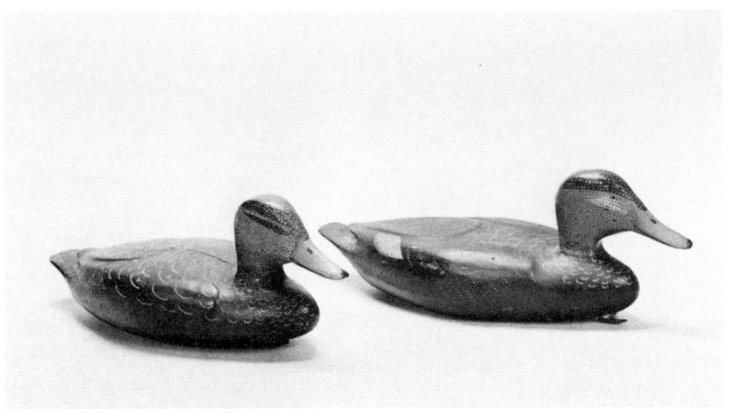

65 Hen and Drake Blackduck

Gold River, Lunenburg County
Original carved and painted softwood
Made by Blair Kaizer (1912-)
Circa 1935
Dimensions: right — 42.5 × 15.2 × 15.2 cm ($16^{3}/_{4}$ × 6 × 6 inches)
left — 41.2 × 15.0 × 16.0 cm ($14^{3}/_{16}$ × $5^{15}/_{16}$ × $6^{5}/_{16}$ inches)
Collection of Blair and Pearl Kaiser, Gold River, Nova Scotia

Blair Kaiser started hunting at twelve years of age, and quickly became a well known hunter. In 1930 Stan Sawler (1887-1966) made a merganser for him which he used as a model for carving a rig of decoys for his own use. Eventually Blair began using shot birds as models, carving mergansers and about a dozen black ducks. He has also carved bluebills, whistlers, and one seagull. His blackducks are noted for the painting of the heads, and decorated with dots using a pointed stick.[1]

Structure: Both decoys are carved from solid blocks of softwood with the heads nailed to the bodies.

Published: Dale and Gary Guyette, *Decoys of Maritime Canada,* (Exton, Pennsylvania: Schiffer Publishing Company Ltd, 1983), p. 20-21.

1. Dale and Gary Guyette, *Decoys of Maritime Canada,* (Exton, Pennsylvania: Schiffer Publishing Company Ltd., 1983), p. 20-21. The same pair of decoys is illustrated on page 79.

66 Merganser Drake and Hen

Little Tancook Island, Lunenburg County
Carved and painted softwood
Made by Lindsey Levy (1892-1980)
Circa 1930-1940
Dimensions: Drake — 40.5 × 16.0 × 17.0 cm (15 15/16 × 6 5/16 × 6 11/16 inches)
Hen — 40.0 × 16.5 × 17.0 cm (15 3/4 × 6 1/2 × 6 11/16 inches)
Private collection

Lindsey Levy, who lived on Little Tancook Island, began carving with his father and grandfather around 1910. Although he was influenced by both these men, he soon developed a distinctive style of carving all his own, creating a more flowing body and head form and changing the design of the tail. His decoys were noted for their careful painting and detail. Many of the decoys that Lindsey produced were made for selling or trading.[1]

Structure: Both birds are in their original painted decoration with the bodies and heads carved from single blocks of softwood. The heads are pegged onto the bodies.

1. Dale and Gary Guyette, *Decoys of Maritime Canada,* (Exton, Pennsylvania: Schiffer Publishing Ltd., 1983), p. 18, a similar pair of merganser decoys carved by Lindsey Levy are illustrated on p. 70.

Refer to colour plate IX, page 16

67 Seagull and Blackduck

Eastern Passage, Halifax County
Both carved and painted softwood
Made by Clyde Edwards (1899-1976)
Circa 1930-1940
Dimensions: Seagull; 57.1 × 30.5 × 17.8 cm (22 1/2 × 12 × 7 inches)
Blackduck; 40.6 × 13.5 × 15.2 cm (16 × 5 5/16 × 6 inches)
Collection of Maurice Edwards, Eastern Passage, Nova Scotia

Clyde Edwards was a fisherman who also carved. His subjects included old squaws, blackducks, blue bills and scoters, and one oversized seagull, which is illustrated. As with all of Edwards' decoys, both the gull and blackduck are hollow-bodied. He is not only known for his expert and realistic carving, but his painted decoration as well.

Structure: Both decoys are hollow-bodied and made from softwood. The paint is original and in excellent condition. The blackduck has shot in the body and neck, indicating that it was used for hunting. The gull was probably not used for hunting, although seagull decoys were employed as confidence birds to help attract waterfowl.

Published: Dale and Gary Guyette, *Decoys of Maritime Canada,* (Exton, Pennsylvania: Schiffer Publishing Ltd., 1983) p. 22, p. 88 (seagull), p. 89 (blackduck)

68 Bird Carving of a Robin

Mader's Cove, Lunenburg County
Original carved and painted softwood
Signed Colin Langille on the underside of the base
Circa 1890-1920
Dimensions: 19.0 × 13.3 × 5.1 cm ($7\frac{1}{2} \times 5\frac{1}{4} \times 2$ inches)
Private collection

This carving of a robin is a delightful piece of folk art. Similar bird carvings are known from Lunenburg County, and they also appear in Pennsylvania-German folk art both as individual birds and in groupings in bird trees,[1] a form also found in Nova Scotia.

Structure: Carved from the solid block of softwood, the bird is attached to the base by means of two metal pins acting as legs.

1. Beatrice B. Garven, *The Pennsylvania German Collection,* (Philadelphia: Philadelphia Museum of Art, 1982), see pages 80-81 for similar examples.

69 Miniature Bird Carving

Indian Point, Lunenburg County
Original carved and painted softwood
Artist unknown
Circa 1910-1920
Dimensions: 13.0 × 13.5 × 3.8 cm ($5\frac{1}{8} \times 5\frac{5}{16} \times 1\frac{1}{2}$ inches)
Collection of Murray E. Stewart, Berwick, Nova Scotia

After the introduction of rubber and plastic birds most decoy makers turned to small miniature bird models, sometimes as toys for children, or simply as decorative items for sale. This example is one of two similar carved and painted birds from Indian Point by the same unknown maker. Although there appears to be a pencilled signature or initials on the reverse of the base, it is not legible.

Structure: Carved and painted softwood with wooden legs inserted into the separate base painted the same colours as the bird itself.

70 Weathervane of Rooster

Halifax, Halifax County
Pierced and riveted sheet iron
Artist unknown
Circa 1790-1810
Dimensions: 59.5 × 42.0 cm ($23\frac{3}{8}$ × $18\frac{1}{2}$ inches)
Collection of the Nova Scotia Museum, Halifax, Nova Scotia

This weathervane is from the Little "Dutch" church located on Brunswick Street in Halifax. Built by the "foreign Protestants" in 1760, the rooster which presently sits atop the steeple is a replacement.

Structure: The rooster is made from heavy gauge sheet iron which is pierced and riveted.

71 Weathervane

Mahone Bay, Lunenburg County
Hand-forged copper with yellow mustard paint
Artist unknown
Circa 1825-1840
Dimensions: 37.5 × 41.5 × 30.0 cm ($14\frac{3}{4}$ × $16\frac{5}{16}$ × $11\frac{13}{16}$ inches)
Collection of Murray E. Stewart, Berwick, Nova Scotia.

This weathervane was purchased by Earle Rhodenizer from a family in Mahone Bay. The elderly sisters who sold it stated that they were given the vane by their father as a toy when they were children, and that it had come from one of the churches in Mahone Bay. A check of information in the Public Archives of Nova Scotia did not reveal any suitable photographs to support this claim. Rooster or weathercocks are probably one of the most common and popular weathervane forms to be found in Nova Scotia.[1]

Structure: This three dimensional vane is made of hand-forged copper with rivited tail and legs. It may have had directionals at one time. The yellow is an early overpaint used to simulate gilt.

1. For further information on rooster weathervanes see, Robert Bishop and Patricia Coblentz, *A Gallery of American Weathervanes and Whirligigs,* (New York: E.P. Dutton, 1981), pp. 27-37.

Refer to colour plate XII, page 18

72 Weathervane of Rooster*

Stellarton, Pictou County
Carved and painted softwood
Attributed to John Oliver (1813-1881?)
Circa 1860-1880
Dimensions: 38.1 × 56.0 × 15.2 cm (15 × 22 × 6 inches)
Collection of John Marshall, New Glasgow, Nova Scotia

A very folky rooster weathervane attributed to John Oliver, a New Glasgow carver who worked between 1855 and 1881 making figureheads, billetheads, trailboards and stern ornaments (either plain or gilt).[1] According to the owner, this vane was used on a church in the Stellarton, Nova Scotia area.

Structure: Laminated softwood with carved tail and carved and painted head. Part of the beak is missing and the legs are damaged.

1. George MacLaren, *The Woodcarvers of Nova Scotia,* (Halifax: The Nova Scotia Museum, Occassional Paper No. 10, 1971), pp. 14-15, p. 25.

*This piece will be on view in Halifax only.

73 Horse Weathervane

Margaretsville, Annapolis County
Painted sheet metal
Artist unknown
Circa 1890-1910
Dimensions: 56.0 × 68.6 cm (22¹⁄₁₆ × 27 inches)
Collection of Jerry and Debbie Vidito, Kentville, Nova Scotia

An example of a weathervane depicting a prancing horse. The overall colour is a light brown with the horse's mane painted in a darker shade of brown.

Structure: The vane is cut from a piece of heavy gauge sheet metal which is "sandwiched" between two strips of wood held together with four nuts and bolts. The end of this forms the shaft which is then hafted into the base and rotates in the wind.

74 Weathervane*

Boutilier's Point, Halifax County
Painted sheet metal
Attributed to Cecil Langille
Circa 1920-1930
Dimensions: 50.0 × 45.8 cm (19¹¹⁄₁₆ × 18¹⁄₁₆ inches)
Collection of Murray E. Stewart, Berwick, Nova Scotia

This whimsical weathervane of a dachshund and puppy is an example of a dog weathervane, which are uncommon in Nova Scotia, the horse and weathercock being the more popular forms. This weathervane is still a working instrument, dating from the first quarter of the twentieth century, at which time it was important to man's knowledge and understanding of winds and weather patterns. By watching the weathervane, usually perched on top of a barn or other building, a farmer could estimate by experience, the direction and perhaps relative velocity of the wind, and what kind of weather system to expect, particularly important during planting and harvest seasons.[1]

Structure: The vane is cut from heavy gauge sheet metal which has been painted a dark orange-brown on the bodies, white for the eyes, and black ground strip and mounting shaft. The vane is two-sided with an additional ground strip and applied legs only on the parent dog which is attached with metal rivets and gives depth perspective when viewed from either side.

1. For further information on dog weathervanes see, Robert Bishop and Patricia Coblentz, *A Gallery of American Weathervanes and Whirligigs,* (New York: E.P. Dutton, 1981), pp. 19, 66.

*This piece will be on view in Halifax only

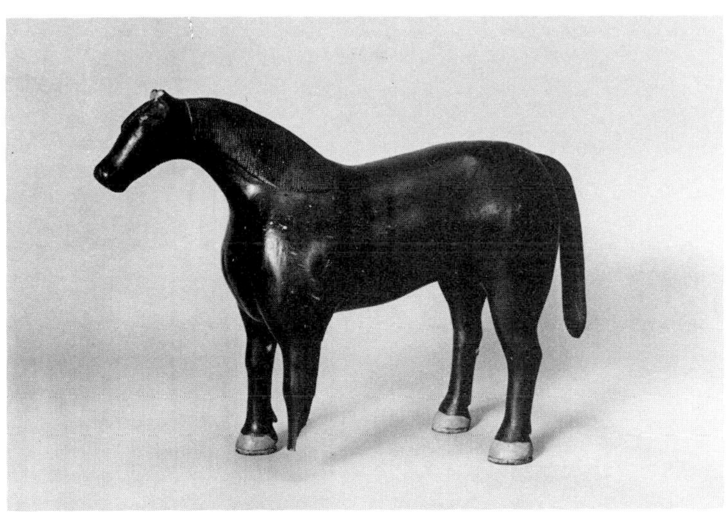

75 Horse "Blackie"

Kings County

Original black and grey painted and carved softwood with leather horseshoes

Artist unknown

Circa 1860-1880

Dimensions: 35.6 × 26.0 × 10.0 cm (14 × 10$^{3}/_{16}$ × 3$^{15}/_{16}$ inches)

Collection of Jerry and Debbie Vidito, Kentville, Nova Scotia

This is one of the finest animal carvings known from Nova Scotia. No doubt made as a child's toy, the carving is probably meant to represent a Clydesdale horse, the draft animal so commonly seen in the mid to late nineteenth century pulling the plow during spring planting in the rural countryside of Nova Scotia. The carving is well executed, although the body is not in proportion with the horse's head and neck. The mane is particularly appealing, carved in slight relief on one side of the neck only and given texture with a series of lightly incised lines. The horse is painted black, with the hooves painted grey, as are small leather horseshoes attached to the feet.

Structure: The horse is carved from a single block of softwood. The tail appears to be carved as part of the whole and not added. The leather shoes are attached with small round nails which could be replacements. If original, the carving would date circa 1900-1920. Unfortunately the front left leg of the carving has been broken and long since lost, and there is some minor damage to the ears.

76 Rocking Horse

Bridgewater, Lunenburg County

Original carved and black painted softwood with leather saddle, manilla tail and iron stirrups

Artist unknown

Circa 1863

Dimensions: (overall) 122.5 × 61.5 × 25.7 cm (48$^{1}/_{4}$ × 24$^{3}/_{16}$ × 10$^{1}/_{8}$ inches)

Collection of the DesBrisay Museum, Bridgewater, Nova Scotia

The function of a hobby-horse is evident in an advertisement placed in the *Pennsylvania Packet* in 1785 by a London cabinetmaker, "He makes Rocking-Horses in the neatest and best manner to teach children to ride and give them a wholesome and pleasing experience."[1]

This particular example was used by Robert Dawson of Bridgewater as a young boy of about five years of age (around 1863). One can easily picture a young Robert Dawson riding this swift horse created with such style and grace by its maker.

History: This horse was donated to the DesBrisay Museum in 1973 by descendents of Robert Dawson.

Structure: The body of the horse is made from several planks of softwood carved and laminated to a core block of softwood and joined with square, and what appears to be, forged nails. The legs are tenoned into the body and nailed, the complete horse attached to the ash rockers by screws countersunk from under the rockers into the four legs. The mane is missing, but was attached with small square nails which are still in place. The tail is probably a later replacement, but the saddle of leather, and stirrups appear to be original. The rockers are held in place with two tenoned dowels and two square-nailed cross stretchers.

1. Anita Schorsch, *Images of Childhood: An Illustrated Social History,* (New York. Mayflower Books, 1979), p. 71.

Sandra Brant and Elissa Cullman, *Small Folk. A Celebration of Childhood in America,* (New York. E.P. Dutton, 1980), pp. 128-129.

Refer to colour plate X, page 17

77 Rocking Horse

Queens County
Carved and painted softwood with hardwood rockers
Artist unknown
Circa 1890-1920
Dimensions: (overall) 140.0 × 67.0 × 34.0 cm (55⅛ × 26⅜ × 13⅜ inches)
Collection of Queens County Museum, Liverpool, Nova Scotia

This rocking horse shows signs of use, and one can picture a happy boy or girl riding this swift steed across the finishing line.

Structure: The head, body and legs are all made from separate pieces of wood. The legs are tenoned into the rockers and held in place with round nails that could be later additions. The mane and harness straps are missing. The saddle is made from rough fabric similar to sofa coverings and fringed with red material.

Boy in Plaid

New England
Oil on canvas
Artist unknown
Circa 1845
Dimensions: 78.4 × 64.8 cm (30⅞ × 25½ inches)
Photograph courtesy of Colonial Williamsburg, Abby Aldrich Rockefeller Folk Art Centre, Williamsburg, Virginia

This lively composition shows a young boy with his hobbyhorse and a riding crop in his hand.

This piece is not included in the exhibition

78 Whirligig

Pictou County
Painted and carved softwood.
Artist unknown
Circa 1860-1880
Dimensions: 9.5 × 41.0 × 5.5 cm (3¾ × 16⅛ × 2⅛ inches)
Collection of Gerald Ferguson, Halifax, Nova Scotia

Although this whirligig is missing both its feet and arms, it is still a fine example of this form, with expressive face and comical hat. The eyes are inset marbles and the original red paint has been brushed with an overcoat of silver.

Structure: The body and hat of the whirligig were carved from a single block of softwood. The nose is missing and was probably inset into the face. A hole in the mouth suggests there might have been a pipe or cigarette.

80 Whirligig of Man with Moustache

West Dublin, Lunenburg County
Original painted and carved softwood
Made by Zenas Publicover
Circa 1920-1930
Dimensions: 38.1 × 38.1 × 12.0 cm (15 × 15 × 4¾ inches)
Private collection

This whirligig of a man with moustache and strange hat may represent a soldier from World War I. It is a very lively wind toy and one of the better examples of a whirligig from Nova Scotia. Zenas Publicover is known for his carvings, mostly dating from the first quarter of this century.

Structure: The man is carved from a solid block of softwood with arms attached through the body by a wooden dowel. The paddles are attached to the end of the arms with round nails. The paint is original. The legs are pegged into the base.

79 Whirligig of Man in Hat*

South Shore
Original painted sheet metal
Artist unknown
Circa 1910-1920
Dimensions: 15.2 × 40.6 cm (6 × 16 inches)
Collection of Patricia and Tom Lackey, Toronto, Ontario

This metal whirligig of a man in a hat was once painted with a face, black pants, and red shirt.

Structure: The surface of the metal is pitted, the paint almost completely lost. The right arm has been repaired and is not in its original functioning position.

*This piece will be on view in Halifax only

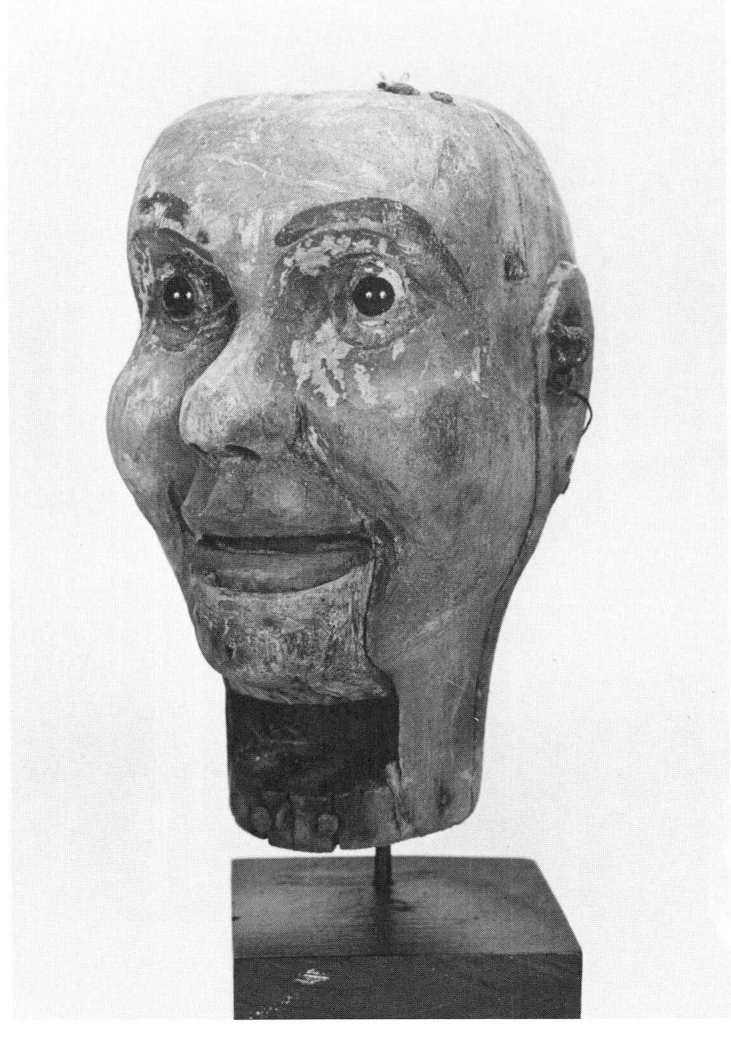

81 Sailor Whirligig

Halifax or Guysborough County
Original painted softwood
Artist Unknown
Circa 1930-1950
Dimensions: 15.0 × 27.5 × 16.0 cm (5⅞ × 10¹³⁄₁₆ × 6⁵⁄₁₆ inches)
Collection of Carole Collins, Hamilton, Ontario

Although nineteenth and early twentieth century whirligigs are not that common to Nova Scotia, it seems appropriate that of those known several are of sailors, reflecting the strong maritime tradition of the province. This example, from the Eastern Shore, was probably made in the last thirty or forty years, and is included in the exhibition to demonstrate the persistence of folk traditions found in Nova Scotia. This example is a fine reminder of the continuation of our material folk culture.[1]

Structure: The figure is carved from a solid block of softwood with attached arms and signal flags, and set on a wooden base. Both the body and arms turn with the wind.

1. For other examples of sailor whirligigs see Robert Bishop and Patricia Coblentz, *A Gallery of American Weathervanes and Whirligigs,* (New York: E.P. Dutton, 1981), pp. 105, 116.

82 Ventriloquist's Dummy Head

Pictou, Pictou County
Original carved and painted softwood
Made by Twitter Johnson
Circa 1920-1930
Dimensions: 15.5 × 7.6 × 11.0 cm (6⅛ × 3 × 4$^{5}/_{16}$ inches)
Collection of Gerald Ferguson, Halifax, Nova Scotia

This is the head of a black man, which was used as part of a ventriloquist's dummy. Although it is possible that a few of the black heads and figures were used by black performers, most of them were made for white actors who did solo routines in the nineteenth century minstrel shows and carnivals. These minstrels, who usually featured Negro songs and dances while in blackface makeup, were part of the North American theatrical scene throughout the nineteenth century, which lasted until 1928 when the last of these troupes, Al G. Field Mistrels, went out of business.[1]

Twitter Johnson was one of the carvers who made these heads, and who, according to the family, worked for the Barnum and Bailey Circus. To date four heads and a skeletal torso have been found, which are directly attributive to his hand.

Structure: The head is carved from two pieces of pine which form the front and back of the head. The working mechanism which made the mouth move up and down when operated by the ventriloquist is located in the hollowed out halves of the head. The eyes in this example are stationary but were often made to move in some examples by other carvers. No heads by Johnson found thus far have eyes that can be operated. The applied hair is missing from this head but present on the other examples in the exhibition. The eyeballs are made from inset black glass marbles. The head was originally painted, but only traces of paint on the lips and eyebrows remain.

1. Marian Klamkin and Charles Klamkin, *Wood Carvings: North American Folk Sculptures*, (New York: Hawthorn Books, Inc., 1974), p. 73.

83 Ventriloquist's Dummy Head*

Pictou, Pictou County
Original carved and painted softwood
Made by Twitter Johnson
Circa 1920-1930
Dimensions: 12.5 × 23.0 × 14.0 cm (4$^{15}/_{16}$ × 9$^{1}/_{16}$ × 5½ inches)
Collection of Gerald Ferguson, Halifax, Nova Scotia

A very dramatic head of a blackman carved by Twitter Johnson. Again this is an example of a ventriloquist's head used in a minstrel show or carnival.

Structure: The head is carved from two pieces of softwood joined at the middle. The hollow interior was used to place the operating mechanism for the mouth. The hair is applied and the paint is original.

* This piece will be on view in Halifax only.

84 Ventriloquist's Dummy Head

Pictou, Pictou County

Original carved and painted softwood

Made by Twitter Johnson

Circa 1920-1930

Dimensions: 39.0 × 12.2 × 15.2 cm (15⅜ × 4$^{13}/_{16}$ × 6 inches)

Private collection

An example of a ventriloquist's dummy head of a white man executed by Twitter Johnson, who according to the family, worked for the Barnum and Bailey Circus. Heads of this type were used by actors and performers in the minstrel shows of the nineteenth century, and in the sideshows of the Big Tops of the early twentieth century. Twitter Johnson is probably one of the most important Nova Scotia folk sculptors of this century.

Structure: The head is carved from two pieces of softwood which form the front and back. The hollow interior was used to place the operating mechanism for the mouth which is controlled by the lever on the shaft. The hair is applied and the paint original.

Refer to colour plate XI, page 18

85 Profile of a Gentleman

Clementsport, Annapolis County

Carved and painted softwood

Artist unknown

Circa 1820-1850

Dimensions: 31.0 × 61.0 cm (12 × 24 inches) Measurement does not include the iron mounting pole.

Collection of Jim and Susan Snowdon, Kentville, Nova Scotia

This tavern sign was found in the basement of the Ditmars' house in Clementsport by the owner. It is one of the rare examples of a flat profile carving, painted and carved on both sides, showing a gentleman in black coat and ruffled shirt. The "Ditmars" is listed as a stage stop or road-house in the Nova Scotia almanacs which became obsolete with the advent of the railway.[1]

Structure: Carved from a single plank of softwood with painted features, the sign may have been cut at an early date and the upper portion attached to the mounting pole.

1. Communication with Professor Jim Snowden, June 5, 1985.

86 Figurehead of the Earl of Dalhousie*

Possibly Halifax, Halifax County
Carved and repainted softwood
Artist unknown
Circa 1820-1821
Dimensions: 61.0 × 80.0 × 35.6 cm (24 × 31½ × 14 inches)
Collection of the Maritime Museum of the Atlantic, Halifax, Nova Scotia

It is very difficult to positively identify figureheads that were carved in Nova Scotia. This example was perhaps installed on the "Earl of Dalhousie" built in Londonderry, Nova Scotia in 1817. Although she did not have a figurehead when launched, this vessel was registered in Greenoch, Scotland by 1820, and it is possible that this figurehead was carved there.[1] The "Earl of Dalhousie" was wrecked off Anticosti Island in October, 1821.

Structure: Carved from blocks of softwood that have been laminated. The present painted surface is recent.

1. Communication from David B. Flemming, Director of the Maritime Museum of the Atlantic, August 6, 1985.

*This piece will be on view in Halifax only.

Refer to colour plate VII, page 15

87 Bust Carving of Samuel Kempton

Milton, Queen's County
Carved and painted softwood
Made in 1853 by George Crouse (1835-1866)
Dimensions: 30.5 × 46.0 cm (12 × 18⅛ inches)
Collection of the Queen's County Museum, Liverpool, Nova Scotia

This bust of Samuel Kempton of Milton was carved when he was five years of age by George Crouse in 1853, the brilliant young woodcarver who was then making figureheads for the sailing vessels being built in Liverpool. Crouse was born in 1835 and died in 1866. This is the only known example of his work to survive. The boy, Samuel Kempton, grew to manhood and went to sea, sailing for many years between Liverpool, the American ports, and the West Indies. In his latter years he became Collector of Customs at Liverpool.

Structure: The paint has weathered on the body and face, and part of the nose and a portion of the right hand are missing. Regardless, this bust has both presence and great folk appeal.

Published: George MacLaren, *The Woodcarvers of Nova Scotia,* (Halifax: The Nova Scotia Museum, 1971), figure 6.

88 Sir Fenwick Williams

Hantsport, Hants County

Original carved and painted softwood on painted and molded mounting board

Carved by David Ells North (1856-1943)

Circa 1880

Dimensions: 29.3 × 68.5 × 10.0 cm (11$^{9}/_{16}$ × 26$^{15}/_{16}$ × 3$^{15}/_{16}$ inches)

Collection of Jerry and Debbie Vidito, Kentville, Nova Scotia

On the back of the mounting board is an inscription that identifies the subject of the carving as Sir Fenwick Williams, who was born at Annapolis Royal, and was the defender of Kars in the Crimean Peninsula during the war of 1854-1856. The relief was carved by David Ells North (1856-1943) who was a shipbuilder at Hantsport, and who is referred to as being "young" when he made this work, suggesting that it was executed while he was an apprentice. The details of the carving show Sir Fenwick in his regimental red uniform with high black boots. His hands are by his side and he stares straight into the distance, which even in this profile carving suggests an officer in the service of his country, loyal, steadfast and indeed heroic.[1]

Structure: The carving is made from a single block of softwood and is attached to the mounting board with square nails. The figure probably stood on a block which is now missing.

1. The town of Port Williams was named after Sir Fenwick in honour of his being not only a native of Annapolis County, but also for his exploits at the Battle of Kars in the Crimean War (1853-1856). From 1866-1867 Sir Fenwick was Governor of Nova Scotia. This information from *The Port Remembers: The History of Port Williams and Its Century Homes* published by the Port Williams Women's Institute, (Kentville, 1976, pp. 20-22). On page 20 there is a photograph of Sir Fenwick which bears a strong resemblence to the relief carving exhibited.

89 Man Fighting Bear*

River John, Pictou County

Carved softwood figures set in glass-fronted case with dried moss and conifer needles

Made by Alf Johnson

Circa 1910-1920

Dimensions: 16.5 × 16.0 × 5.5 cm ($6\frac{1}{2} \times 6\frac{5}{16} \times 2\frac{3}{16}$ inches)

Private collection

Groups of figures combining men, women and animals in various domestic and outdoor scenes are often found in the folk art sculpture from Nova Scotia.[1] This particular example shows a bearded lumberman in combat with a brown (?) bear. The man is in the act of reaching for his sheath knife strapped to his belt while grasping the neck of the bear with his other hand attempting to hold him back. The sculpture is very realistic and well carved.

Structure: The figures are set into a glass-fronted case and glued to the base board which is decorated with dried moss and conifer needles. The case is painted brown with butt corners reinforced with small round nails. The backboard is nailed and screwed into place and the figures are reached by removing this panel.

1. For other examples of groups of sculptured figures in various settings see Wesley Mattie (*et al*), *From the Heart*, (Toronto: McClelland and Stewart Limited in cooperation with the National Museum of Man, Ottawa, 1983), pp. 165, 182-183.

*This piece will be on view in Halifax only

90 Armorial Achievement of Nova Scotia

Wallace, Cumberland County

Original carved and painted softwood

Made by Hudson Langille (1876-1965)

Circa 1910 1930

Dimensions: 22.5 × 30.0 cm ($8\frac{7}{8} \times 11\frac{13}{16}$ inches)

Collection of Pascal and Angela Dinaut, Great Village, Nova Scotia

This hand carved rendition of the coat of arms of Nova Scotia may have been made for a lodge, or some type of ceremonial purpose. The maker, Hudson Langille, was the son of Captain George Langille and Margaret Weatherby.

Structure: There is some breakage along the edges of the piece. The paint is original and in good condition, and the proper colours for the Nova Scotia coat of arms. The plaque is mounted on a support block with round nails.

91 Figure of a Man in a Grey Suit

Wallace, Cumberland County
Original carved and painted softwood
Made by Hudson Langille (1876-1965)
Circa 1930
Dimensions: including base — 18.0 × 12.1 cm (7¼ × 4¾ inches)
Collection of Pascal and Angela Dinaut, Great Village, Nova Scotia

This small carving of a man with outstretched arm is typical of early twentieth century folk sculpture from Nova Scotia in that it exhibits the simple and direct style of untrained artists who work for their own enjoyment, shunning direct function for decoration.

Structure: The figure is carved from a solid block of softwood, the feet still attached to the block which in turn is set into the round softwood base. The hair and feet remain the natural wood colour while the suit and hands are painted grey.

92 Sculptured Hand

Kings County
Carved and painted softwood
Artist unknown
Circa 1860-1880
Dimensions: 4.3 × 11.0 × 3.5 cm (1 11/16 × 4 5/16 × 1⅜ inches)
Collection of Jerry and Debbie Vidito, Kentville, Nova Scotia

It is difficult to determine exactly the purpose of this small carving of a hand with pointing index finger. There is no evidence that it was ever mounted or hafted onto a base. It was first thought it was a fineal for a gravestone, or even the handle of a cane, but there is nothing to support this suggestion. Most likely it is a decorative carving, perhaps even a small practice model to establish proportions and technique for a larger version as illustrated in the following entry.

Structure: The hand is carved from a solid block of softwood and painted white, and shows signs of use and/or weathering.

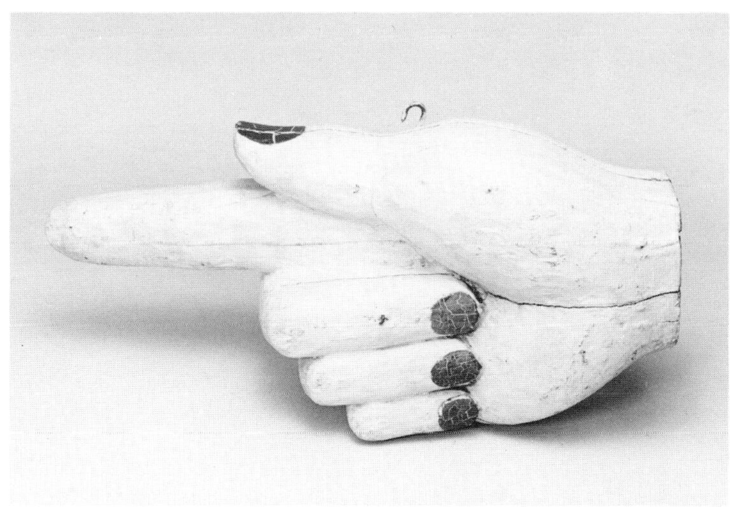

93 Sculptured Hand

Found in Annapolis County
Painted and carved softwood
Artist unknown
Circa 1860-1880
Dimensions: $30.0 \times 61.0 \times 20.0$ cm ($11\frac{13}{16} \times 24 \times 7\frac{7}{8}$ inches)
Collection of the Art Gallery of Nova Scotia, Halifax, Nova Scotia

This large pointing finger was either used inside a store or as the fineal on a church steeple pointing the way to heaven. A large hook on the side of the hand suggests that it was used as a hanging device to mount the finger in a pointing position. However, there is some evidence on the underside of the hand, to suggest that it was hafted with the finger pointing toward heaven, although it seems small in scale to serve as a church fineal. It is entirely possible that this particular example served both functions.[1]

History: The hand was donated by Mrs Betsy Harwood in 1982 to the Art Gallery of Nova Scotia.

Structure: Although slightly weathered, the hand is in good condition and made from four laminated and square nailed blocks of softwood. The surface is painted white and the finger-nails painted red, with an under layer of gesso used to fill the cracks.

1. The pointing finger toward heaven is also called the Hand of God. For more information on this form see C. Kurt Dewhurst, Betty MacDowell and Marsha MacDowell, *Religious Folk Art in America: Reflections of Faith,* (New York: E.P. Dutton, Inc., 1983), p. 150 (figure 209 is an illustration of a Hand of God which is 50 inches in height with a very long arm. The form is somewhat different and larger than this example).

94 Diorama of the Sloop "Jane"*

Halifax, Halifax County
Carved and painted wooden vessel in glass case
Artist unknown
Circa 1870-1880
Dimensions: $39.0 \times 31.7 \times 11.0$ cm ($15\frac{3}{8} \times 12\frac{1}{2}$ $4\frac{5}{16}$ inches)
Collection of Dr and Mrs Charles Armour

A very early example of a ship diorama showing a single masted sloop under sail, passing a small boat which has the word BUS painted on the bow. The backboard is painted to simulate sky and the vessels are set on painted plaster shaped to imitate waves with white caps.

Structure: Plank constructed case with butt joints. The backboard is attached with square nails. The front of the case is glazed and the molding attached with round finishing nails.

*This piece will be on view in Halifax only

95 Ship Diorama of Three Masted Vessel Passing a Lighthouse*

Shelburne, Shelburne County

Softwood half-model of three masted vessel mounted on board with lighthouse and two masted steam-sail vessel

Artist unknown

Circa 1880-1890

Dimensions: 68.5 × 47.0 × 9.5 cm (27 × 18½ × 3¾ inches)

Collection of the Shelburne County Museum, Shelburne, Nova Scotia

A very detailed example of a diorama showing a three masted vessel entering a port. The vessel is flying both the American and French flags, and is displaying various signal letters subordinate to the American flag which is being flown on the monkey gaff. The ship is sailing past a lighthouse with flagpole displaying the tricolour and is being passed by a two-masted sail-steamer. The vessel is entering a French port.

The model has a small figurehead and the name of the vessel is partially legible on the bow as "Lawrence." This diorama undoubtedly depicts the "William D Lawrence," built in Maitland, Nova Scotia in 1874. The "William D Lawrence" was a ship of 2458 tons, the largest vessel built in the Maritimes.[1]

Structure: Carved and painted softwood was used to make the vessel, sails and lighthouse. These are attached to a backboard of softwood, which is painted to depict sea and sky. Cotton was used for the smoke from the sail-steamer. The case is made from softwood with plank construction and butt joints that are nailed with small square brads. The molding around the base is painted gold.

1. Charles A. Armour and Thomas Lackey, *Sailing Ships of the Maritimes,* (Toronto: McGraw-Hill Ryerson, Limited, 1975), pp. 126-127.

*This piece will be on view in Halifax only

96 Ship Diorama of the Barque "Annie"*

Inverness County

Original softwood box with glass front and models of sailing vessels and lighthouse

Artist unknown

Circa 1880-1890

Dimensions: 45.7 × 37.5 × 12.4 cm (18 × 14¾ × 4⅞ inches)

Collection of Mr and Mrs Francis Coutellier, Moncton, New Brunswick

This is a wonderful ship diorama of the "Annie" which was built in Port Hawkesbury in June, 1885. The master was Isaac Reynolds, the builder R. McVicar, and the owner Alfred Bissett. The model is very complete and flys a masonic pennant from the spanker gaff.

Structure: Plank construction, softwood case with mitered joints screwed in place. The case is presently painted a dark brown.

*This piece will be on view in Halifax only

98 Ship Diorama of the "Bluenose"*

Greenfield, Colchester County

Softwood half model of schooner mounted on board and enclosed in a glass fronted case

Made by Oliver Tupper

Circa 1910-1920

Dimensions: 41.3 × 28.0 × 8.0 cm (16¼ × 11 × 3⅛ inches)

Collection of Carl Boswick, Halifax, Nova Scotia

An excellent example of a small ship diorama of the original "Bluenose" schooner.

Structure: Carved and painted softwood was used to make the vessel and sails, which was then attached to a backboard of softwood. The case is plank construction with butt joints that are round nailed. The outer frame of the case is painted gold.

97 Frame with Photographs and Diorama

Digby, Digby County

Softwood, glass and paper with cardboard backing

Artist unknown

Circa 1880-1900

Dimensions: 24.0 × 28.0 cm (9$\frac{7}{16}$ × 11 inches)

Private collection

A very interesting and unique work of Nova Scotia folk art. The frame is made in a fashion similar to tramp art construction, with carved pieces of softwood shaped into a wreath design. Within the frame are two tintypes of a seated man wearing a cap, and a woman standing wearing a fancy hat. Directly underneath these images is the small diorama of a three masted sailing vessel suggesting that the man was a sailor. Information from the owners of this work indicate that the man and woman are husband and wife, and that he is the maker of this piece.

Structure: The frame is made from shaped pieces of softwood which have been linked in a wreath design. Inside this is set a second frame containing a glass case housing the tintypes and the diorama. This in turn is backed with cardboard. Between the tintypes and the vessel are borders cut from blue and white paper.

99 Ship Diorama of Schooner*

Lunenburg, Lunenburg County
Carved and painted softwood in glass case
Artist unknown
Circa 1920-1930
Dimensions: 72.0 × 54.6 × 12.0 cm ($28\frac{3}{8} \times 21\frac{1}{2} \times 4\frac{3}{4}$ inches)
Private collection

Another fine example of a ship diorama of a schooner under sail.

Structure: Plank constructed case with butt joints that are nailed and screwed. The molding is painted black with a gold liner giving depth to the piece. The sails are carved from softwood.

*This piece will be on view in Halifax only

100 Ship Model in Glass Case

Wards Brook, Cumberland County
Carved and painted softwood ship model in softwood case with glass sides
Artist unknown, but initials W.H.M. are painted on the stern of the model
Made in 1908
Dimensions: 32.5 × 17.5 × 12.5 cm ($12\frac{13}{16} \times 6\frac{7}{8} \times 4\frac{15}{16}$ inches)
Collection of Gerald Ferguson, Halifax, Nova Scotia

Although the full name of the maker of this model is unknown, his initials are painted on the stern of the vessel as W.H.M. The model was made in Wards Brook in 1908 and is a fine example of a detailed three dimensional model. The inside of the case is painted sky blue with clouds, to further the illusion of a ship under sail on the open sea.

Structure: The case is plank construction with butt joints and round nails. The ship is carved and painted softwood. The base on which the ship is mounted is a hard clay or plaster-like substance which is painted to resemble the sea with waves. The sides and top of the box are painted to represent a sky with clouds.

101 Ship Model of the "Marie Maie"
Belliveau Cove, Digby County
Carved and painted softwood
Made by August Gaudet
Circa 1920
Dimensions: 170.0 × 76.0 × 20 cm (66 15/16 × 29 15/16 × 7 5/8 inches)
Collection of the Yarmouth County Museum, Yarmouth, Nova Scotia

This model was built by Mr Gaudet and named after his wife.

History: This model is on loan from Mr Elie Belliveau to the Yarmouth County Museum.

Structure: The model is made mostly of softwood.

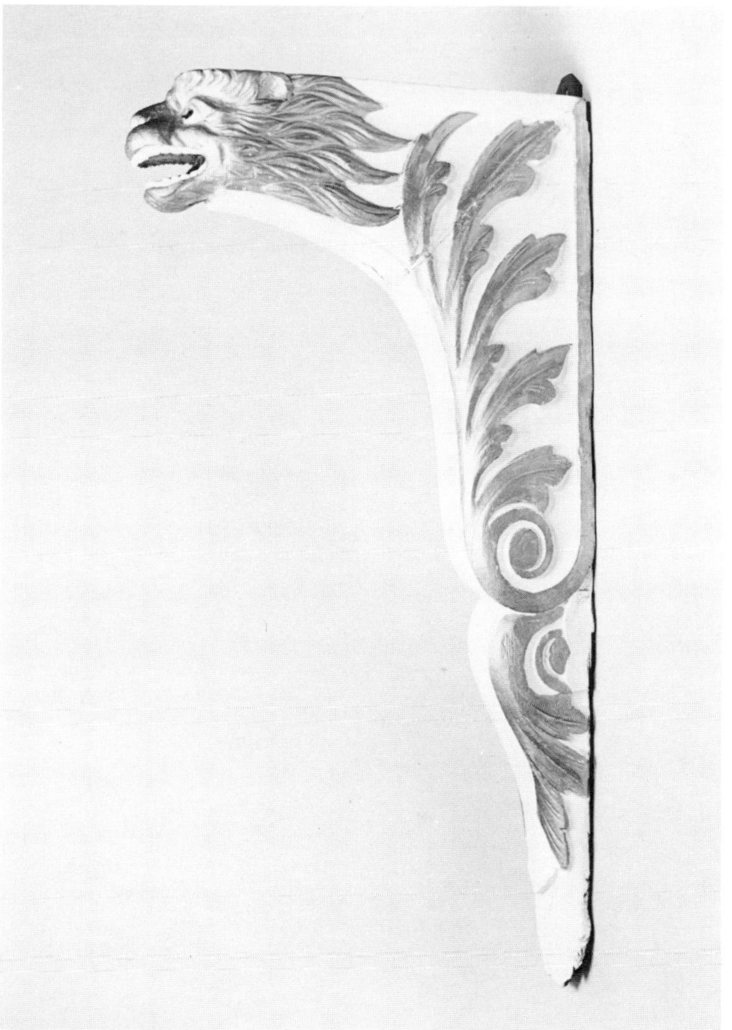

102 Carved Ship's Knee
Probably Yarmouth County
Carved and repainted softwood
Artist unknown
Circa 1850-1880
Dimensions: Length — 141.0, Projected horizontal section — 67.0, Width — 18.0 cm (55 1/2 × 26 1/2 × 7 inches)
Collection of the Yarmouth County Museum, Yarmouth, Nova Scotia

A carved ship's knee with sea lions (?) head and gcanthus leaves. The mouth is open showing teeth, some of which are damaged. This is an external knee used to support a poopdeck overhang. There would have been two knees on each side of the ship. Judging from the slanted camber top this particular knee would have been on the starboard side of the vessel.

History: This knee was purchased by the museum from the McInnis collection.

Structure: The ship's knee is carved from several blocks of softwood. Unfortunately it was repainted white and gold after it was acquired by the museum.

103 Billethead*

Indian Point, Lunenburg County
Carved and painted softwood
Artist unknown
Circa 1870-1890
Dimensions: 10.0 × 23.5 × 9.0 cm ($3^{15}/_{16} \times 9^{1}/_{4} \times 3^{9}/_{16}$ inches)
Collection of Leslie J. Langille, Lunenburg, Nova Scotia

As the nature of shipbuilding started changing around the end of the nineteenth century, figureheads began being replaced with billetheads on ship's prows. This beautifully carved and painted example is from the Whynot (Whynacht) family and may never have been used on a vessel. Painted blue, white and red, the billethead is in the form of a volute scroll with egg-and-dart and acanthus leaf details.

Structure: The billethead is in excellent condition and is carved from a solid block of softwood.

Published: Michael Bird and Terry Kobayashi, *A Splendid Harvest: Germanic Folk and Decorative Arts in Canada,* (Toronto: Van Nostrand Reinhold Ltd., 1981), illustrated on p. 36.

* This piece will be on view in Halifax only.

Refer to colour plate VIII, page 16

104 Nameboard of the "S.S. Edna R."

Yarmouth County
Carved and painted softwood
Artist unknown
Carved in 1892-1893
Dimensions: 146.0 × 48.0 × 3.5 cm ($57^{1}/_{2} \times 18^{7}/_{8} \times 1^{3}/_{8}$ inches)
Collection of the Yarmouth County Museum, Yarmouth, Nova Scotia

This nameboard was placed on the front of the wheelhouse of the steamer/tug "S.S. Edna R.", which was built in 1893 at Arcadia. The vessel was used to transport lobster and fish, and as a tug, running between Yarmouth and Argyle. The prominent placement of the Masonic symbol indicates that the owner and/or master of this vessel was a mason.

History: The nameboard was donated to the Yarmouth County Museum by Mr. William Utley of Goderich, Ontario in 1969.

Structure: The nameboard is carved from two planks of softwood. The black and gold is a recent overpaint.

105 Deckhouse Nameboard*
Lunenburg, Lunenburg County
Carved and painted softwood
Artist unknown
Circa 1910-1920
Dimensions: 83.0 × 9.0 × 1.0 cm (32 11/16 × 3 9/16 × 3/8 inches)
Collection of Richard Henning Field and Deborah Field, Halifax, Nova Scotia

This small name board was used to identify the port of origin for a small fishing vessel, and was probably located on the deckhouse. The name Lunenburg, the initials N.S. and two five pointed stars were carved into the softwood slab and painted black, the rest of the sign painted white to highlight the name and decorative motifs.

Structure: The sign has weathered but it is in good condition. The paint appears to be original.

*This piece will be on view in Halifax only.

106 Ship Nameboard
Lunenburg County
Original painted and carved softwood
Artist unknown
Circa 1920-1940
Dimensions: 114.0 × 13.0 × 2.3 cm (40 15/16 × 5 1/8 × 7/8 inches)
Collection of Gerald Ferguson, Halifax, Nova Scotia

A rather whimsical takeoff on the name of the famous "Bluenose" fishing schooner. This nameboard was probably attached to the deckhouse of a fishing vessel.

Structure: The nameboard is carved from one piece of plank softwood. Some of the original paint is missing due to weathering.

INTRODUCTION

Paintings, Watercolours and Drawings

Richard Henning Field

Painting is one of the easiest categories of decorative folk art to recognize. Works which exhibit a naïve or primitive style can be readily accepted as products of untrained artists. But it is more difficult to label paintings which combine naïve elements such as flat perspective with some obvious academic techniques, suggesting that the artist had some knowledge or training in the subject of painting or drawing.

In terms of this exhibition the scope of decorative folk art has been purposely broad in definition believing that folk art cannot simply be defined as art alone, but must include the cultural context in which it was produced and used. From another standpoint this approach forces the acceptance of a broader definition and interpretation of what constitutes folk art, enlarging the present meaning beyond the descriptive (naïve, provincial) to include a scale of folk painting ranging from the obviously primitive to those works which exhibit a combination of folk and academic technique.

At first glance the "Man with Pen" portrait appears as an academic work painted by a trained artist. If examined carefully elements of what constitutes a folk style are evident, particularly in the modeling of the body and shoulders, the way the hand is drawn and painted, and the perspective of the face. This artist had problems in drawing the human figure and this portrait is an excellent example of the combination of folk and academic elements. In this respect this painting falls at one end of the academic scale of folk painting preceding the full academic style of professional portraiture.

By comparison the examination of the Eisenhauer and Payzant portraits, or the "Girl in the Red Dress", reveal a painterly style falling within the mainstream of what is generally accepted as folk painting. This same criteria can be applied to all types of painting including the sub-categories in this exhibition, ranging from folk and ship portraits to landscapes, seascapes and townscapes.

However, throughout the four years of research into the material in this show, it was always assumed that there actually existed a folk painting tradition in Nova Scotia, which would become evident once there was a large

INTRODUCTION

enough body of works to examine and compare. Unfortunately this has not proven to be the case, and at this point it can only be suggested that there is simply no tradition of folk painting in this province which can be defined as Nova Scotian existing between the years 1780-1930. Certainly there are folk paintings, but no patterns are yet discernable in terms of attributions to the same artist (except for Joseph Brown Comingo) or school of artists, region or ethnic group. Isolated works do exist (such as the Payzant portrait, or the MacKay house portrait) which suggest the existence of such a tradition, but further research must be conducted into this category before trends become evident.

In terms of the works that are included the question is often asked how do these paintings have a function if traditional folk art is defined as the marriage of function with decoration. In many instances decoration can be considered function when the painting was used to indicate social status and station in life. Many landscapes and seascapes were hung not only to decorate the parlour, but to suggest to guests and visiting family that they were prosperous enough to afford such embellishment.

However, the most important function of folk, ship, house and animal portraits, townscapes, landscapes and farm scenes, was as a form of documentation. Folk portraits were painted to record the likeness of family members the same way we use photography today. Ship owners and Captains wanted a painting of their vessel to admire and show off, but it had to be accurately rigged and drawn. Proud owners of prize bulls and horses often had these animals painted. Some landscapes, townscapes and farm scenes, and particularly house portraits, were commissioned to be hung on walls as decoration, and to record a particular place, time or event, preserving important memories.

Today's enthusiasm for folk painting may help to raise the level of appreciation for this art form, and at the same time uncover works which will help to define a tradition of folk painting in Nova Scotia.

Aspects of Nova Scotia Folk Portraiture

Susan M. Foshay

Susan M. Foshay received her MA in Folklore/Folklife from the University of Pennsylvania in Philadelphia, Pennsylvania in 1983. Foshay, a native of Nova Scotia, lectures on various aspects of folklife and is a resident of Halifax.

your Repreſentatives in the laſt General Aſſembly--I am induced to come forward and offer myſelf as a Candidate at the enſuing Election --hoping that my conduct has been ſuch that I may again meet with your approbation--If I do my beſt abilities ſhall be exerted for your intereſts.

I am, Gentlemen,
Your very humble ſervant,
WILLIAM LAWSON.

Halifax, Auguſt 19, 1811.

Portraits & Miniatures.

J. Brown Comingo,

ACQUAINTS his friends and the public, that he has taken a Convenient room, in the Jeruſalem Tavren (Madden's) where he takes Portraits and Miniatures; from 10 to 15 Dollars.--Miniatures likewiſe on vellum paper done at one ſitting from 2 to 5 dollars.

He ſolicits thoſe Ladies & Gentlemen who wiſh to favor him with ſitting for their likeneſſes to apply as early as poſſible, as he intends to leave the Town ſoon.

Auguſt 19, 1811.

Notice.

ALL perſons having any juſt demands againſt

Newspaper Advertisement

Joseph Comingo placed this advertisement in the Halifax Journal, 19 August 1811, for his services as a portrait painter.

Collection of the Public Archives of Nova Scotia, Halifax, Nova Scotia

This piece is not included in the exhibition

Since the founding of Halifax by the British in 1749 and the subsequent settlement of Nova Scotia, lifestyles and attitudes began merging, influenced by many social and cultural factors. Immigrants arrived from Ireland, Scotland, England, Germany and Holland, with the greatest proportion from the New England colonies.

By 1800 the hardships associated with the pioneering of the previous century were becoming memories, as the once-struggling settlements developed into bustling centres. The demand for decoration increased. "No significant resident artists were in the Atlantic region until after 1800 . . . Officials in the new capitals [Halifax, Fredericton, Charlottetown] had their portraits painted to substantiate their prestige, and bare walls of fine new houses required decoration. There was a growing demand for paintings. Portraits were a first interest, as they had been in the United States."[1] Academically trained portrait painters were most certainly available to fulfil this need for those who could afford the expense.[2]

For those with more limited budgets a variety of ambitious artists was available. With limited experience and little or no training, they tailored their prices to meet their clients' circumstances. These non-academic portrait painters flourished between 1800 and 1842, after which time photography became available in Nova Scotia.[3] A photographer could produce an exact likeness of a person for a fraction of the cost and the time it took an artist to paint a portrait. The limited number of folk portraits from the second half of the nineteenth century and early twentieth century is the result of many portraitists turning to the cheaper process of photography.

This article focusses on the non-academic artists who painted portraits of ministers, merchants, sea captains and their loved ones in towns around Nova Scotia. Some of these artists painted signs and houses as a livelihood, and others travelled from community to community, staying until their skills were no longer required. It is very difficult to identify most of these artists since very few of them signed their work. It is somewhat easier, though often inconclusive, to identify their subjects.

The study of early Nova Scotia folk art generally, and folk portraiture specifically, is still in its infancy. How, then, is a portrait identified as Nova Scotian? Three criteria for inclusion in this exhibition were established: that the painting be attributable to a Nova Scotian artist; or, that the portrait be of a person known to have been a Nova Scotian; or, that the portrait has been found in Nova Scotia, and through the owner's oral records believed to be that of a Nova Scotian ancestor.

Defining *folk* poses more of a problem. There are so many definitions of the word that it is perhaps easier to point out what it does not mean in relation to folk portraits. It is not a style in the sense of "Gothic" or "Queen Anne" but it does consist of a number of factors: a tendency toward flatness or two-dimensionality, difficulty with perspective, problematic draftsmanship, for example, with hands and limbs, a deficient use of light and shadow, assisting in identifying a folk portrait and contributing to each artist's individual style as a painter. We have, therefore, a descriptive formula for defining the individual folk artist's style in executing portraits to which some or all of the above factors are appropriate. The folk painter is self-taught, or perhaps has little training, unaware of or uninterested in the academic conventions of portrait painting, and places considerable emphasis on the subject, often outlining objects and then filling in colour, and thereby becoming a master of line and colour.[4]

The portraits represented here cover a broad range of technical accomplishment and academic awareness. On the one hand, we have the portrait of Sarah Elizabeth Eisenhauer, a painting executed by an unidentified and untrained artist. On the other, is the Blood portrait, exhibiting considerable technical detail and accuracy, by an artist with some academic training and skill.

Other than being painted by Nova Scotians, of Nova Scotians, what then constitutes a Nova Scotian folk portrait? Have values and criteria been established which render a portrait clearly Nova Scotian?

Portraiture in eighteenth and early nineteenth century Britain was an art form popular among the aristocracy, employing well-trained academic portrait painters. It was also popular, though to a lesser extent, among the lower classes, who employed the skills of untrained itinerant painters to reproduce their likenesses. Portraits by these artists tended to place the subject in identifiable surroundings, in a garden with a familiar river flowing by, or perhaps in a parlour with a large window overlooking a village, thereby establishing the subject's status within a community and at the same time vesting the subject with a sense of place.[5]

On the other hand, American folk portrait painters of the eighteenth and nineteenth centuries, for the most part, placed their subjects in nondescript rooms, adding details to inform the viewer of the subject's status, but rarely providing the notion of identifiable space. Most portraits are of subjects in the three-quarter pose employed by the academics (both American and British) in their formal portraits. Many portraits are of a single individual.

Nova Scotian folk portraiture is so similar to the American tradition that without knowing the details of artist and/or subject, identification as Nova Scotian is impossible. However, the portraits in this exhibition have now provided a base for further study. Research may yield more information on the artists represented in it, and perhaps undiscovered Nova Scotian folk portrait painters will be identified in the future. Before examining the portraits it is important to consider that these paintings, out of their original context, are being dealt with in isolation and should be examined from their decorative standpoint rather than from a cultural or sociological standpoint.

Joseph Brown Comingo, an itinerant artist, was born in 1784 in Lunenburg, Nova Scotia, a town populated largely by Germans and Dutch, who began arriving in Lunenburg in 1753. His grandfather, Bruin Romkes Comingo (1723-1820), arrived in Lunenburg from Holland in 1753, and in 1770 became the first Presbyterian minister ordained in British North America. Joseph's father, Romkes (1754-1825) married Jane Margaret Bailly (1753-1836). In 1808, according to the Fredericton *Royal Gazette,* Joseph announced himself as an itinerant painter of portraits and miniatures.

In October, 1810, Joseph Brown Comingo placed an advertisement in the Halifax *Weekly Chronicle* stating that he would do portraits and miniatures at his studio in the Jerusalem Tavern in Halifax.[6] He married Elizabeth Winslow Reynolds in Halifax in 1812 and they had three children.

In 1814-1815 Comingo was in Saint John, New Brunswick, painting portraits and miniatures on paper and ivory and watercolour landscapes. He visited Yarmouth in southwestern Nova Scotia in 1817 and there painted landscapes and portraits. Among his subjects were Joseph Ellis (1779-1851), a minister, and his wife, Ruth Porter Ellis (1782-1865). The Ellises, who lived in Chebogue, just outside Yarmouth, were both devoted to their religion, and in 1815 established the first Sunday school in Yarmouth County. In 1821 Joseph Ellis became minister of the Congregational Church in Chebogue and preached there until his death in 1851.

By 1820 Comingo was painting in Baltimore, where he evidently did several paintings, and in 1821 moved on to Nassau and died later that year.[7]

No information on Comingo's education or art instruction has surfaced, but a possible influence has been identified. In 1808 in Halifax, the eminent artist Robert Field commenced work in oils and watercolours, producing large portraits as well as miniatures. Field, born in England about 1769, was educated and worked in London; he immigrated to the United States in 1794. His advertisements do not state that he taught painting, but close observation of the work of Comingo and Field suggests that Field did influence Comingo.

Ellis is painted, head held high, in the three-quarter pose, seated beside a table with an ink well, a quill pen and a book, all informing us of Ellis' erudition. The table suffers from problems with perspective, and Ellis' facial structure is less than perfectly executed. The green background paint is applied to the paper in such a way as to simulate the painted ivory background of the more expensive miniatures popular at the time, which Comingo also painted.

The portrait of Ruth Ellis, though not signed or dated, has been attributed to Joseph Comingo. Both portraits are painted on the same paper, and both exhibit very similar styles and paint application. Judging by the style of her hair and clothing it would be reasonable to assume that Ruth Ellis' portrait

Joseph Comingo

Copy of a photograph of a self portrait of the artist. Location of original unknown

Collection of the Public Archives of Nova Scotia, Halifax, Nova Scotia

This piece is not included in the exhibition

Elizabeth Winslow Comingo

Copy of a photograph of Joseph Comingo's wife. Location of original unknown.

Collection of the Public Archives of Nova Scotia, Halifax, Nova Scotia

This piece is not included in the exhibition

Jane Margaret Bailly Comingo

Copy of a photograph of Joseph Comingo's mother. Location of original unknown.

Collection of the Public Archives of Nova Scotia, Halifax, Nova Scotia

This piece is not included in the exhibition

Romkes Comingo

Copy of a photograph of a miniature of Joseph Comingo's father. Location of original unknown.

Collection of the Public Archives of Nova Scotia

This piece is not included in the exhibition

was painted around 1817. Her portrait is from the waist up. She sits or stands immobile and upright, her face suffering from the same slight distortion as that of her husband. The treatment of light and shadow is less detailed for Ruth Ellis, and shading and perspective from the neck down in no way match the painstaking detail of Joseph Ellis' garments, where even the buttons on his jacket are handled with technical finesse. The background is painted with similar delicacy of colour, though with no attempt at the ivory simulation effect that the background of Joseph's portrait suggests. Unlike Joseph, Ruth is placed outdoors, with shrubs and a cloudless aqua sky. Both subjects are identified by their names in block letters. Comingo did not customarily identify his subjects in this manner, and it has been impossible to determine whether the printing was done by the artist or by another hand, perhaps at a later date.

The portrait of Margaret Ratchford DeWolf is neither signed nor dated, but clearly has been executed by an artist with some obvious training. The portrait has been painted to represent unmistakably the likeness of Margaret DeWolf, with considerable attention given to perspective, light and shadow, and replication of the lace-edged bonnet and collar ruff. Her body, on the other hand, is undetailed, and her black dress has been painted with a limited number of brush strokes. The dark monochromatic background, barely distinguishable from Margaret's black dress at this point in conservation time, emphasizes the fact that the artist and the viewer concentrate on the subject, who stares at us impassively.

Margaret Ratchford was born in 1762, the daughter of Captain Thomas Ratchford of Cornwallis, Kings County, Nova Scotia. In 1779 she married Elisha DeWolf, who had been born in Saybrook, Connecticut, in 1756 and later immigrated to Kings County with his parents Nathan and Lydia Kirtland DeWolf. From 1784 to 1789 Elisha was High Sheriff of Kings County, and by his death in 1837 had been postmaster, Collector of Customs and a Justice of the Peace. In 1799 Judge DeWolf, as he was fondly called, built a home in Wolfville later known as Kent Lodge, which evidently was the seat of much grand entertaining. Elisha and Margaret had 13 children.[8]

Margaret died in 1852 at the age of 90, and though her portrait is not dated, she appears to be in her 60's, corroborating speculation of the general date of the portrait as "first quarter of the nineteenth century".

In 1818 William Valentine (1798-1849) came to Halifax from England and immediately began advertising himself as a painter, earning a living as a house painter and decorator.[9] His expertise at portrait painting became established through Joseph Howe, one of Nova Scotia's leading political figures and statesmen of the nineteenth century. Howe maintained that Valentine was self taught, and while he did not sign his work, attributions are relatively numerous. By 1833 Valentine began seeking commissions for his portraits throughout the Atlantic Provinces. In the late 1830's Valentine made at least one trip to England where he is said to have copied portraits by academic artists there, thus honing his skills and changing his style of brushwork and choice of pigment. His early portraits appear to have been executed with dark monochromes and flat flesh tones while his later work used warmer redder tones.[10]

Like many other professional portraitists in the 1840's Valentine became a photographer. He died in Halifax in 1849.

The portrait included here, attributed to Valentine and dated around 1830, has an overall effect suggesting an artist aware of the conventions of academic art but, in this instance, failing to make the grade. Valentine has given each feature considerable attention, and there can be little doubt that the portrait resembles the subject. We are told the subject is an educated man by the small red leather bound book he holds in his right hand. The man's hand, with forefinger marking his place, is professionally and realistically executed. Shadow and light details in his coat suggest a well-trained eye. Each facial feature is carefully undertaken, with considerable detail given to light and shadow in the hair, and the effective execution of the three-quarter pose. Considerable detail is given to the book, clearly identifying both binding and individual pages. His right arm rests on the back of a wooden chair characteristic of the style of chair made in Halifax County in the nineteenth century.[11] However, the effect of the painting as a whole gives the impression of a subject who has suffered deformities in the translation from artist's eye to canvas. The subject's head is far too large for the shoulder width and arm length, his hand is too large in proportion to his arm length, and his nose is almost the same size as his hand.[12] The intense gaze of the subject and the accuracy of details in addition to the disjointed perspective, have produced an appealing portrait. Had these features been executed conventionally, the resulting portrait could have been a rather uninteresting and dull likeness of an unidentified gentleman, accurate in detail but otherwise hardly noteworthy.

The second DeWolf portrait, an oil painting of a young woman, is appealing because of the highly individualized and skilfully executed facial features attached to the stiffly posed body and wooden neck that appear to have been painted with a minimum of paint and few brush strokes. Attention has been given to her hair, yet its execution falls short of the technically accurate face. Her long string of jet beads has been hastily applied with minimal attention to detail. The subject wears a black dress with very full puffed sleeves, low neck and wide belt, and her hair is carefully curled and plaited, indicating a highly fashionable woman of the 1840's.

The artist has neither signed nor dated the work, and there is some confusion as to the subject's identity. The painting is on loan from the Wolfville Historical Society, and is identified in their records as Elizabeth Brown, wife of Edward DeWolf who died in 1796. However, the subject in the painting is dressed in the style fashionable in the 1840's. The painter of this portrait appears to be the same artist who painted Thomas Andrew Strange DeWolf (1795-1878), in the collection of the Wolfville Historical Society's Randall House. He married his first cousin Nancy Ratchford (1798-1883) and had 14 children.[13] While Thomas DeWolf's portrait is neither signed nor dated, it appears to have been painted around 1840, from the hairstyle and clothing. Both paintings have an unidentifiable monochromatic background similar to the majority of Nova Scotian folk portraits.

In 1832, when he was 82, John Payzant of Liverpool had his portrait painted, probably by an itinerant painter. The portrait, oil paint on wood panel, is not signed, but is dated in pencil on the back, information doubtless added some time after the portrait was completed. We see a rather gruff-looking, balding old man with shaggy hair, piercing eyes and no teeth. Local lore informs us that Payzant had wooden dentures which caused him a great deal of discomfort; consequently he rarely used them. It is interesting that he chose to be represented here so obviously without the teeth rather than with them. Payzant is dressed in the black top coat, vest and white chin collar and bow similar to that worn by Joseph Ellis, the Valentine sitter and the "Man with Pen".

The painting has been done by someone who is perhaps a professional and conforms with the style of composition of many American folk portraits of the time, filling in every corner of available space with visual information: dark red drapery; a chair with brass tack detail; a shelf of books including the Bible, School Lessons, and a scroll document; a small table — doubtless used for a candle — with two drawers each with two brass pulls in the American Federal style; a table in the foreground with ink well, pen, a stack of papers with handwritten alphabets, books, and manuscript; a small book held in the hand. The drapery is painted with little detail and a thin application of paint while Payzant's face has been given the greatest concentration of detail. The paint has been heavily applied in even strokes and with rather pasty looking pigment, resulting in a muddy complexion, although this could appear quite different after proper cleaning. However, the artist has failed to achieve the academic conventions of perspective. We see the several pieces of furniture from several angles giving an impression of distortion to the room in which this conventional and dour-looking man sits.

The book on the table is clearly identified "Tract and Bible Society London 180[4?] Printed Shand and N . . .". Tract societies were associations established to publish and/or circulate religious treatises or books in the eighteenth and nineteenth centuries.[14] There is no record of a Tract and Bible Society in London in 1804, although a Religious Tract Society was founded in London in 1799, and five years later the British and Foreign Bible Society was founded. It is possible that the artist felt the precise details of title and organization unnecessary for conveying to the viewer the essence of Reverend John Payzant. The information that we have been provided by yet another anonymous itinerant artist in Nova Scotia indicates that John Payzant is an educated man devoted to his religion and to education.

John Payzant was born in the Jersey Islands in 1749 and arrived in Lunenburg County with his parents, Marie and Louis Payzant, who had previously fled to the Jersey Islands as Huguenot refugees. Rather than settle in close proximity to the other immigrants with whom they had arrived in Nova Scotia, Louis chose to settle his wife and four children on Covey's Island in Mahone Bay. In 1756 Louis was killed in an Indian raid of the island, and his wife and children were abducted and turned over to the Jesuits in Quebec City. John and his younger brother Louis attended Jesuit's College where they were educated in Latin and Greek. Following the British taking of Quebec in 1759 the Payzants were granted freedom to return to Nova Scotia. John arrived in Halifax in 1760 and in 1761 moved to Falmouth, Hants County. He lived and apprenticed with William Allin who had arrived in Falmouth from New England in 1760. The Allins had five children, Francis, Henry, Rebecca, Elizabeth and Mary.

John Payzant married Mary Allin, or Alline as the family name became, in 1774. In the following year, Henry Alline began his ministry with the Congregational Church of Nova Scotia, preaching salvation, reviving the dying churches of Nova Scotia and leading the New Light Movement in Nova Scotia communities populated by New England immigrants.

Reverend Bruin Romkes Comingo

Copy of a photograph of Joseph Comingo's grandfather. Location of original unknown.

Collection of the Public Archives of Nova Scotia, Halifax, Nova Scotia

This piece is not included in the exhibition

Payzant committed himself to Henry's church and gospel. While neither had formal theological training, Payzant had been well educated by the Jesuits and was familiar with English, French, Latin, Greek and Micmac. John preached in Hants and Kings counties until he took over the foundering Congregationalist Church in Liverpool, Queens County, in 1793. The Liverpool congregation had been established by Simeon Perkins, a New England Congregationalist who had arrived in Liverpool from Norwich, Connecticut, in 1762. Payzant remained in Liverpool, leading the congregation, and actively preaching the gospel until his death at 85 in 1834.[15]

"Josefina" and the P.E.H. portrait are works about which we know very little. Josefina is a reverse glass painting revealing a clarity of features and of brush strokes not usually found in other media.

Josefina's dress and hairstyle indicate the fashion of around 1830. We know nothing about her except her name. The portrait originated in the Annapolis Valley, suggesting the possibility that Josefina is of British ancestry.

The artist has provided many details with Josefina's coiled hairstyle, her gold ear bobs, lace collar and wide belt with gold buckle. The artist also displays skill in shading Josefina's features, but she appears pasted to the monochromatic unshaded background. Her head is at an uncomfortable angle and her mouth is strangely placed in relation to her eyes and nose. Josefina's posture, the writing of her name, and the fact that it is a reverse glass painting, indicate tht the portrait may have been copied from a print.[16]

The P.E.H. sketch in pencil and charcoal, and the portrait in pencil and pastel, are initialled and dated. The initials "P.E.H." have been carefully incorporated into the folds of the subject's left sleeve in both, and the sketch dated 1849. It is believed that these two fine works come from the Annapolis Valley. Here we have another virtually anonymous artists who gives considerable attention to the subject's lace collar, small gold beads, and flowered cap. Again we view a subject in the stiff and formal three-quarter pose with little distinction made between arms and body, and hands not shown. Again we see the nondescript background which seems to be characteristic of the portraits represented here.

Nova Scotia's coastal communities were home ports for fishing and trading vessels in the nineteenth century. Captain Joseph Hogg of Shelburne was commander of one such vessel. His portrait, neither signed, dated nor identifying the subject, matches the ship portrait. The painting of the ship *Kurramanny of Calcutta* is identified on the canvas as "Laying in Blenheim Reach River Tigris China 10th August 1849 Josh Hogg Commander". The artist remains anonymous, but both paintings were executed by the same hand, and are classified as port paintings.[17] That Captain Hogg's portrait was painted at the same time as his ship, in 1849, is substantiated by Captain Hogg's clothing. His high chin collar with black bow tie, white shirt, white vest with collar, white trousers secured under the arches, black square-toed shoes and high collared top coat conform to the style popular about 1845.[18]

Both paintings are oil on canvas; however the canvas is of a very fine texture, of either silk or cotton fabric rather than the linen canvas generally found in oil paintings on canvas. Neither is mounted on the standard stretcher, and the dimensions of each are identical, the ship's portrait being horizontal and that of Captain Hogg, vertical.

The artist uses clear pigment and the finest of brush strokes; the result is a freshness in colour and detail seldom seen with oil paints. The fine canvas and almost imperceptible brush strokes together produce a very polished finish.

Hogg is seated with legs crossed at the knee in an armchair resembling a Duncan Phyfe chair in production from 1768-1854. His green eyes and bearded face reveal a man relaxed and content. In his right hand he holds a blue leather-bound book, indicating that he is a man of knowledge and education. The book rests on what appears to be a chest draped with dark green velvet. Behind Hogg on the right of the painting is heavy red drapery. On the extreme left is a column and tasselled gold cord often found in nineteenth century American folk portraits. Little attention has been given to details of shading to relieve the two-dimensionality of Hogg himself. However, light enters the painting from behind, casting minimal shadow yet producing a ghostly effect in the painting, suspending Hogg in opaque light.

While the artist has mastered his technique of painting drapery, his execution of perspective is poor. Hogg's head is large, round and smooth, but the rest of his body diminishes in size, resulting in distortion of body image.

The charming portrait of Sarah Elizabeth Eisenhauer, painted in 1856, is clearly the work of an amateur, yet the artist has successfully vested his subject with personality and individuality. The unknown artist knows nothing of proportion, perspective and draftsmanship, yet has provided us with details of Sarah's lifestyle and status. She is dressed in a dark dress with small white collar, no jewellery other than a large bow and pin, and the severe hairstyle popular at that time. She holds a book, indicating that she is an educated woman, and is seated as rigid as her whalebone stays can keep her, epitomizing the young Victorian woman. The sofa suggests the Empire style popular in New England between 1820-1840.[19]

A Sarah Eisenhaur (there are several local spellings of the name) died in 1873 in Mahone Bay, a few miles from the community of Chester where the portrait was discovered in the possession of a descendant of the subject. The census does not give her birth date, her age, or her parents' names. This Sarah Eisenhaur died unmarried at the age of 35. However, both the name Sarah and the surname Eisenhauer are common in Lunenburg County and may not refer to the subject. The family could provide no details other than the subject's name, her birth date, and her age at the time the portrait was painted.

A specific Canadian or Nova Scotian tradition of portrait painting appears to be, at best, elusive. Nova Scotian folk portraits do exist, but little, if anything, distinguishes them from their American or British counterparts. The nineteenth century portraits represented here served as testaments of love and devotion, rather than as visible demonstrations of worldly success so important in the more defined British class structure. As one generation succeeded another and portraits of remote ancestors were replaced with photographs of loved ones, the painted portraits went into attics and basements, and subsequently to the auction block or flea market.

As the cultural and historical value of these paintings is recognized by their owners, and the works brought out for public attention and study, it will become increasingly possible to identify a tradition of Nova Scotia folk portraiture.

1. Russell Harper, *Painting in Canada. A History*, (Toronto: University of Toronto Press, 1966), p. 99. A preference for portraits is also mentioned by Beatrix Rumford, *American Folk Portraits. Paintings and Drawings from the Abby Aldrich Rockefeller Folk Art Center*, (Boston: NY Graphic Society, 1981), p. 20.
2. Harry Piers, "Artists in Nova Scotia", *Collections*, Nova Scotia Historical Society, V. XVIII, (Halifax: Wm. McNab, 1914).
3. Scott Robson, and Shelagh Mackenzie, *An Atlantic Album. Photographs of the Atlantic Provinces, Before 1920*, (Halifax: Nimbus Publishing Limited, 1985), p. 11 note that N.S. portrait painter William Valentine began his photographic business in Halifax in January 1842. It was probable he had learned the process in Boston and then returned to Halifax via Saint John, N.B.
4. John Ebert, and Katherine, *American Folk Painters*, (N.Y.: Charles Scribner's Sons, 1975), and Beatrix Rumford, op. cit.
5. James Ayres, *English Naive Painting 1750-1900*, (London: Thames and Hudson, 1980).
6. L. B. Jensen, *Vanishing Halifax*, (Halifax: Petheric Press, 1968) describes the Jerusalem Tavern as follows: The Jerusalem Warehouse, now Morse's Tea, rests on the site of William Fury's Crown Coffee House of 1770. After a period as a town house of great luxury and known as Saul's Folly, it was converted to the Jerusalem Coffee House and burnt down in 1837. The present building was erected in 1841."
7. Public Archives of Nova Scotia (PANS) Biography File.
8. A. W. H. Eaton, *The History of Kings County*, (Salem, Mass.: The Salem Press Company, 1910), p. 492.
9. Piers, op. cit., p. 127.
10. Mentioned by both Russell Harper and Harry Piers.
11. George E. G. MacLaren, *Antique Furniture by Nova Scotia Craftsmen*, (Toronto: McGraw-Hill Ryerson Limited, 1961), p. 55.
12. Harper states that Valentine's accentuation of his subjects' noses is a curious characteristic of his later years, op. cit., p. 103.
13. Eaton, op. cit., p. 492-4.
14. *Encyclopedia Britannica*, 1888.
15. PANS Biography File.
16. Discussion with Scott Robson, Curator of History, Nova Scotia Museum, 1985.
17. Discussion with Richard Henning Field, 1985, based on information supplied by the Shelburne County Museum.
18. Elisabeth McClellan, *Historic Dress in America 1607-1870*, (N.Y.: B. Blom, 1969).
19. Wallace Nutting, *Furniture Treasury*, (N.Y.: Macmillan Publishing Company, Inc., 1976).

Additional information and assistance have been provided by Susan Whiteside, Libarian and Scott Robson, Curator of Historic Furnishings at the Nova Scotia Museum, by Lloyd Melanson, Librarian at the Atlantic School of Theology, and by the staff at the Public Archives of Nova Scotia.

Aspects of Nova Scotia Ship Portraiture

Eric Ruff

Eric Ruff is the Curator of the Yarmouth County Museum in Yarmouth, Nova Scotia where he resides.

Most of the ship portraits in this exhibition can be called "decorative art". While all the portraits are described as "Nova Scotian", this term needs some explanation. Some of the portraits can be attributed to painters from the province. Others are unsigned, but probably come from Nova Scotia. Several were definitely painted elsewhere, but are classed as Nova Scotian because the vessels portrayed are of local origin and/or ownership, and their portraits hung in homes, offices — and, more recently, museums in this province.

These ship portraits differ very little from those of New Brunswick and Prince Edward Island, and indeed from those originating in the United States, Great Britain, or even Germany. The variations arise from the difference in time periods, and in the type and nature of the ships portrayed. Compare, for example, the ship portraits in the Peabody Museum in Salem, Mass, with those in the Yarmouth County Museum, Nova Scotia. The Roux family of Marseilles painted many portraits of the Salem fleet, which was well developed in the early years of the nineteenth century and often engaged in the Mediterranean trade. The Yarmouth County Museum has no portraits by these prolific French artists because the port's deep-sea fleet was not developed until many years later. Many of Yarmouth's ships, however, were painted by artists whose work is found in Bath, Maine (Maine Maritime Museum), Liverpool, England (Merseyside Maritime Museum) and Oslo, Norway (Norsk Sjöfartsmuseum). Fleets from these ports traded to areas of the world where the ships of Yarmouth also went.

Ship's portraits can be divided into four separate, but sometimes overlapping categories: owners' and captains' portraits; portraits relating to a specific story or event; shipping office and advertising portraits; and general seascapes and folk art.

The life of many communities in Nova Scotia was tied to the sea in the nineteenth century. The type of seagoing activity would decide which kinds of portraits hung in the offices and homes in the communities.

Owners' and Captains' Portraits

These portraits are almost always of deep-sea vessels employed in transoceanic trading, and are the type most commonly seen in museums in Nova Scotia. Towns with a deep-sea tradition — Halifax, Yarmouth, Shelburne, Bridgewater, Hantsport and Pictou — have this type of painting in their collections. Lunenburg, a fishing port, does not.

Ships, barques, brigs, the larger brigantines and, later, barquentines were built for deep-sea trading not coastal trading. Very often they never returned to their home port.

County of Yartmouth, built in Belliveau's Cove, Digby County, in 1884 for William D. Lovitt, one of Yarmouth's leading shipowners, was towed to Saint John, New Brunswick, to be rigged. There she picked up a cargo of timber and sailed for Liverpool, England. In her first two years, *County of Yarmouth* visited Cardiff, Rio de Janeiro, Java and Falmouth, England. Until she was sold in 1895, the ship traded to such places as New York, Buenos Aires, Montevideo, Shanghai, Port Townsend and San Francisco — but never touched her home port of Yarmouth.

The absence from the home port is the very essential element behind ship portraiture. Proud owners of such absentee vessels as *County of Yarmouth* wanted reminders of her at home. When built, this vessel, at 2,154 tons, was the second-largest ship built in Nova Scotia — and the largest ever to be owned in Yarmouth. The pride of ownership in such a vessel must have been immense and the profits she earned must have endeared her to her owner. A portrait, then, meant much more to the owner than the occasional letters from the master, or the ship's name in the ledger. And a painting of the vessel in the place of business would impress business associates and customers!

Captains — and even crew members — liked to have portraits of their ships. Thus painters in Liverpool, London, Belfast, Le Havre, Antwerp, Leghorn, Naples, Boston, New York, Melbourne, Hong Kong, Calcutta and other ports painted pictures of Nova Scotian ships. Work by artists from African and South America are hard to find, even though Nova Scotian vessels often visited their major ports. The Canadian ports were represented by E. J. Russell of Saint John and John O'Brien of Halifax — Nova Scotia's only ship portrait painter of note.

The ships' owners tended to stay at home, so the masters usually had the responsibility for commissioning the portraits, and this had an important influence on the style of painting. Captains were seamen, not art connoisseurs, and demanded accurate renderings of their vessels, not artistic interpretations. Proportions had to be right, and rigging and sails correct in every detail. Otherwise the captain would not purchase the painting.

Many ship portrait painters were self-taught, and worked as house or sign painters, listing themselves as "also producing ship portraits" in directories. Among the Roux of Marseilles, the Walters of Liverpool, and the Weyts of Antwerp, the painting of ship portraits ran in the family and certain skills and knowledge were passed on to successive generations. Portrait painters such as Antonio Jacobsen and John O'Brien had academic backgrounds, and Thomas Buttersworth even exhibited in the Royal Academy. John Henry Mohrmann, perhaps the most unusual ship portrait artist, rounded Cape Horn before he turned 14 and spent more than 10 years at sea before receiving his formal art education in Antwerp. In Mohrmann's paintings, the figures on the deck seem to be actually working, and he includes details in his portraits that never appear in more formal ones — such as Dennis the pig, in his sty on deck.

Because the captains demanded accuracy in their ship portraits, those that have survived offer a very useful tool for the study of marine history. Photographs do not give the same precision in the rigging. Nor do they often show the ships under sail, which the painted portrait usually does. Such portraits tell whether or not the vessels had "built" masts, carried stunsails or spencers, etc. They also provided information on deck layouts, type and sex of the figurehead, company houseflags and details that cannot be found in other sources.

Such questions as: Why are some sails absent or furled in certain situations? Why is a child on deck with her parents? What is the function of such-and-such a line? do not come to mind while reading a book or researching the history of ships in the registers.

Look at the painting of the ship *Kurramanny* lying in the River Tigras on August 10, 1849, and see if questions do not arise. Try the same for the de Clerke painting of the barque *Brothers*. To answer one question on the *Kurramanny* — the sails are drying before being furled; this was necessary to ensure that mildew would not damage the canvas. The barque *Brothers* does not have her upper sails set due to the heavy weather indicated by the stormy sea. The answer to the most frequently asked question "Why are the flags flying the wrong way?" is simply that artistic licence allowed the artist to paint them this way since, if they were flying the correct way, they could not be read. As well, the flags blowing astern gives the vessel a sense of speed. Also, in the case of a houseflag, the owner's ego will be boosted if he can see his initials or even his whole name prominently spelled out.

While a great deal can be learned from these owners' or captains' portraits we can also learn from paintings from the next category.

Portraits which Relate a Specific Event

This type of portrait invariably illustrates an event involving danger, potential damage and sometimes partial or total destruction. Early European paintings are a direct descendant of votive models or paintings commissioned to be placed in churches by captains thankful to God for saving their vessels from the dangers of the sea. Many of these votive models and portraits can still be seen in coastal churches, particularly in the Latin countries.

A number of ship portraits of this type exist in Nova Scotian homes offices and museums. They range from scenes showing the dangers of a stormy sea to ones portraying rescues from sinking vessels and complete losses.

The most notable artist specializing in "storm scene" portraits was Edouard Adams of Le Havre, France. His paintings are often captioned with the ship's name and the occasion. "*Autocrat* hove down in a gale of wind, February, 1884" (Maritime Museum of the Atlantic) or "Barque, *George B. Doane Cap' Corning* entering Havre in the gale of the 25th January, 1878" (Yarmouth County Museum). Sometimes these portraits, as in the case of the Autocrat, show blown-out sails and broken spars; at other times, they show vessels flying an upside down ensign, an international signal of distress.

Occasionally, a portrait illustrates the aftermath of a collision, such as one in private hands in Yarmouth portraying a sailing vessel with a broken bowsprit and foremast in disarray with the steamer involved in the collision standing by.

Another Yarmouth portrait of the famous "ship of many rudders", the *Research*, shows her hove to in the North Atlantic in heavy seas with her mate, Aaron Flint Churchill, slung over the stern attempting to install a new rudder.

Still other portraits show rescue attempts, with a boat's crew pulling towards a burning vessel or one nearly awash.

The Browse Island portrait tells the complete story of a shipping disaster, although it is not a true "ship portrait". A Yarmouth vessel, the barque *Carleton*, left Melbourne, Australia, on November 21, 1877, and was loading guano from the tiny Indian Ocean islet of Browse Island when she was driven ashore and wrecked. This picture shows the entire process of this trade right from the birds hovering above the island to the imported labour, probably Chinese, digging and transporting the guano to the shore, where it was carried to the ships outside the reef by ships' boats. Also shown in this picture is the wreck of the *Carleton*, which was driven across the reef and wrecked by a severe hurricane, as well as the scattered remnants of the 1300 ton ship *Matterhorn*, which lost all but four of her crew. The whole tragic incident was related by a passenger to a friend in Yarmouth who passed it on for publication in *The Yarmouth Herald*.

Shipping Office or Advertising Portraits

The *SS Alpha* portrait is an example of this third type of ship portrait. Just as today a travel agency may have a model of a Boeing 747 aircraft in its windows with Air Canada posters, in olden days model steamers and portraits of vessels were displayed. Posters and paintings of the company's steamships would hang inside the offices of the various steamship lines which invariably, at least in small towns, had their offices and ticket counters in their wharfside buildings.

While some artists specialized in "storm scenes" others worked mainly on portraits of steamers. Among these was Antonio Jacobsen of New York, a prolific artist, who is reputed to have employed his mother and sister to paint his backgrounds. Most of the Jacobsen portraits give the standard side view of the vessel. But one dramatic bow view portrait, owned by Mystic Seaport Museum, and currently on display in the Yarmouth County Museum, was undoubtedly commissioned to hang in company offices where it would without a doubt sell tickets. This portrait, as well as a more standard one of the same vessel, the *SS Prince George,* was likely commissioned by the Dominion Atlantic Railway for their offices in New York, Boston or Yarmouth. Perhaps the company was content with a copied portrait in one office since a third one, unsigned, exists in Yarmouth. While the style is that of Jacobsen, his attention to detail and clarity are missing.

At some time, the Boston and Yarmouth Steamship Company, a subsidiary line of the Eastern Steamship Company, must have decided to commission a number of portraits of former Yarmouth steamers which plied the Yarmouth to Boston run. A number of these portraits exist, some signed "J.E. Baker," a Yarmouth artist who flourished in the 1920's and 1930's. The *SS Alpha* is one such example. This vessel was originally purchased by L.E. Baker for the Yarmouth Steamship Company and was later sold with the remainder of the fleet to the Dominion Atlantic Railway around the turn of the century.

This third category of ship portraits was usually paintings of steamers and as they were most often found in shipping offices they are geographically restricted to coastal trading towns or villages.

This category of portraits was most likely to be transferred into advertising posters, since the vessels always plied to two or more ports and the companies would naturally like to advertise in more places than simply their ticket office. Sometimes these posters would be coloured but usually they were two-tone mezzotints.

General Seascapes and Folk Art Portraits

Paintings in this category can be termed "general art on a nautical subject" and have been done by artists ranging from Joseph Turner through Pablo Picasso to Maude Lewis. Their range is immense, and the exhibition offers excellent samples of such works.

"Liverpool Bay", painted in 1888 by John Grant, is a fine portrayal of a brigantine running before the wind. The handling of sea and sky is much better than that of most ship portrait artists, revealing this artist's formal training. The ship is clearly a brigantine, but not a painting of a specific vessel for there are no details of rigging or other shipboard elements.

Sometimes a vessel is added to a seascape, just to provide atmosphere, as in the painting of the entrance to Yarmouth Harbour, showing Sunday Point in the foreground and the Cape Forcher light in the distance. The schooner sailing seaward is a correct, but not detailed, portrait of the vessel, providing the only human element in a nice little seascape.

Marine folk art consists of work done by artists who were usually untrained, but had a love of the sea and ships, if not a first-hand knowledge of them. Those paintings which do demonstrate real knowledge fall into the category of "sailors' folk art", for they show correctly the nautical elements of the vessels. They were often painted on the inside lids of seamen's trunks or on canvas mats. Sailors also made models of their ships, or shadow-box models, which showed a ship in relief on a painted background.

Some who painted ships because they loved them did not know the proper shape of the sails or how they were set. Any sailor worth his salt would know that an eight-masted schooner was fiction — there would not be enough days in the week to name the masts after! A closer look at this painting reveals that the artist did know about schooners and their sails. The cut of the topsails is correct, and the painting does include a certain amount of detail. Perhaps this painting is a sailor's fantasy.

Nova Scotia's history is intertwined with the seas around her coasts. Our communities depended on the seas for employment, food and trade, and a few still continue to do so. This exhibition records the love and pride that Nova Scotians had for their ships. It should entice the viewer into taking a closer look at the province's collections of ship portraits, marine art and her maritime history.

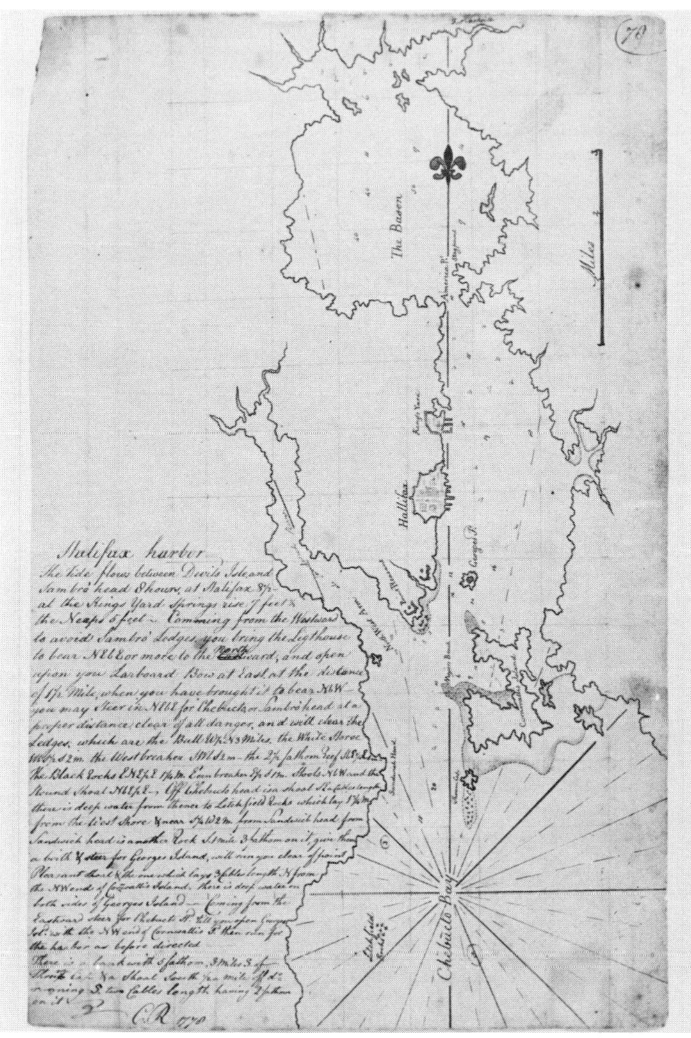

107 Map of Halifax

Found in New York City, New York

Watercolour and ink on paper

Drawn by Captain Charles Randle (Active 1775-1813), initialed CR in the lower left corner

Dated 1778 in the lower left corner

Dimensions: 20.0 × 31.0 cm ($7\frac{7}{8} \times 12\frac{3}{16}$ inches)

Collection of Gerald Ferguson, Halifax, Nova Scotia

Captain Randle was an eighteenth century topographical artist and a British Naval officer who served on Lake Champlain in 1776 and off the coasts of Eastern Canada as Captain of the HMS Peggy, sailing between Quebec City and Halifax in 1778. The written information concerns the tide flows and shoals in and around Halifax Harbour, and shows Halifax with wharves and defense works only 29 years after its founding.

Structure: Watercolour and ink on paper. There are some small tears and one hole in the upper left and lower right corner of the map, all in margin areas.

108 Self-Portrait of Joseph Partridge

Halifax, Halifax County

Watercolour on paper

Painted by Joseph Partridge (1792- circa 1833)

1819

Dimensions: 16.0 × 18.0 cm ($6\frac{1}{4} \times 7\frac{1}{8}$ inches)

Collection of the Nova Scotia Museum, Halifax, Nova Scotia

Partridge was born in England, arriving in Halifax in 1817 where he set up a drawing school. He sent this self-portrait to Mrs Currie on July 27, 1819 as a gift for her friendship and attention before he left Halifax for Boston and Providence, Rhode Island.[1]

Structure: Watercolour on paper. The work is in excellent condition.

Published: "Joseph Partridge, painter", In *The Magazine Antiques*, Antiques, Volume CXXVI, No 3 (September, 1984), pp. 582-589.

1. Based on a letter attached to the reverse of the painting written by Partridge.

109 Portraits of Ruth Ellis and Joseph Ellis

Yarmouth County
Watercolour on paper
Joseph Ellis is signed Comingo[1] in lower right corner.
Ruth Ellis is attributed to Comingo.
Joseph Ellis is dated 1817 in lower right corner.
Ruth Ellis probably 1817.
Dimensions: Ruth Ellis — 8.2 × 10.2 cm ($3\frac{1}{4}$ × 4 inches)
Joseph Ellis — 8.5 × 10.0 cm ($3\frac{5}{16}$ × $3\frac{15}{16}$ inches)
Collection of the Yarmouth County Museum, Yarmouth, Nova Scotia

Ruth (nee Porter) Ellis, wife of Joseph Ellis and daughter of Nehemiah Porter, Jr and Mary Porter of Yarmouth, was born December 9, 1782 and died September 3, 1865. The first Sunday School in the County of Yarmouth was organized in the Ellis home at Chebogue in 1815. Ruth Ellis donated the land on Main Street in Yarmouth for the Tabernacle Church. She is a descendent of Lieutenant John Ellis of Sandwich, Massachusetts.

Joseph Ellis, son of Phillip and Rebecca (nee Perry) Ellis was born on March 10, 1779, and died at Chebogue on December 29, 1851. He was adopted by his aunt Mrs Anna (nee Perry) Clements and her husband Captain Clements of Chebogue.

Structure: Both works watercolour on paper with some minor foxing.

1. For detailed information on Joseph Comingo and these two portraits see the catalogue essay by Susan Foshay.

110 Portrait of a Gentleman

Probably Halifax, Halifax County
Oil on canvas
Painted by William Valentine (1798-1849)
Circa 1820
Dimensions: 42.8 × 37.4 cm ($16\frac{7}{8}$ × $14\frac{3}{4}$ inches)
Collection of the Art Gallery of Nova Scotia, Halifax, Nova Scotia

William Valentine was born in 1798 at Whitehaven, Cumberland, England. He came to Halifax in 1818 and until 1824 worked as a house painter and decorator in the firm Bell and Valentine. After 1824 Valentine worked alone. His workshop was at Starr's wharf until 1827 when he moved to a building on Bell's Lane.

About 1836, Valentine visited London where he painted portraits of three presidents of the Royal Society. When he returned to Halifax, Valentine received several commissions for portraits. In 1844 he introduced the new daguerreotype process into Halifax, thus becoming the first Nova Scotia photographer, although he still continued to paint houses, signs, and ornamental work.

A fire broke out in his studio a few years before his death, which destroyed much of his work and left Valentine weakened. He died on December 26, 1849.

History: Donated by Mrs David Murray, Scotsburn, Nova Scotia, 1976.

Structure: Oil on canvas.

111 Portrait of John Payzant

Liverpool, Queens County

Oil on wooden panel

Artist unknown

Dated 1832 on reverse

Dimensions: 70.0 × 92.0 cm ($27\frac{9}{16}$ × $36\frac{3}{16}$ inches)

Collection of Queens County Museum, Liverpool, Nova Scotia

This is the finest folk portrait found to date in Nova Scotia. The gentle man in the painting is Reverend John Payzant (1744-1834), a follower of Henry Alline and a leader in the New Light Movement in Nova Scotia. Because Payzant had wooden teeth he often kept his mouth tightly closed as shown in this revealing portrait. Payzant is seen in his study surrounded by his library with the Bible shown prominently on the shelf over his right shoulder. In the foreground, next to the quill pen, is a book from the Tract and Bible Society London, 180(4)?

This painting has all of the qualities associated with folk portraiture, and is discussed in detail in the essay contribution by Susan Foshay.

Structure: The painting is oil on wooden panel. The frame is period and probably original to the work.

Refer to colour plate XIII, page 19

112 Portrait of Woman in White Bonnet-Hat
Portrait of Lady with Black Dress and Brooch

Wolfville, Kings County

Both oil on canvas

Artist unknown

Circa 1820-1850

Dimensions: Woman in bonnet-hat; 61.0 × 72.4 cm (24 × $28\frac{1}{2}$ inches)
Lady with black dress; 61.0 × 72.4 cm (24 × $28\frac{1}{2}$ inches)

Collection of the Wolfville Historical Society (Randall House), Wolfville, Nova Scotia

For detailed information on these portraits consult Susan Foshay's essay on folk portraiture in this catalogue.

Structure: Both works are oil on canvas. Lady with black dress has been recently cleaned by the conservation staff at the Art Gallery of Nova Scotia.

113 Lady with Flowers on Bonnet

Preliminary Sketch and Final Portrait

Victoria Harbour, Kings County

Charcoal and pencil (preliminary sketch)

Charcoal, pencil and pastel on paper (final portrait)

Artist unknown but the sketch is initialed PEH, as is the final portrait (but less clearly), both in the lower right

The preliminary sketch is dated 1849 in the lower right

Dimensions: Sketch — 25.0 × 28.5 cm (9¹³⁄₁₆ × 11¼ inches)
Final Portrait — 25.5 × 29.0 (10¹⁄₁₆ × 11⁷⁄₁₆ inches)

Collection of Jerry and Debbie Vidito, Kentville, Nova Scotia

The unknown woman in this sketch and final portrait boasts an impressive array of finery that includes a flowered bonnet, a necklace and a very delicate, intricate collar of lace on her black dress. Although the artist is unknown, these works are two of the finest examples of Nova Scotia folk portraits known. The pose and drawing technique are related to those artists with some knowledge of academic conventions, although the overall execution and perspective of the portraits characterize the best of those painters defined as folk artists. The artist in making the sketch drew a finer face with well defined lips and nose, and gave the sitter a portly quality by drawing more defined arms and dress sleeves. In the final portrait, which is coloured with pastel, the face is more sensitive, softer and younger, and the body less massive with no arm or sleeve definition. It is possible that these changes were suggested by the woman to give her a more youthful and slimmer appearance.

Structure: The sketch is charcoal and pencil on paper while in the final portrait the artist also added pastel.

114 Girl in Red Dress

Lunenburg County

Watercolour on paper

Artist unknown, but the portrait was found in the house of Mr. Niran Begin in an old album

Circa 1840-1850

Dimensions: 14.0 × 16.0 cm (5½ × 6⁵⁄₁₆ inches)

Collection of the National Museum of Man, Canadian Centre for Folk Culture Studies, Ottawa, Ontario

This portrait is one of the gems of this exhibition. The subject is a girl standing in a red dress with white bloomers, black hair parted in the centre with blue ribbons, who holds a flower in one hand and a basket in the other. The flat perspective and lack of facial modelling and detail is typical of the best in folk portraiture, reflecting the simple, direct style of untrained artists. Although found in Lunenburg County, this work is isolated in that it does not form part of a larger group of Nova Scotia works in a folk portraiture genre, and could be of American origin.

Structure: Watercolour on paper. There is some scattered foxing, discolouration, wrinkling and creasing of the paper.

Published: Blake McKendry, *Folk Art: Primitive and Naïve Art in Canada,* (Toronto: Methuen Publications, 1983), Frontispiece

Refer to colour plate XVI, page 21

115 Sarah Elizabeth Eisenhauer

Chester, Lunenburg County
Watercolour and pencil on paper
Artist unknown
Circa 1856
Dimensions: 10.2 × 13.3 cm (4 × 5¼ inches)
Collection of Murray E. Stewart, Berwick, Nova Scotia

This portrait is of Sarah Elizabeth Eisenhauer at 18 years of age who was born in 1838, dating the work circa 1856. According to family tradition the painting was executed by an itinerant artist who stayed with the family for a few days, and did the portrait as payment in return for lodging.[1]

Sitting on what appears to be a sofa with high wooden back and curving arms, Sarah is holding a book in her right hand. She is wearing a dark dress with lace collar and a bow, with what appears to be a cameo pinned in the centre. Sarah's serene countenance suggests a young lady of educated upbringing, and captures the fragile and delicate beauty of an adolescent approaching womanhood and possibly marriage.

Structure: The artist has used a combination of watercolour and pencil for outlines of hands, arms, head and body.

1. Based on discussions Paul Killowee had with the family from whom he purchased the portrait.

116 Josefina

Found in Annapolis County
Reverse painting on glass
Artist unknown
Circa 1840-1860
Dimensions: 15.0 × 20.0 cm (5⅞ × 7⅞ inches)
Collection of Barbara Doiron, Black Point, Nova Scotia

This small painting was probably a companion piece to a set of family portraits, and is possibly of American origin. Similar examples of reverse painting on glass are also known from the nineteenth century folk art tradition in England. Its Nova Scotia origins are based on the fact that it was found discarded in a garbage dump in Annapolis County, one must presume by a local resident.

Structure: Reverse painting on glass. There is some paint loss in the green background due to scratching. The work appears to be in the original frame.

*This piece will be on view in Halifax only

117 Man with Pen

Found in Chester, Lunenburg County

Oil on wooden panel

Artist unknown

Circa 1830-1840

Dimensions: 55.0 × 75.0 cm (21⅝ × 29½ inches)

Collection of Jerry and Debbie Vidito, Kentville, Nova Scotia

This portrait is an example of a work that borders on that fine line between folk and academic art. It is included in this exhibition to help illustrate the range of folk art and to show how some paintings can exhibit qualities of both a trained and untrained hand in a single work. There is little question that the upper portion of the sitter, including his clothing, face and head form, has been painted by someone with training. However, when one examines the simplified modeling of the shoulders and arm, and in particular the hand holding the pen, it is evident that the artist still had problems with perspective, body form and shape, as well as some difficulty in painting hands, probably one of the most problematic human aspects to draw. The pen is held awkwardly, too far back from the normal index-thumb grasp, and is poorly drawn and undefined. The hand itself is too large with oversized fingers, and out of proportion, creating an awkward perspective between hand and face. In addition the glasses are not correct, with the right lens too far forward, creating a poor alignment between lens and eye.

This work however, demonstrates a level of competence not usually found in folk painting. The articulate definition of facial features, skillful modeling of the head, and convincing rendering of fabric folds, reflect a hand with some proficiency in studio techniques. Although the artist is unknown, the work is probably of American origin, brought to Nova Scotia by immigrants to the province in the early nineteenth century.

Structure: Oil on wooden panel. The painting has been cleaned by the conservation staff at the Art Gallery of Nova Scotia.

118 Ship Portrait of the "Kurramanny of Calcutta" Folk Portrait of Joseph Hogg, Commander of the "Calcutta"

Shelburne, Shelburne County

Both oil on canvas

Artist unknown

"Kurramanny of Calcutta" is dated 1849

Portrait of Commander Hogg — circa 1850

Dimensions: "Kurramanny of Calcutta" — 59.0 × 45.0 cm (23¾ × 17¾ inches)

Portrait of Commander Hogg — 45.7 × 59.7 cm (18 × 23½ inches)

Collection of the Shelburne County Museum, Shelburne, Nova Scotia

The information along the bottom of the ship portrait reads "Kurramanny of Calcutta, 1206 tons laying in Blenheim Reach, River Tigras, China, 10 August 1849. Josʰ Hogg Commander." Information from the Shelburne County Museum, and the family to whom these portraits still belong, indicates that they are both port paintings executed while the vessel, under the command of Joseph Hogg, was in the Far East.

The ship portrait painter who was commissioned to produce a "likeness" of a vessel was usually an artist who specialized in this type of work, being familiar with the construction of ships and rigging. In many instances it was the ship that travelled and not the artist. Both Canadian and American vessels had their portraits done in the ports of Europe, the Mediterranean, and the Far East.[1] In this particular painting, the artist portrayed the vessel with the sails set for drying.

Refer to colour plate XIV, page 20

The portrait of Joseph Hogg was perhaps executed by the same artist, or someone trained in a similar style. The perspective is awkward, as is the foreshortening and proportions of the body, which lend a very folky quality to this work. Perhaps it was painted by someone more familiar with ships than human figures. Hogg sits in what is best described as a studio setting in an empire style armchair. His right hand holds a book bound in blue cloth which rests on a chest either painted or draped with royal blue fabric.

Commander Hogg was one of nine children of Alexander and Agnes Hamilton. Alexander was born in Glasgow, Scotland. He was with the 4th Regiment of Scottish Highlanders, disbanded at Annapolis. He later moved to Clyde River, Shelburne County where he married Agnes Hamilton, daughter of James Hamilton, on February 10, 1796. Joseph was lost at sea, his brother Phillip settled at Clyde River, East Side, Alexander at Barrington Passage. They were both coopers. Other brothers were Robert, who lived in West Barrington and was a shoemaker, John who remained on the old river homestead, Nathaniel who lived in Yarmouth, and William in Shelburne.[2]

Even though these port paintings were not executed in Nova Scotia, they are included in the exhibition because they form part of the history and material heritage of the province.

Structure: Both works are oil on canvas. They have been recently cleaned by the conservation staff at the Art Gallery of Nova Scotia.

1. John and Katherine Ebert, *American Folk Painters,* (New York; Charles Scribner's Sons, 1975), p. 97.
2. Based on written correspondence from Sandra Burke, Shelburne County Museum, July 22, 1985.

119 Barque "Brothers"

Liverpool, Queens County
Watercolour on paper
Signed A.de Clerk in lower right corner
Dated 1874 in lower right corner
Dimensions: 73.0 × 59.0 cm (36 × 30 inches)
Collection of the Yarmouth County Museum, Yarmouth, Nova Scotia

The 437 ton Barque "Brothers" was built in 1871. At the time this portrait was painted, Captain Edgar Jenkins was master. The ship was wrecked on Cape Sable in 1883 on a voyage from Dublin to Yarmouth.

Structure: Watercolour on paper. The work is in good condition.

120 Ship Portrait
Liverpool, Queens County
Watercolour and pencil on paper
Artist unknown
Circa 1875-1885
Dimensions: 89.5 × 61.0 cm (35¼ × 24 inches)
Collection of Gerald Ferguson, Halifax, Nova Scotia

Although the ship is not named and the artist unknown, this is one of the finest examples of a folk art ship portrait found to date in Nova Scotia. It is flying the Canadian Merchant ensign; an American flag, indicating it is sailing into an American port of call; the ship name pennant which unfortunately does not carry the ship's name; and the houseflag, under whose authority and ownership the vessel is registered. This ship is accompanied by three other vessels which are drawn totally out of perspective and scale, adding to the folk quality of this ship portrait.

Structure: Watercolor and pencil on paper. The work is in good condition.

121 The Sail-Steamer "S.S. Alpha"
Probably Yarmouth County
Oil on board
Attributed to J.E. Baker
Dated 1884
Dimensions: 76.2 × 48.2 cm (30 × 19 inches)
Collection of the Yarmouth County Museum, Yarmouth, Nova Scotia

Purchased in 1886 for Yarmouth S.S. Company, the "Alpha" ran between Boston and Yarmouth, along with the "S.S. Dominion". Originally built in Prince Edward Island, the ship was wrecked on November 24, 1876 at West Head, Cape Sable. It was refloated and brought to Yarmouth on February 23, 1877, and repaired by Burrell-Johnson Iron Company, and sold to Captain Ramsey of Prince Edward Island for $4700.00.

Structure: Oil on board. The work is in excellent condition.

122 Ship Portrait

Possibly Halifax or the South Shore
Oil on sail-cloth
Artist unknown
Circa 1880-1890
Dimensions: 38.0 × 28.0 cm (15 15/16 × 11 inches)
Collection of Murray E. Stewart, Berwick, Nova Scotia

On the reverse of this painting are pasted newpapers, the last date being 1887, which helps to place this work in the last quarter of the nineteenth century. Although the ship is executed with some obvious attention to detail, its proportions and overall perspective speak of an untrained artist perhaps working from memory of a vessel on which he served.

Structure: The work is oil on sail-cloth.

123 The Barquentine "Stranger"

Lunenburg, Lunenburg County
Watercolour and pencil on paper
Artist unknown
Circa 1893-1915
Dimensions: 64.2 × 48.7 cm (25 1/4 × 19 inches)
Collection of the Maritime Museum of the Atlantic, Halifax, Nova Scotia

An absolutely wonderful folk painting of the Barquentine "Stranger" showing sailors on the deck passing a community on the shoreline behind. The vessel was built at Yarmouth, Nova Scotia in 1893 and sailed until 1915. The 540 ton vessel was owned by Thomas A. Wilson of Lunenburg and this painting is attributed to one of their crew.

Structure: Watercolour and pencil on paper. The work is in excellent condition.

Published: J. Russell Harper, *A People's Art: Primitive. Naïve, Provincial and Folk Painting in Canada,* (Toronto: University of Toronto Press, 1974), p. 131.

J. Russel Harper, *People's Art: Naïve Art in Canada,* (Ottawa: The National Gallery of Canada, 1973), p. 126.

Exhibited: People's Art: Naïve Art in Canada, National Gallery of Canada, Ottawa, Ontario, November 30, 1973 January 6, 1974.

124 Ship Portrait

Shelburne, Shelburne County
Watercolour, oil and pencil on paper
Artist unknown
Circa 1900-1920
Dimensions: 61.0 × 38.0 cm (24 × 14$^{15}/_{16}$ inches)
Collection of Chris Cooper, Dartmouth, Nova Scotia

This painting is by the same artist as the work shown in the following entry, which is in the Art Gallery of Nova Scotia permanent collection. Purchased from a house in Shelburne, this particular example of this unknown artist's work may be earlier than the Art Gallery painting based on the simpler shore line with less detail, and the lack of rigging and seamen on the ship. Until it was discovered that these two paintings were by the same artist it was assumed that they were simply isolated works of imaginary sailing vessels. It is possible that there are other works by this same painter yet undiscovered, which may eventually lead to the identity of this turn of the century folk artist.

Structure: The work is painted using a combination of watercolour, oil and pencil, the latter used to draw the rigging.

125 Five-Masted Ship Portrait

Probably Yarmouth County
Oil and pencil on paper
Artist unknown
Circa 1890-1920
Dimensions: 84.5 × 34.0 cm (33¼ × 13⅜ inches)
Collection of the Art Gallery of Nova Scotia, Halifax, Nova Scotia

This is a fine example of a folk ship portrait, showing men on the deck of the five-masted vessel which seems to be in the vicinity of a busy port community, judging by the buildings, lighthouse, and other vessels in the background. This work is probably by the same artist as the one preceding. Until work on this exhibition began, it was assumed that this piece was an isolated work of folk art. It is possible that other paintings by this same artist may be found, which could lead to his/her identity.

Structure: Oil and pencil on heavy green paper.

Refer to colour plate XV, page 20

126 The "County of Yarmouth"

Probably Yarmouth County
Oil on canvas
Signed Ed Adams in lower right corner
Dated 1900 in lower right corner
Dimensions: 91.0 × 58.0 cm (37 × 25 inches)
Collection of Yarmouth County Museum, Yarmouth, Nova Scotia

The "County of Yarmouth" was the largest ship built in the County and was launched in 1884 at Belliveau Cove. This painting depicts the ship as it appeared in 1887, only three years after it was launched. In December 1895, the "County" was demasted and damaged at sea. It was towed into Crimsby and eventually sold to the Argentine government for use as a training ship.

Adams painted another version of this ship, also in the collection of the Yarmouth County Museum, but which is far less "folky" in character.

History: The painting was donated by Mr Albert Raymond of Douglas, Georgia to the Yarmouth County Musuem.

Structure: Oil on canvas. The work has recently been cleaned by the conservation staff at the Art Gallery of Nova Scotia.

127 Ship Painting of a Vessel in a Storm

Hadden Hills, Lunenburg County
Oil on academy board
Signed B.D. in lower right corner
Dated 1905 in lower right corner
Dimensions: (measurements include frame) 66.0 × 48.5 cm (26 × 19⅛ inches)
Collection of David L. Beck, Mahone Bay, Nova Scotia

Although the identity of the artist and vessel in this painting are unknown, it is a good example of a work combining both folk and academic elements. The nautical detail of the frame is integral to the theme of this work.

Structure: Oil on academy board. The knotted rope is attached to the frame with round-headed tacks.

128 Ship Portrait of the Five Masted Barque "Potosi"

Lunenburg, Lunenburg County
Ink and watercolour on paper
Signed A. E. Ringman in lower right corner
Dated 1917 in lower right corner
Dimensions: 50.0 × 36.0 cm ($19\frac{9}{16} \times 14\frac{3}{16}$ inches)
Collection of Leslie J. Langille, Lunenburg, Nova Scotia

No information has been located in helping to identify the artist of this fine folk art ship portrait, however, it is known that the five masted steel hulled Barque "Potosi" of 4020 tons was built in 1895 in Geestemudel, Germany by J. C. Teccklen. In 1899 it was registered in Hamburg and owned by F. Laersz. The flag flying from the spanker gaff is the tricolour for the Netherlands, suggesting that in 1917, when this portrait was painted, the "Potosi" was either under Dutch registry or entering a Dutch port.[1]

The painting was purchased by the owner from a family in Lunenburg. On the cardboard backing is written in pencil, "Victor, many happy returns of the day, May 24, 1926, from the Metzlers". This would indicate that the painting was given as a birthday present, and that perhaps Victor sailed on this vessel at one time.

Structure: Ink and watercolour on paper. The work is in excellent condition.

1. This information provided by Dr. Charles Armour, Archivist at the Dalhousie University Archives, Halifax, Nova Scotia.

129 Browse Island

Yarmouth County
Oil on canvas
Artist unknown
Circa 1878-1880
Dimensions: 66.0 × 49.0 cm ($26 \times 19\frac{1}{4}$ inches)
Collection of Yarmouth County Museum, Yarmouth, Nova Scotia

Browse Island in the Indian Ocean was the scene of the wreck of the Barque "Carleton" of 742 tons with Captain Robert W. Allen Master. On voyage from Melbourne, Australia, the "Carleton" stopped at Browse Island to load Guano, but was caught in a hurricane March 11, 1878, and dashed on a reef where she was abandoned. The captian, his wife, and crew were saved and lived on the Island — the crew in tents and the Captain and his wife as guests of the Governor — until removed by the U.S. Barque Niphon. Three other ships were wrecked at the same time. This painting depicts the events of this shipwreck showing the demasted vessel, and boats on shore set up as quarters for the crew of the "Carleton"

History: This painting was donated to the Yarmouth County Museum by Mrs Henry Waterman.

Structure: Oil on canvas. The work is in excellent condition.

130 Seascape of Sunday Point, Cape Forcher

Yarmouth County
Oil on canvas
Artist unknown, but the painting is initialed LL in lower right corner
Dimensions: 29.5 × 17.8 cm (11⅝ × 7 inches)
Collection of the Yarmouth County Museum, Yarmouth, Nova Scotia

This small painting depicts Sunday Point on Cape Forcher with houses, lighthouse and schooner leaving the harbour, probably at sunrise.

Structure: Oil on canvas. The painting has been cleaned by the conservation staff at the Art Gallery of Nova Scotia.

131 Mission at Aneiteum in the New Hebrides*

Round Hill, Annapolis County
Pencil and ink on paper
Artist unknown
Circa 1850
Dimensions: 38.7 × 31.0 cm (15¼ × 12³⁄₁₆ inches)
Collection of Richard Henning Field and Deborah Field, Halifax, Nova Scotia

This is one of the most exciting and important historical works in the exhibition relating to the history of the mission work[1] of the Presbyterian Church of Nova Scotia in the New Hebrides. Spearheaded by the Rev. John Geddie, who was born in the old Scotch town of Banff on April 10, 1815, and moved with his family[2] to Pictou, Nova Scotia in 1816, he was the driving force behind the establishment of a foreign mission by the Presbyterian Church of Nova Scotia, small and poor as she was at the time. After considerable trouble within the Church to establish the Mission, Geddie finally triumphed[3] leaving Newburyport in January of 1847 to set up a Mission on the island of Aneiteum which he reached on July 29, 1848.

In his journal,[4] Geddie describes the island of Aneiteum as the most southerly of the New Hebrides group, shaped like a pear with a circumference of about forty miles. Volcanic in origin, it is mountainous and rugged, with the interior rising to about 3000 feet above sea level. Dividing the island into five divisions, Geddie established his station in Anelcauhat and it is this location that this drawing represents.

The inscription reads, "Mission premises of the Presbyterian Church of Nova Scotia, on the island of Aneiteum, New Hebrides group. No. 1 Mission Chapel, No. 2 Native teacher's house, No. 3 Schoolhouse and printing office, No. 4 Mission house occupied by Mr Geddie, No. 5 Servants house. Mission boat at anchor in front of the premises." It is difficult to establish whether this drawing was done from memory by someone who either had served on or visited Aneiteum, or was perhaps loosely based on the inset engraving of the Mission,[5] which shows the station at Anelcauhat, but with the buildings and their function in a different relationship than in the drawing. The frontal perspective of the drawing also differs from the engraving, which places the observer to the left of the village with a view down the shoreline of the island. It is interesting to note that all the houses in the drawing have plain front facades, except for the Mission house occupied by Geddie, its arbors and vines framing the windows and door.

Structure: Pencil and ink on paper. The work is in excellent condition, although the ink has faded with time.

1. Rev. George Patterson, D.D., *Missionary Life Among the Cannibals: The Life of Rev. John Geddie, D.D., First Missionary to the New Hebrides,* (Toronto: James Campbell & Son, 1882), pp. 17-51.
2. His father was a clockmaker by trade (Patterson: *Ibid,* pp. 17-19)
3. Rev. George Patterson, *Ibid,* pp. 29-50.
4. Rev. George Patterson, *Ibid,* p. 173.
5. This engraving is taken from Patterson, page 3.

*This piece will be on view in Halifax only.

Taken from Rev. George Patterson, D.D., *Missionary Life Among the Cannibals: The Life of Rev. John Geddie, D.D., First Missionary to the New Hebrides,* frontispiece. *This piece is not included in the exhibition.*

132 Micmac Indians in Native Dress

Probably Halifax County or South Shore
Watercolour on paper
Painted by Elizabeth S. Ladds (1837-1922)
Circa 1865-1870
Dimensions: 13.2 × 10.8 cm ($5\frac{3}{16}$ × $4\frac{1}{4}$ inches)
Collection of the Nova Scotia Museum, Halifax, Nova Scotia

This watercolour of three Micmac Indians depicts two standing males and one sitting female beside a tepee on a shoreline. The woman has a papoose in her lap while one male is holding a canoe paddle. The front of a birchbark canoe is showing to the left of the group of figures, who are all dressed in traditional Micmac clothing.

Structure: Watercolour on paper. The work is in excellent condition.

133 Micmac Woman in Native Dress

Probably Halifax County or South Shore
Watercolour on paper
Painted by Elizabeth S. Ladds (1837-1922)
Circa 1865-1870
Dimensions: 9.3 × 14.0 cm ($3\frac{5}{8}$ × $5\frac{1}{2}$ inches)
Collection of the Nova Scotia Museum, Halifax, Nova Scotia

This painting depicts a Micmac woman carrying a papoose on her back, and two baskets in her hand with decorated lids. The dress is traditional Micmac, including the peaked hat. Note the Christian cross hanging from what appears to be a bead necklace.

Structure: Watercolour on paper, the work remains in good condition.

Exhibited: "From Women's Eyes: Women Painters in Canada", organized and circulated by the Agnes Etherington Art Centre, Queen's University at Kingston, Ontario, December 12, 1975-January 31, 1976.

134 Micmac Woman with Sewing Basket

Cape Breton County
Watercolour on paper with pressed (embossed) border
Artist unknown, but the initials M.I.H. are pencilled in the lower right.
Circa 1880-1890
Dimensions: 15.2 × 20.3 cm (6 × 8 inches)
Private collection

An interesting example of a watercolour showing a Micmac woman in native dress, holding a lidded sewing basket. She is wearing a Christian Cross. The border is embossed in an intricate design, which includes pineapple motifs in the four corners.

Structure: Watercolour on embossed paper. This paper is similar to card stock used for valentines which were often embossed with various designs at the turn of the century.

135 View of Clementsport, Nova Scotia

Digby County
Watercolour on paper
Attributed to Mrs Finney[1]
Circa 1860-1880
Dimensions: 40.0 × 34.4 cm ($15\frac{1}{2} \times 13\frac{9}{16}$ inches)
Collection of the National Museum of Man, Canadian Centre for Folk Culture Studies, Ottawa, Ontario

This view of Clementsport combines both folk and academic elements.

Structure: Watercolour on paper. The work is in good condition.

1. According to National Museum of Man file data

136 Bridgewater, Nova Scotia

Lunenburg County

Pencil on paper

Signed J. Liechte in the lower right corner

Dated July 28, 1889 in the lower left corner

Dimensions: 33.0 × 22.8 cm (13 × 9 inches)

Collection of the National Museum of Man, Canadian Centre for Folk Culture Studies, Ottawa, Ontario

This pencil sketch shows a complex of buildings along the LaHave River on which the town of Bridgewater is located.

Structure: Pencil on paper with some discolouration and foxing.

137 Davison Lumber Company

Bridgewater (LaHave River), Lunenburg County

Watercolour on paper

Painted by F.W. McKinnon

Dated April 6, 1901

Dimensions: 67.0 × 44.0 cm ($26\frac{3}{8} \times 17\frac{5}{16}$ inches)

Collection of the DesBrisay Museum, Bridgewater, Nova Scotia

The scene in this watercolour shows the Lower Mill of the Davison Lumber Company on the LaHave River during spring flood on April 6, 1901. The artist, F.W. McKinnon, was originally from Prince Edward Island and lived in Bridgewater where he met and married Miss Dolliver, the cousin of Oliver and George Dolliver.[1]

History. This work was donated in June, 1970 by Mrs E.D. Killam to the DesBrisay Museum permanent collection.

Structure: Watercolour on paper. There is some paper damage and foxing.

1. This information was supplied to the DesBrisay Museum on June 11, 1972 by Mrs Horace Jones, formally Pauline McKinnon.

138 East End Station, Sable Island

Sable Island

Oil on wood

Artist unknown

(The date 1885 is written in ink on the backing board)

Dimensions: 21.5 × 19.7 cm ($8\frac{7}{16} \times 7\frac{3}{4}$ inches)

Collection of DesBrisay Museum, Bridgewater, Nova Scotia.

This small painting depicts the East End Station on Sable Island just after sunset, judging by the waning red streaked clouds and darkening sky. Probably painted in 1885, the harvested fields and shock of corn stalks suggest autumn, and the family living there preparing for the long Nova Scotia winter. On the hill to the left is a windmill while several small figures can be seen working in the barnyard.

History: This painting belonged to the Reverend W.A. DesBrisay.

Structure: Painted with oil on wood, the work has been recently cleaned and is in good condition.

139 Streetscape of Milton Pond

Milton Pond, Yarmouth County

Oil on academy board

Artist unknown, but on reverse of painting is written "for Joseph C. Killam — B.W. Harris"

Dated 1856 on reverse

Dimensions: 39.2 × 17.3 cm ($11\frac{1}{2} \times 7$ inches)

Collection of the Yarmouth County Museum, Yarmouth, Nova Scotia

This small painting of a streetscape shows a private residence, a store, and what appears to be a church or meeting house along a main road. The information on the reverse of the work suggests that perhaps it was painted by B.W. Harris for Joseph Killam who lived in the handsome house with the red roof.

Structure: Oil on academy board. The painting has recently been cleaned by the conservation staff at the Art Gallery of Nova Scotia. The date 1856 is legible on a paper label on the reverse.

140 Painting of Church

Probably Lunenburg or Shelburne County
Oil on canvas
Artist unknown
Circa 1870-1880
Dimensions: 14.0 × 16.5 cm (5½ × 6½ inches)
Collection of the DesBrisay Museum, Bridgewater, Nova Scotia

The design of this church suggests that it is Anglican in denomination. Set in an open field surrounded by small pine or spruce trees, bordered by a wooden fence, and facing small hills and perhaps the main road, this church is typical of many still found today in the pastoral countryside of Nova Scotia. The Church was more than a place to worship the Lord, however, often acting as a meeting place for the community on festive days and occasions such as Church suppers, as well as on days of tragedy to mourn the loss of a friend or loved one, or to deal with emergencies faced by the community. The two figures standing outside the Church suggest the minister offering comfort and advice to one of his parishioners.

Structure: Oil on canvas.

141 House Portrait

Found in Oxford, Cumberland County
Oil on canvas
Signed F.D. MacKay in lower right corner
Circa 1850-1860
Dimensions: 40.0 × 29.0 cm (15¾ × 11 7/16 inches)
Collection of Murray E. Stewart, Berwick, Nova Scotia

Portraits of houses and farm scenes can be considered a more personal form of architectural painting than town views, and were often painted by members of the family as well as trained and untrained artists.[1] This particular house portrait is signed F.D. MacKay who, judging by the detail and perspective of the work, probably had some training as a painter. A search of various archival records and lists of painters has failed to identify the artist beyond that of knowing his name. In many respects this painting embodies some of the best qualities found in folk art: strong design, beautiful colour and fascinating details, all executed with the intention of uniting decorative qualities with documentary function.

Structure: Oil on canvas. This work remains in excellent "as found" condition.

1. John and Katherine Ebert, *American Folk Painters*, (New York: Charles Scribner's Sons, 1975), pp. 127-128.

142 Farm Scene

Berwick, Kings County
Oil paint on cardboard
Artist unknown, signed Grandma Small on reverse
Dated 1912
Dimensions: 71.0 × 43.5 cm (27¹⁵⁄₁₆ × 17⅛ inches)
Collection of Murray E. Stewart, Berwick, Nova Scotia

On the reverse of this painting in pencil is written "Ivy Cottage, 1912 Grandma Small".

Structure: The work is painted on 1/4 inch cardboard which has been cut into an oval shape. It is doubtful if this work was ever framed. A grey painted border around the edge of the work acts as a painted frame.

143 Landscape with Horse-Drawn Carriage

Probably Annapolis County
Oil on canvas
Artist unknown
Circa 1860-1870
Dimensions: 36.0 × 27.5 cm (14³⁄₁₆ × 10¹³⁄₁₆ inches)
Collection of Murray E. Stewart, Berwick, Nova Scotia

If it were not for the horse-drawn carriage and human figures, this painting would be bland and rather uninteresting, similar to so many other landscapes of lakes and mountains executed during the latter half of the nineteenth and early part of the twentieth century, as nonpersonalized work simply for decoration.[1] Many landscapes of similar style and subject matter were either painted from imagination, or perhaps a printed source. This particular example is difficult to place geographically but has long been considered by the owner to represent an area around Annapolis Royal where it was found.

The addition of the human figures in the foreground and background add a certain measure of personalization to this work. The figures in the left of the foreground show a woman standing beside a man who has a spade resting over his shoulder, while the figures in the carriage show a man and woman, the woman holding a parasol, being driven by a coachman dressed in black and cracking his whip over the head of the white horse. The scene suggests that the couples are on a Sunday outing or perhaps are going rowing on the lake.

Structure: Oil on canvas. The painting has been cleaned and restored by the conservation staff at the Art Gallery of Nova Scotia.

1. John and Katherine Ebert, *American Folk Painters*, (New York: Charles Scribner's Sons, 1975), p. 130. Even in the role as wall decoration a painting serves a function of embellishing the domestic interior while also suggesting social position and status.

144 Landscape with Farm Scene

Chester Basin, Lunenburg County
Oil on academy board
Signed A. Kirk in the lower right hand corner
Circa 1875-1885
Dimensions: 30.0 × 19.0 cm (11¹³⁄₁₆ × 7½ inches)
Collection of Leslie J. Langille, Lunenburg, Nova Scotia

The farm depicted is probably local to the region, however, its exact location is not known. The buildings, particularly the Cape Cod style structure with an extension in the middle of the picture, and the house with single gable directly behind, are both typical of the Chester-Mahone Bay, area, set as they are in a rolling summer landscape. The identity of the artist, other than his name, is not known, however further research may reveal other works by this same hand. The painting was purchased by the owner at a house auction in Chester Basin.

Structure: Oil on academy board. The work has been cleaned by the conservation staff at the Art Gallery of Nova Scotia.

145 Birth and Baptismal Record *Edward Hughey Conrad*

Crousetown, Lunenburg County
Watercolour, ink and pencil on paper
Artist unknown
Dated 1817
Dimensions: 33.0 × 20.0 cm (13 × 7⅞ inches)
Collection of Judy and Earle Rhodenizer, Pleasantville, Nova Scotia

This is only the second birth and baptismal record of this type to be found in Nova Scotia, although no doubt others survive in private hands. The Frederick Corkum record dated 1826 was found several years ago in the province and is now in the permanent collection of the Nova Scotia Museum.[1] This work which notes the birth and baptismal dates and sponsors for Edward Hughey Conrad is dated nine years earlier (1817) and definitely by the same hand as the Corkum record.

Both of these records exhibit strong Lunenburg-German decorative traditions in the style of lettering, design and motifs. The names of the sponsors are equivilant to godparents.

Structure: The record is watercolour, ink and pencil on paper with some foxing. There is little fading of colours which remain bright suggesting it was hung out of direct sunlight.

1. For information and illustration of the Corkum record See Michael Bird and Terry Kobayashi, *A Splendid Harvest: Germanic Folk and Decorative Arts in Canada,* (Toronto: Van Nostrand Reinhold Ltd., 1981), pp. 46-47.

   See also Deborah A. Young, *A Record for Time,* (Halifax: Art Gallery of Nova Scotia, 1985), p. 18.

Refer to colour plate XVIII, page 22

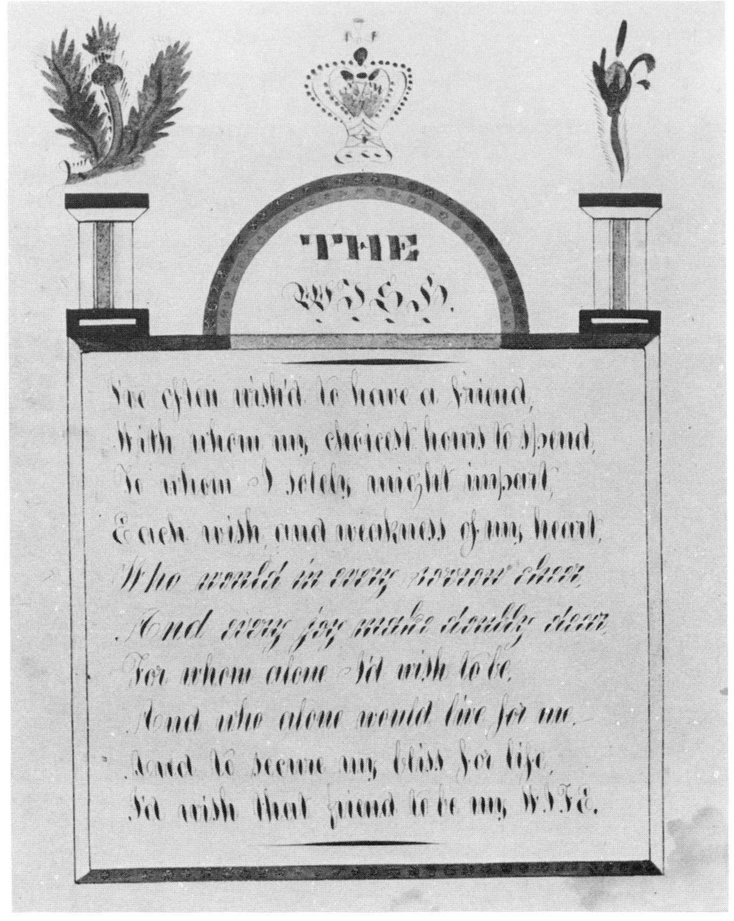

146 The Marriage Wish

South Shore or Annapolis Valley
Watercolour and ink on paper
Artist unknown
Circa 1840-1860
Dimensions: 20.0 × 24.2 cm (7⅞ × 9½ inches)
Collection of the National Museum of Man, Canadian Centre for Folk Culture Studies (Gerald Ferguson Collection), Ottawa, Ontario

This marriage wish is a proposal in the form of a poem from a hopeful suitor. It relates to a series of family records known from Nova Scotia dating between the years 1838 and 1847 all done by the same hand, and containing similar decorative motifs, including the crown (sometimes with the word "Victoria" above it) as well as the arch, pillars, rose and thistle. Although the identity of this artist is unknown some of the records are signed J PW, and this Marriage Wish is attributed to the same artist.[1] The poem reads as follows:

I've often wish'd to have a friend
With whom my choicest hours to spend
To whom I solely might impart
Each wish a weakness of my heart
Who could in every sorrow cheer
And every joy make doubly dear
For whom alone I'd wish to be
And whom alone would live for me
And to secure my bliss for life
I'd wish that friend to be my wife.

Structure: Watercolour and ink on paper. The work is in its original painted frame.

1. See Richard Henning Field, *From Birth To Mourning: Nineteenth Century Family Records and Memorials from Nova Scotia and New Brunswick,* (Halifax, 1984), unpublished manuscript.

147 Lodge Painting, "Onward IOOF"

Lunenburg County
Painted and decorated sail-cloth
Artist unknown
Circa 1880-1890
Dimensions: 88.0 × 48.2 cm (34⅝ × 19 inches)
Private collection

This lodge painting from the Independent Order of Oddfellows contains most of the important motifs of the Order. A heart carved on the palm symbolized the friendship of an "unselfish giver whose hand is always extended to a brother". Heart and hand carvings were important in the ceremonies and rituals of the I.O.O.F., an organization that appealed mostly to the middle and industrial classes, offering them sick and death benefits in time of family need. During a candidate's initiation he was asked to practise friendship, love and truth, represented by the three links of the Oddfellows chain in the upper right and left corners of this painting. The F.L.T. in each link stand for these three principles of initiation.[1]

The ten Roman numerals, in the open book on the right, stand for the Ten Commandments, while the book on the left contains the words "Love ye one another" on the left page, and "Thou Shalt have no other Gods before Me" on the right page. The all seeing Eye of God sits above the heart in hand, while the scales represent equality and justice and the sword and hatchet stand for support and brotherhood in time of distress and tragedy.

Structure: The painting is decorated with oil-based paint on sail-cloth. Close examination reveals that there is probably an earlier version of this painting under the present one.

1. Cynthia V.A. Schaffner and Susan Klein, *Folk Hearts: A Celebration of the Heart Motif in American Folk Art,* (New York: Alfred A. Knopf, 1984), pp. 78-79.

Refer to colour plate XVII, page 22

148 James Hamilton *"British Standard"* Inn Sign

Shelburne, Shelburne County
Painted softwood sign within molded and turned hardwood frame
Artist unknown
Circa 1823
Dimensions: 76.2 × 96.0 cm (30 × 37¾ inches)
Collection of the Nova Scotia Museum, Halifax, Nova Scotia

According to tradition this sign was used by John Hamilton on his inn which he built at Clyde River beside the Tusket Road. Named Wood Hall for his home in Scotland, this signboard is one of the very few known from Nova Scotia,[1] and retains its original paint on both sides. The turned and molded frame is in a later green. Attached are two forged "eye-hooks" from which the sign can be hung.

Structure: The sign is made from two softwood planks with tongue and groove joint. Both boards are mortised into the molded cross frames, which in turn are mortised into the two turned posts.

1. Based on information supplied by the Shelburne County Musuem, July, 1985, and on the *History and Folklore of Shelburne County* by Marion Robertson (1962). James Hamilton's will was probated in 1823. The age of the sign is based on that date, as well as construction technique and form.

INTRODUCTION

Decorated Utilitarian Objects

Richard Henning Field

This is the largest category of objects in the exhibition, and includes a vast array of artifacts falling within many sub-categories reflecting the function of these items. Ranging from several types of storage containers including splint, document, wall, candle, knife and blanket boxes to crooked knives, gameboards, footstools, table looms and canes, this is perhaps the most comprehensive collection of small decorated objects ever assembled in Canada.

These objects epitomize the best in traditional folk art, combining specific function with decorative embellishment often determined by the shape of the object. Many of the items reflect both the occupation and ethnic background of their makers, and in some cases the object will probably be new to many viewers who have never seen spruce gum boxes, needle cases or busks.

Many of the items in this category come from the South Shore of the province which is rich in artifacts of this nature. This results mostly from the fact that both the seafaring and farming traditions were important in this region, the population substantial, and the area (Lunenburg County) settled in part by German immigrants with a strong tradition of decorative art. Most importantly this region has been heavily visited by antique dealers and collectors over the past 50 years.

For some the true *spirit* of the province will be found here in these objects which reflect most strongly the domestic and community environment of their makers and owners. It is easy to envision the candle box hanging on the wall by the hearth, or the decorated document box containing important family papers sitting on the desk or chest of drawers.

In many respects this was the most difficult category in which to select material. Many examples were rejected due to lack of firm provenance, or because they had been tampered with in some fashion. Yet this was the most satisfying section to compile because of the uniqueness and decorative character of many of these items. This is not to suggest that the textiles, paintings, and sculpture chosen for the show are not as important, it is simply that they are more accepted as a form of decorative folk art. In this category we are dealing with objects that often are overlooked because they are either too functional or utilitarian, or are considered antiques. Unfortunately this attitude seldom prevails as objects of this type are very important to the understanding of decorative folk traditions within a particular province or region.

The decorative aspect of the items in this category ranges from what could be called the "plain style" as exemplified by the stack of three graduated splint boxes with worn paint, or the round splint box painted blue with no carving or further embellishment, to the ornately carved powderhorn with tulip motifs and incised compass stars. The magnitude of the folk expression of this province is manifested in these objects as they combine all the elements which define traditional decorative folk art: function, decoration, reflection of occupation, ethnic tradition and domestic/communal use.

In many respects this category will more easily explain the life-styles of the Nova Scotians of the late eighteenth through early twentieth centuries. Textiles, paintings, and sculpture form only part of the picture. Because many of the purposes for which these objects were made are now obsolete, they help give us insight and understanding into the complexity of many tasks which have now disappeared. Sometimes the problem of identifying just what an object was used for remains a mystery. But the fact that the object exists, and we may not know what its purpose was or how it was used, is simply further indication of how our knowledge about our past heritage is slowly slipping away. It is time that we place the serious study of our material folk culture on a higher priority, and take a look at just what makes us Nova Scotians and Canadians.

The Traditional Folk Arts of Lunenburg County

Terry Kobayashi
and
Michael Bird

Terry Kobayashi is an author and researcher who lectures on various aspects of Germanic and ethnic folk art in Canada. Kobayashi is a graduate in art history from the University of Toronto and teaches art at Eastwood Collegiate Institute in Kitchener, Ontario.

Michael Bird is a noted and published authority on Germanic Folk Art in Canada. Bird is Associate Professor at Renison College, University of Waterloo, Ontario where he teaches in the area of religion and the arts. Michael and Terry have co-authored five books on aspects of Canadian folk art.

The increasing use of the word *Lunenburg* in folk art discussions to describe a particular body of decorated utensils, furniture and accessories brings into question the advisability of using regional definitions for objects. Many pieces that look as if they come from Lunenburg County actually originate in other parts of Nova Scotia. And not all folk art from Lunenburg resembles the dominant objects.

Yet the designation reflects what the general public associates with the settlements of German origin on the South Shore. This informal working designation is a matter of emphasis rather than of uniqueness. The tulip, for example, is found on Lunenburg gravemarkers, but also on a painted chest from the Guilford-Saybrook area of Connecticut. Traditional design elements in Nova Scotia furnishings and accessories show related motifs from Yarmouth to Cape Breton. Nevertheless, one finds distinctive clusters of motifs where Scots, French, Germans and other ethnic groups settled in the province.

Both traditional and contemporary forms of folk art are strongly represented in Lunenburg. The works in *Spirit of Nova Scotia* are drawn mainly from the earlier tradition. These folk art forms tend to be variations on a theme, rather than unique expressions of creativity. Contemporary folk art in Lunenburg is marked by greater individuality of expression.

The known artifacts indicate that Lunenburg folk art flowered between 1850 and 1925, when the material displayed a recognisable predominance of forms, techniques and motifs. There is a significant, though smaller, body of artifacts dating from the late eighteenth century. The first German immigrants arrived in Halifax in 1750 and in Lunenburg in 1753. Not until the last quarter of the century does a substantial body of folk art expression emerge. A small but noteworthy body of ornamental details in architecture — carved whorls, hearts and other motifs on door trims and mantelpieces — have survived from this period. And so have some smaller objects. A few simply inscribed and decorated books indicate a passing familiarity with the fraktur tradition in the late eighteenth century. Carved and painted flax heckles, all apparently the work of one individual, and other decorated utensils also survive from this period. Powder horns were sometimes inscribed with tulips and other motifs typical of Lunenburg folk expression. The furniture of the time resembles English Chippendale. In rare circumstances these pieces were decorated, with hearts and geometric designs appearing on a few cupboards. The most striking Germanic decorative work appears in the motifs and inscriptions carved into gravemarkers of the last decades of the century, forms which proclaim their own dates. The gravemarkers of George Jung (d.1793), Elisabeth Meissner (d.1803) and Johan Eisenhauer (d.1805) show significant Germanic decorative details.

Folk art motifs are found on many objects made throughout the nineteenth century. The perpetuation of traditional design conventions, colours and ornamental embellishments is predictable, in an area somewhat isolated from the emerging English centre of Halifax. While this city became the political centre of Nova Scotia, its main port of entry and principal link with Great Britain, settlements on the South Shore experienced a slower rate of growth. The use of the German language and the religious bonds in Lunenburg County kept the area out of the English mainstream, and contributed to its cultural conservatism. In such settings, folk art often takes the form of variations upon traditional themes. At the same time, the region was open to external influences and contact with groups as diverse as the English in Halifax and the Micmacs in the rural areas. The English influence can be seen in the New England gravestone motifs in Lunenburg cemeteries; Micmac influences can be seen in motifs borrowed from them on furniture and accessories. Sometimes these encounters produced eccentric results. Lunenburg cabinetmakers used all the dominant English styles from Chippendale to Sheraton and Hepplewhite, as well as the heavy American Empire forms, popular in Canada in the mid-nineteenth century. Lunenburg furniture often reveals traditional decorative enhancement through painting, inscription or carving. A Sheraton chest of drawers will feature carved geometric designs on its drawer-fronts. An American Empire bonnet chest exhibits a decorative painted finish, its complex detail fighting with the piled-up structural ornamentation of the piece.

The blending of German decorative detail with English forms is not unique to Nova Scotia. Decorated furniture from southeastern Pennsylvania, made in the nineteenth century, shows the same characteristic. Waterloo County in Ontario was settled by two distinct Germanic groups. The first came from Pennsylvania after scouts had looked over the land in 1799. The second arrived from the continent in several migrations from the 1820's to the 1850's. The furniture produced by the first group is English in contour, like that still made in Pennsylvania. The furniture of the continental Germans retains baroque design elements derived from Europe.

The most striking examples of Lunenburg folk art are in the decoration of such utilitarian articles as knife handles, walking sticks, planes, powder horns and butterprints. Most of the work is by "untrained" artisans, although this term suggests a wider separation of function and experience than actually seems to have been the case. In the German settlements in Pennsylvania and Waterloo, a modest degree of professionalism existed. These areas had trained weavers, potters, and some fraktur artist schoolteachers. Apart from cabinetmakers, no Germanic tradition of professional craftsmen has been identified to date in Lunenburg County, which had no weavers, potters or fraktur practitioners. Most Lunenburg folk art is of the "made-at-home" variety, with a strong emphasis on the decoration of everyday objects, which were painted and carved. Chip-carving is very common, although some forms of ornamental woodworking, such as inlay work, are virtually unknown in Lunenburg County. The amount of decorative chip-carving surpasses that of the Germanic settlements of southern Ontario, where most of the work is attributed to Fred G. Hoffman (1845-1926) and his followers.

Butterprints are among the most dramatically decorated pieces from Lunenburg County. They were carved to print designs on butter set out on special occasions. But some were possibly carved by woodworkers as a challenge to their skills. Tulips, hearts, compass stars and geometric designs characterize many Lunenburg butterprints, and these motifs resemble those of Pennsylvania German folk art. It is easy to confuse them especially as large quantities of Lunenburg County folk art have been shipped out of the province, lost its provenance, and been sold as Pennsylvania folk art.

Crooked knives, used for a variety of purposes, were decorated on their heavy wooden handles which extend at an oblique angle to the blade. Many of the handles are elaborately carved with geometric designs; others have been sculpted, sometimes in the form of animals. Mackerel ploughs, squid jig holders, fish string winders and other wooden objects used in the fisheries were also inscribed or carved.

The makers and owners of decorated objects can rarely be identified. But a small document or trinket box is an exception. It has a dramatic painted decoration in strong colours, showing multi-coloured compass stars on a deep red background. Pencilled inside the lid are the words: "Abraham Hirtle, First South, Lunenburg County, N.S."

Familiar motifs and techniques in Lunenburg folk art continued into the twentieth century. Newer objects such as spruce-gum boxes, sail-cloth mats, and gamesboards were decorated. Some of these objects were made before 1900, but the largest number seem to have been made in the first 30 years of this century. Small boxes, often in the form of books, were hollowed out to hold spruce gum. Elaborately decorated and occasionally inscribed with mementoes of the "Remember Me" kind, these boxes appear to have been regarded by makers and recipients as love tokens. Several dated examples from the early twentieth century suggest that the custom of making them had become popular then. The sail-cloth mat also seems to have fascinated many folk artists in the first decades of this century. The designs may have been inspired by the emerging interest in rug-hooking which became widespread during and after the 1880's. While some painted sail-cloth mats used designs and subjects from popular sources, several used the traditional motifs of stars, hearts and whorls. Many Lunenburg craftspeople made their own gamesboards, even though commercially made ones were available. In fact, handmade, painted gamesboards may well be an example of handcrafted products coming after, rather than being supplanted by, the commercially made item. The manufactured product provided new raw material for folk art expression, rather than hindering it. Makers of Lunenburg boards, especially for parcheesi, used stars and other geometric forms from their own design tradition. Their use of local motifs on such objects follows the same principles whereby their eighteenth and nineteenth century ancestors gave their particular decorative nuances to Anglo-American architecture and furniture.

The continuing vitality of culture in Lunenburg has been sustained by the continual pressures from inside and outside the community, a dynamism reflected in the folk art of Lunenburg County.

Background, Interpretation and Function of Decorated Utilitarian Objects in Early Nova Scotia Households

Murray E. Stewart

Murray E. Stewart is a well known Nova Scotia dealer and collector of early furniture, accessories and folk art whose long standing interest has been in the material history of this province. Stewart is a resident of Berwick, Nova Scotia.

Many of the objects selected to be included in *Spirit of Nova Scotia* were made to fulfill definite, practical purposes. They therefore need to be interpreted differently from purely decorative forms of folk art. The term *folk art* is often used in an all-inclusive manner because form, decoration and function are closely interrelated and sometimes difficult to separate and define. Two broad categories of objects emerge. Some were born out of a need to express strong personal vision and feeling, and designed to be seen and appreciated rather than used. The second category includes objects made for practical use, decorated in a way that gave special meaning to the piece for the maker or owner. The untrained individuals who decorated these objects almost certainly did not consider themselves as artists, yet they created folk art in the truest sense.

These utilitarian objects, although now collected and displayed purely for their decorative qualities, once served everyday needs in early Nova Scotian households. Someone so cherished these articles that they deliberately carved, painted or applied decorations to them, combining beauty with utility. The ethnic and cultural origins of the makers of these objects, their social and economic history, values and traditions, and even their successes and failures all nurtured the seeds of creativity that generated the "folk process". This art form, created by ordinary people, helps us to understand the experiences of Nova Scotians of the past. They reveal how uprooted and transplanted peoples fought against severe odds to transform a harsh, hostile wilderness into a prosperous new homeland. The objects show how these settlers added beauty to everyday objects while they struggled to establish themselves and transform their new environment. As they became Nova Scotians, they expressed the spirit of their new land and of their new lifestyles in the objects that make up this exhibition.

The history of Nova Scotia has been that of successive waves of settlers who brought with them some of the objects they needed to survive, making others as the need arose, and learning all the time to adapt the resources of the new land to create the articles necessary for maintaining and sustaining life in a difficult environment. The Micmac Indians had learned to exploit the resources of Nova Scotia by moving around with the seasons. They were skilled canoe and basket makers long before the arrival of the European settlers.

Samuel de Champlain and his company of soldiers and artisans founded Port Royal in 1604. Characteristically, this first European settlement took the form of a fort. Between 1632 and 1640, about 300 new settlers arrived in Acadia. Because the home government concentrated its attention on Quebec, the newcomers were left on their own. The settlers, ancestors of the present day Acadians, were mainly farmers and fishermen. Poorly educated in the formal sense, these robust, courageous peasants began to carve homes and farms from the wilderness. By 1663, most of them had established themselves near Port Royal, with others scattered in fishing outposts along the Annapolis Basin and in other parts of Acadia which then included what is now Nova Scotia, New Brunswick, Prince Edward Island and part of Maine. These earliest colonists lived in crude log huts with thatched roofs and the most basic of furnishings. When the British acquired Acadia in 1713, they left the Acadians alone. But as these people flourished and their numbers grew to exceed 10,000, the British conquerors offered them a choice of signing the Oath of Allegiance to their new rulers — or expulsion. The Acadians refused to sign the oath — and were expelled from their homes and farms with great brutality. When the Acadians were allowed to return home in 1763, they found their lands occupied by English-speaking settlers. They moved to other parts of Nova Scotia, and began the hard task of making a new life — and to make their unique contribution to the culture and folk art of this province.

To populate the new colony after the founding of Halifax in 1749, the British offered land to the "foreign Protestants" of Germany, Switzerland, the Netherlands and France who were anxious to escape religious wars and persecution. About 3000 of these settlers came to Nova Scotia, and in 1753 about 1500 of them founded Lunenburg. These frugal and industrious people worked hard to improve the land, and began to add another component to the culture and folk art of Nova Scotia.

The next wave of settlers arrived between 1759 and 1763. The "Planters" came from Massachusetts, Rhode Island, Connecticut and New Hampshire to settle in many parts of western Nova Scotia and to farm, fish, cut down the trees for timber, build ships and trade.

After the American Revolution came the largest group of immigrants to arrive in Nova Scotia at any one time — the United Empire Loyalists. At Shelburne, then known as Port Roseway, the newcomers tried to create a new centre of commerce in British North America. But this dream died in that rocky and infertile place, and the Loyalists dispersed to other parts of Nova Scotia where they farmed and traded.

In the last half of the eighteenth century, small numbers of Irish settlers, a group from Yorkshire, and Scots settled in Nova Scotia, and after the War of 1812, British soldiers took up land.

As the newcomers arrived and began to establish themselves and to adapt their ways and their culture to new conditions, life in Nova Scotia became increasingly stable and prosperous. Permanent homes, churches, schools and businesses arose as communities established themselves throughout the province. People of varied origins, languages and cultures learned to live together and to share resources.

The homes of farmers and fishermen in the late eighteenth and early nineteenth centuries began to reflect a certain rude prosperity. The large kitchen or "keep-room" formed the centre of family life. A large open fireplace and hearth, with a built-in bake oven, dominated the room. The implements and utensils for daily use hung, or were stored, nearby. A large pantry for storing food and supplies was located off the kitchen.

Butter and cheese were made in the kitchen, and meals prepared and eaten here. In this central place in the home, herbs were dried, wool and flax spun, clothing, candles and soap made and the leisure time of the family spent in warmth and comfort.

A formal parlour or "good room", rarely used, lay at one side of the house. Better finished than other rooms, and furnished with the best the family could afford, the parlour was used to entertain visitors, to hold family celebrations, and for weddings and funerals. The "good room" might contain a built-in wall cupboard or corner cabinet to display the family's best dishes and ornaments, and might also have an attractive mantel and decorative architectural mouldings.

At the other side of the house, a bedroom opened off the kitchen. Sometimes used as a "borning-room," it benefitted from the heat of the fireplace that circulated through it.

The fireplace also heated the upper storey or half storey of the house, which served as a sleeping loft and was reached by a steep staircase. If the family could afford it, this part of the house would be closed off and divided into separate bedrooms.

Colour and decoration enlivened the interior of the homes. The pine panelling and the wainscotting around the lower interior walls, the fireplace mantel, doors, the mouldings around windows and even the softwood floor were painted in strong and striking shades of reds, greens, blues, yellows and other basic colours that contrasted beautifully with the whitewashed walls and ceilings.

The furniture, often of plain or primitive construction, was also painted in the same basic shades as the woodwork of the homes. Some pieces were decorated with two or three colours, worked to simulate the grain of fancier woods, or sponge decorated. Paintings with feathers or fingers in fanciful designs enhanced other pieces of furniture.

The day-to-day life of settlers was demanding and dreary in many ways. They used bold colours inside their homes and added more vitality through the use of brightly-coloured fabrics and floor and bed coverings, and by decorating utensils, containers, implements and other possessions in everyday use.

Containers came in all shapes and sizes for use in kitchen, pantry, parlour and bedroom. Boxes with tightly fitted covers held butter, cheese, salt, grains and other foods, while wall boxes contained candles, cutlery, pumice blocks for cleaning knives and other handy items. Open boxes on the kitchen table held cutlery.

The "work box" of elaborate design in the parlour stored sewing supplies and fancy needlework. Here too might be found a box for holding writing supplies, and others for documents and money and perhaps a fancy box for liquor bottles and glasses. In the bedroom, large blanket boxes stored quilts, blankets, and clothing, and smaller containers held hats, toilet articles and jewellery. Throughout the house other boxes held games, toys, pills, combs, tea and many other household items.

Amateurs and craftsmen made boxes from "splint", finely shaved strips of ash or oak, soaked in water to make them pliable, then formed on wooden moulds. The sides of the split boxes were fastened with a straight nailed seam or fancy long "fingers". Bottoms and covers were usually made of white pine, and occasionally of maple or birch. Trinket boxes and "bandboxes" for men and women to hold small items of clothing were also made this way. Some craftsmen made boxes in graduated sizes that nested inside each other.

The home-made hanging wall boxes, sometimes graceful and decorative, at other times crude and plain, held spills (pieces of paper to light candles) and the candles themselves so that they did not discolour, dry out, or crack. Pipe boxes, designed to hold long-stemmed clay pipes, and with a drawer to hold tobacco, are rarely found. Equally rare are elaborately carved early spoon racks with a cutlery drawer in the bottom.

Coopers and barrel makers produced buckets, kegs, firkins and tubs for kitchen and pantry. The barrels made by wet coopers held liquids, those of dry coopers, dry goods. The white cooper made smaller items for storing sugar, butter, flour and to carry feed to horses, collect maple sap and hold garden produce, using the same methods of barrel construction as the other coopers.

Other containers would be made at home, while local carpenters, joiners and cabinet makers created fancier boxes. And such elaborate items as tea caddies, fancy lacquered boxes and liquor boxes would have been imported by families who could afford such luxury items. Boxes intended as gifts for brides, and to hold sewing and jewellery, were made with loving attention to construction, detail and finish. Many other kinds of boxes were made for domestic use, including plain square and rectangular ones, often with locks, to hold important papers, cash and treasures. Most household boxes were made of wood. But tin, copper or brass, cardboard, papier-maché, bone and ivory, covered with leather, wallpaper and other material, were also used for making boxes.

The plain surfaces of the finished boxes lent themselves to embellishment. Boxes in the exhibition carry almost every kind of decoration known from the time of the early settlers.

Other kitchen items including butter moulds, bowls, scoops, paddles, churns, spoons, iron and tin utensils were also decorated. Small items of furnishing and other household accessories were brightened up with decorative paint, carving, applied decorations and fancy mouldings. Picture frames were enhanced in this way, as were those of mirrors which were decorated to emulate the more sophisticated ones owned by wealthy city folk. Some wonderful examples of footstools that have been carved or painted — or both — have been found in Nova Scotia. Shelves and cupboards, often decorated with stylized form or fancy painting, hung on the walls of early homes. And folk artists decorated cradles, game boards, fireplace bellows and other articles of household furnishing and equipment to light up their lives and to provide a feast for the eyes of others.

Some of the most finely decorated objects were created by fishermen and those who worked in the woods. The fishermen of Nova Scotia, especially those from along the South Shore, had a strong tradition of finely chip-carving their small hand tools such as mackerel ploughs, fish splitters, fishing line winders, hand reels and hook straightening devices. The owners decorated these small implements with hearts, vines, geometric designs initials, etc. They chip carved and incised the wooden surfaces and inlaid them with lead and coloured spruce gum. Men working in the camps in the woods occupied their spare time in making spruce boxes, carving the flat surfaces of the book-shaped containers hollowed from a single block of wood and fitting them with sliding covers at each end. Given as gifts to wives and sweethearts, the boxes sometimes had inlays of coloured wax.

The folk artists blended "the useful with the agreeable."

While the wealthy could import decorative products, poorer rural people satisfied the urge for brightness and vitality in their lives by creating their own decorations. As Bird and Kobayashi point out in *A Splendid Harvest*, The greatest decorative impulse is sometimes reserved for the smallest objects, perhaps because carving or painting is more easily accomplished on smaller areas. Then, too, there may be fewer inhibitions about decorating objects for personal use. Decorating walls, floors, furniture and other larger home objects was difficult and took a great deal of time — and perhaps was overly ambitious for some folk artists. But enhancing small household and personal objects, a pleasant and playful way to pass time and to experiment with creative impulses was safer. If the decorations turned out less successfully than expected, the articles could still be used.

Much of the decoration on everyday objects, obviously done by untrained hands, is crude and primitive in technique but often shows a natural sense of design, proportion and balance which sometimes borders on brilliance. The sheer joy of creation shines from these objects, whether they have been decorated along traditional lines or in boldly personal styles.

A plain and simple coat of paint was the most fundamental form of decoration. Paint was made by the settlers, using whatever ground pigments were available, mixed into a variety of media. Reds, greens, yellows, blues, white and black paints, made in this way, preserved and beautified the objects on which they used. One or two colours might be used to enhance an object, but more sophisticated techniques imitated fancy woods, and folk artists also painted abstract designs on surfaces. With paint, they created stencilled and freehand designs, as well as traditional motifs such as stars, hearts, compass rosettes, pinwheels, flowers and other forms of design.

Not all folk art was created by amateurs and homeowners. Itinerant and local house painters would often decorate large and small objects inside the house to suit the needs of the occupants and to earn a little extra money. They knew the techniques of grain painting, marbling, stencilling and other decorative touches of the time.

Carving required a steady hand and a reliable eye, especially for chip carving and relief carving. Wooden objects were scratched and incised, punched with a pointed object, or sculptured in three dimensions. Traditional and universal symbols such as hearts, compass stars, flying swastikas, diamonds and other geometric designs were cut into objects. And some carvers used floral motifs, vines, or eccentric designs. Some domestic objects were carved and decorated, and boxes and other articles, especially if used to hold sewing supplies, jewellery or tea, were often inlaid with ivory, bone and metal.

Other forms of decoration include hand-painted wallpapers, gold leaf gilding, painted paper coverings, hand-tooled leathers, painted string work, and designs made with straw. The Micmac Indians decorated boxes with dyed porcupine quills and moosehair and scratched designs on birch bark containers.

The desire to give graceful and sculptural form to an object so that it felt comfortable in the hand and pleasant to the eye is an ancient one. And this exhibition shows the wide range of creativity of the peoples who settled in Nova Scotia.

But why did these people decorate simple domestic objects?

When the settlers arrived in Nova Scotia, they brought with them a heritage of traditional craft definitions, and ideas about form, design and colour. Once they survived the first brutal years and created rough homes in the wilderness, they had time to remember and recover the decorative forms, patterns, motifs and colours of their places of origin. But when they began to use them, they introduced new and subtle differences in the traditional designs. Their rural folk arts became simpler and bolder in colour and design as memories and their experiences of creating a new world in a new land merged. The objects in this exhibition illustrate how the "folk process" operates, changing as the environment, lifestyle, social and economic attitudes of ordinary people changed. A strong craft tradition persists, uninfluenced by sophisticated art traditions or fashionable styles.

This is an unconscious and innocent art form, based on a fascination and delight with colour and design, and on the feelings, artistic inventiveness and instincts of individual craftsmen. The creative impulses often came from within the home, since most decorated articles were used — and often made — there. Decorative styles and influences passed down through generations, especially in isolated communities. In other areas, the traditional styles of different groups sometimes blended through cultural borrowing.

In some cases, decorations show a more individual and eccentric approach. Here someone with an internal vision, driven by a need to satisfy creative impulses, broke away from traditional folk styles and created unique painted or carved decorations.

The objects and their decorations offer insights into the lifestyles of past generations. They also provide a link with the social and human development of our communities, province and nation.

149 Oval Splint Box

Main a Dieu, Cape Breton County

Original green painted softwood (top and bottom) and ash (sides of top and base) with chip-carved and incised decoration, and a mirror recessed into the centre of the top.

Artist unknown, but the name Jean Ayles and the date 1789 is stitched into the side of the lid and base

Dated 1789

Dimensions: 33.5 × 24.2 cm (13⅛ × 9½ inches). Height with lid 11.0 cm (4⅜ inches), height of lid 4.5 cm (1¾ inches), height of base 10.0 cm (3⅞ inches).

Collection of James Denison How, Annapolis Royal, Nova Scotia

Most splint boxes were used for domestic storage purposes to hold either foodstuffs such as herbs and spices, or other family necessities. Before the days of glass jars, tin cans and other commercial packaging, convenient wooden boxes served a variety of needs. Of round or oval form, they came in sizes ranging from 24 inches in diameter and over 16 inches in width, to tiny receptacles for pills or other small accessories.[1]

This particular splint box, however, is the only example known to this author with a name and date added as decoration to the sides of the top and base. Using the same binding material that holds together the overlapping sides of the box, the maker stitched the first name JEAN into the side of the lid and the surname AYLES and the date 1789 into the side of the base.

Boxes which have a woman's name and date incorporated into the decoration are usually referred to as dower gifts suggesting they were presentation pieces for a wedding day, and always include the name of the owner and the commemorative date.[2] This interpretation is reinforced in terms of this particular splint box because of the small mirror which has been recessed into the centre of the lid from the underside.

Structure: The sides of the lid and base are formed by bending strips of ash around the oval form of the top and bottom which are cut from softwood. The ash is overlapped and the joints stitched together with twine or gut. Wooden pins were probably originally used to reinforce the construction and hold the sides to the top and bottom. Secondary nailing with small metal brads occurred at a later date. The mirror is recessed from the underside of the lid and is visible through an oval opening in the top. The top of the lid is decorated with chip-carved and incised geometric motifs, which accentuate the oval shape of the box. The condition of the box is excellent with only minor damage to the rim of the lid and a small chip of wood missing from the top. The paint is original although the mirror is probably an early replacement.

1. Nina Fletcher Little, *Neat and Tidy: Boxes and Their Contents Used in Early American Households,* (New York: E. P. Dutton, 1980), p. 150.
2. Monroe H. Fabian, *The Pennsylvania-German Decorated Chest,* (New York: Main Street Press, 1978), pp. 28-29. For example, according to Fabian in the Pennsylvania-German households ". . . both young men and women received chests at about the time they would have become old enough to be responsible for their own belongings. The young men's chests probably held mainly clothes and whatever small treasures they had managed to accumulate. The girls' storage chests would have been filled with both clothes and other fabrics to be taken along to new homes after marriage." Gifts to children about to be married was a widely practiced custom in the eighteenth and nineteenth centuries.

   Little states (*Ibid,* pp. 98-99) that "In Pennsylvania oval boxes, often referred to as bride-boxes, were traditional marriage gifts to hold delicate finery or trinkets." The tradition of giving a bridebox on a wedding day is certainly not strictly a Pennsylvania custom, but reflects the universal theme of presenting to young people on their marriage day a gift to remember the happiness and significance of the occasion.

150 Oval Splint Box

Feltzen South, Lunenburg County

Original green painted softwood (top and bottom) and ash (sides of top and base) with chip-carved decoration

Artist unknown

Circa 1790-1810

Dimensions: 43.0 × 25.0 cm (17 × 9⅞ inches). Height with lid 15.2 cm (6 inches), height of lid 4.2 cm (1¾ inches), height of base 13.9 cm (5½ inches)

Private collection

The chip-carved decoration on the top of the lid includes two opposing heart motifs separated by a complex series of intertwining incised lines, forming oval geometrics which are sectioned into two compartments. The hearts are located in the two outer sections of these compartments, while the inside sections contain two opposing cross-like designs. The heart is an ancient motif often interpreted in religious terms as the center of life, the soul or spirit of man. The heart is a common design found on European, American and Canadian folk art used to adorn small accessories, furniture, works of art on paper and various textiles, including hooked rugs and sail-cloth mats.[1]

It is difficult to say whether this box with hearts was given to a bride on her wedding day, or was ornamented to make an every day storage box more appealing. In the same manner it is a matter of debate concerning who made these types of splint boxes, specifically in Lunenburg County. Many feel they were produced by the Micmacs while others argue they were made by the Lunenburg-Germans. A third theory suggests that they were made by the Micmacs and decorated by their Lunenburg owners. Certainly the construction of these boxes is similar to other items made by the Micmacs but it is also true that the splint box is a common Continental and Pennsylvania-German form.[2] It seems likely that the Lunenburg-Germans made and used these boxes and that either the craft was copied by the Micmacs or that both groups produced oval and round storage boxes for domestic and personal use, the Micmacs using them as well as trade items.

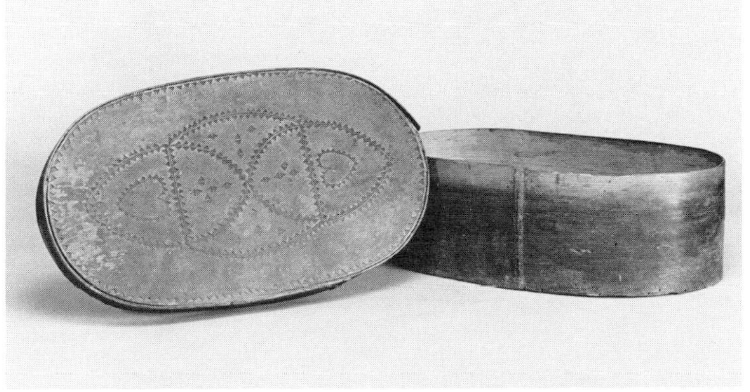

Structure: Typical bentwood construction made by overlapping the sides of ash and sewing them with fine brass wire. Small wooden pins hold the sides of the top and base to the softwood lid and bottom. There is some minor worm damage to the rim and base, but otherwise the box is in original and excellent condition.

1. Cynthia V. A. Schaffner and Susan Klein, *Folk Hearts: A Celebration of the Heart Motif in American Folk Art*, (New York: Alfred A. Knopf, 1984), pp. 7-11.
2. Nina Fletcher Little, *Neat and Tidy: Boxes and Their Contents Used in Early American Households*, (New York: E. P. Dutton, 1980), pp. 98-99.

There is little question that the carved geometric designs often found on the lids of these oval storage boxes are similar to the decorations found on Micmac quillwork. Certainly the heart, star, cross and fylfot ("flying swastika") motifs were worked as designs on quillwork on bark storage containers and other objects. See Ruth Holmes Whitehead, *Micmac Quillwork*, (Halifax: The Nova Scotia Museum, 1982), pp. 133-199, specifically pp. 168-174, pp. 181-185, pp. 193-195. For example, Whitehead states that " 'Compass Work' motifs appear on dated examples of quill boxes about 1830" (p. 183). The compass motif was used as a Lunenburg-German decorative design in the late eighteenth century.

151 Oval Splint Box

Lunenburg County

Original red painted softwood (top and bottom) and ash (sides of top and base) with chip-carved decoration

Artist unknown

Circa 1790-1810

Dimensions: 53.0 × 41.7 cm (20⅞ × 16⅜ inches). Height with lid 18.5 cm (7$^{5}/_{16}$ inches), height of lid 6.3 cm (2$^{7}/_{16}$ inches), height of base 15.3 cm (6$^{1}/_{16}$ inches).

Private collection

The decoration on the lid is mostly composed of a single complex geometric design formed by a series of curvalinear and straight incised lines with chip-carved crosses and single diamonds interspersed throughout the decoration. The design is flanked by two circular geometric motifs.

Structure: Bentwood construction made by overlapping the sides of ash and sewing them together with fine wire. Small wooden pins and square nails originally held the sides of the top and base to the lid and bottom, but many of these have been replaced with secondary round nails.

Published: Michael Bird and Terry Kobayashi, *A Splendid Harvest: Germanic Folk and Decorative Arts in Canada*, (Toronto: Van Nostrand Reinhold Ltd., 1981), p. 45.

152 Oval Splint Box

Lunenburg County

Original green painted softwood (top and bottom) and ash (sides of top and base) with black painted decorative designs

Artist unknown

Circa 1850-1870

Dimensions: 48.2 × 29.0 cm (6$^{15}/_{16}$ × 11⅝ inches). Height with lid 18.4 cm (7¼ inches), height of lid 4.5 cm (1¾ inches), height of base 16.5 cm (6½ inches)

Private collection

This particular splint box is simply painted with two bands of black designs on the original green ground, one band around the outer rim of the lid, the other around the base. This decoration is reminiscent of the designs found on second quarter nineteenth century bandboxes which were made of pasteboard covered with printed or stencilled papers.[1] Perhaps these boxes were the inspiration for the decoration found on this splint box. This motif is also similar to nineteenth century wall paper borders.

Structure: Bentwood construction made by overlapping ash and sewing the ends together with wire. Small wooden pegs and square nails hold the sides of the top and base to the softwood lid and bottom. Except for some secondary round nails, the box is in its original condition. The green paint, now highly patinaed, was probably closer to a robin egg blue as suggested by the upper rim of the base, protected from wear and aging by the rim of the lid.

1. Nina Fletcher Little, *Neat and Tidy: Boxes and Their Contents Used in Early American Households*, (New York: E. P. Dutton, 1980), pp. 98-99.

153 Splint Box Lid*

Liverpool, Queens County

Original carved and painted softwood

The name Nathaniel Rayment (Raymond ?) is carved into the lid which is either the maker's or owner's name

Circa 1780-1800

Dimensions: diameter — 19.0 cm (7½ inches)

Collection of Leslie J. Langille, Lunenburg, Nova Scotia

This is truly an exciting and early piece of decorative folk art. Although only a fragment lid from a splint box (one must wonder what the rest of the piece looked like), it is carved with a series of geometric motifs including hearts, diamonds and solar motifs, with a chip-carved border. The name Nathaniel R (?) Rayment (Raymond ?) and the place Liverpool B (Brook ?) is carved into the lid along with the initials ADV probably standing for Anno Domini (in the year of our Lord), although no date is given. On the reverse are the carved initials NRBR.

Structure: The identification of this piece as a splint box lid is confirmed by the series of small holes along the outside edge (five in all), where this piece would have been recessed and either pegged or nailed to the top inside of the box forming the lid. It is in excellent condition with traces of black paint.

* This piece will be on view in Halifax only

154 Stack Of Three Splint Boxes

Liverpool, Queens County

Original painted softwood (top and bottom) and ash (sides of top and base)

Artist unknown

Circa 1810-1830

Dimensions: bottom box — 18.3 cm (7$^{3}/_{16}$ inches), height with lid 8.6 cm (3⅜ inches) middle box — 16.0 cm (6$^{5}/_{16}$ inches), height with lid 8.6 cm (3⅜ inches) top box — 14.4 cm (5$^{11}/_{16}$ inches), height with lid 6.3 cm (2½ inches).

Collection of Murray E. Stewart, Berwick, Nova Scotia

An example of a graduated set of three splint boxes. Although the paint is well worn, and these three boxes have seen a lot of wear and use, they are examples of a common everyday utilitarian object made for function and not with any particular decorative intent in mind. They fall into what could be considered folk art in a plain style. For even though they are not carved or have painted decoration, their method of construction using finger shaped lapped joints and what at one time were both painted (middle box/red, bottom box/green) and unpainted (top box) surfaces, makes this set of splint boxes almost "pure" examples of Nova Scotia folk art.

Structure: All three boxes are made from bent ash formed around softwood tops and bottoms with finger lapped construction joined with wooden pins and forged nails. It is on the basis of this construction method and hardware that they are given a first quarter of the nineteenth century date, although they certainly could date as late as the second quarter.

155 Round Splint Box

Lunenburg County

Original blue painted softwood (top and bottom) and ash (sides of top and base)

Artist unknown

Circa 1850-1870

Dimensions: 28.0 cm (11 inches). Height with lid 15.7 cm (6$\frac{3}{16}$ inches), height of lid 4 cm (1$\frac{9}{16}$ inches), height of base 14.3 cm (5 $\frac{5}{8}$ inches)

Private collection

Although this storage box is not decorated with geometric motifs, its beauty is in the proportions and simple lines accentuated with a now highly patinaed "blueberry" paint.

Structure: Bentwood construction made by overlapping ash and sewing them together with wire. Small metal brads or nails hold the sides of the top and base to the softwood lid and bottom.

156 Round Splint Box

Lunenburg County

Original softwood (top and bottom) and ash (sides of top and base) with chip-carved decoration.

Artist unknown

Circa 1860-1880

Dimensions: diameter — 29.2 cm (11$\frac{1}{2}$ inches). Height with lid — 14.0 cm (5$\frac{1}{2}$ inches), height of lid 4.1 cm (1$\frac{5}{8}$ inches), height of base — 12.7 cm (5 inches)

Collection of Jerry and Debbie Vidito, Kentville, Nova Scotia

Another example of a splint box with ornate chip-carved decoration on the top of the lid including a central compass star motif. This particular design is identical to the compass work motifs which appear on Micmac quill work boxes. "The Rev. Richard Uniacke recorded the use of the compass by Micmac coopers in the nineteenth century. Quillworkers apparently began using compasses in the first half of the nineteenth century. 'Compass work' motifs appear on dated examples of quill boxes about 1830".[1] This is another indication that some of these splint boxes were made by the Micmacs.

Structure: The box is typical bentwood construction made by overlapping the ash and sewing them with fine brass wire. Small wooden pins hold the sides of the top and base to the softwood lid and bottom. The box appears never to have been painted, or perhaps was stained at one time with most of this colouring worn off through use.

1. Ruth Holmes Whitehead, *Micmac Quillwork*, (Halifax: The Nova Scotia Museum, 1982), p. 183.

157 Round Splint Box

Lunenburg County

Painted and incised softwood (top and bottom) and ash (sides of top and base)

Artist unknown

Circa 1860-1880

Dimensions: 27.0 cm (10$\frac{5}{8}$ inches). Height with lid 13.0 cm (5$\frac{1}{8}$ inches), height of lid 3.8 cm (1$\frac{3}{4}$ inches), height of base 12.1 cm (4$\frac{3}{4}$ inches)

Private collection

An excellent example of a splint box with mottled red, green and yellow painted decoration. A series of concentric circles are carved on the top of the lid with a clover leaf design in the centre, made from four incised hearts.

Structure: Bentwood construction made by overlapping the ash sides and sewing them together with wire. Small wooden pegs hold the sides of the top and base to the softwood top and bottom.

158 Round Splint Box

Lunenburg County

Original painted softwood (top and bottom) and ash (sides of top and base)

Artist unknown

Circa 1860-1880

Dimensions: height with lid 7.0 cm (2¾ inches), diameter 12.5 cm (4$\frac{15}{16}$ inches)

Private collection

This small splint box is painted with red and black graining similar to many examples of furniture found in Lunenburg County dating from the last quarter of the nineteenth century.

Structure: The sides are lapped and tied with brass wire around the round form of the top and bottom. The underside of the bottom is also painted red. There is some paint loss around the rim of the base due to the tight fitting lid.

159 Round Splint Box

Bridgewater, Lunenburg County

Original red stained softwood (top and bottom) and ash (sides of top and base) with chip-carved star or flower motifs on the top of the lid.

Attributed to an Indian named Molly

Circa 1870-1880

Dimensions: 30.0 cm (11$\frac{13}{16}$ inches). Height with lid 12.7 (5 inches), height of lid 5.0 cm (1$\frac{15}{16}$ inches), height of base 11.0 cm (4$\frac{5}{16}$ inches).

Collection of the DesBrisay Museum, Bridgewater, Nova Scotia

According to the information given to the DesBrisay Museum when this box was donated to their permanent collection in 1967, it was made by an Indian named Molly, who lived in Bridgewater, for Enos Spidel of Farmington, Lunenburg County. If this information is correct it helps to support the claim that these types of oval and round splint boxes were made by the local native Micmac population, probably for their own storage use and as trade items.

This particular example has the lid decorated with a series of star or flower motifs arranged in a circular pattern around a central geometric design comprised of an eight pointed star motif.

History: This box was donated to the DesBrisay Museum in 1967 by Russell Haines of Barss Corner, Lunenburg County.

Structure: The construction of this box is similar to most of this design with the ash sides bent around the round form of the softwood lid and bottom. The ash is overlapped and joined with square nails.

160 Splint Box

La Baie de la Riverie, Digby County
Original painted decoration on ash and softwood
Made by Henri LeBlanc
Circa 1848
Dimensions: 12.0 cm (4 11/16 inches). Height with lid 3.5 cm (1 3/8 inches), height of lid 1.2 cm (1/2 inch), height of base 3.0 cm (1 3/16 inches).
Collection of Murray E. Stewart, Berwick, Nova Scotia

The maker, Henri LeBlanc, was a sailor who was occasionally locked in a room in his house with his paints and tools, due to a recurring nervous disorder.[1] During those times he used to carve and paint. His painted decorations always consisted of this multi-coloured dot pattern, and the one carving that is known to exist is an extremely intricate fretwork piece also included in this exhibition. Newspapers pasted inside the lid and bottom are dated 1848.

Structure: The sides of the base and lid are formed by bending thin strips of ash around the round form of the top and bottom which are of softwood. The ash is overlapped slightly and joined with wooden pins. The multi-coloured red and green dot decoration is applied over a yellow-ochre ground. The box is in excellent condition.

1. Personal communication with Murray Stewart and Paul Killowee, April 19, 1985.

Refer to colour plate XXIII, page 26

162 Carved Fretwork Ornament*

La Baie de la Riverie, Digby County
Carved hardwood
Made by Henri LeBlanc
Circa 1850-1870
Dimensions: 74.0 × 54.0 cm (29 1/8 × 21 1/4 inches)
Collection of Paul Killawee and Judy Aymar, Queensland, Nova Scotia

This is the ultimate example of Henri Le Blanc's work, and one of the finest examples of fretwork ornamentation known from Nova Scotia. Its purpose is uncertain, but judging by its structure it was possibly meant to be used as a back on a small chest or bureau.

Structure: The piece is carved from one thin plank of hardwood.

*This piece will be on view in Halifax only

161 Blanket Box Lid

La Baie de la Riverie, Digby County
Original painted decoration on softwood
Made by Henri LeBlanc
Circa 1850-1870
Dimensions: 76.0 × 35.5 cm (29 15/16 × 14 inches)
Collection of Paul Killawee and Judy Aymar, Queensland, Nova Scotia

The inside of this blanket box lid, painted by Henri Le Blanc, has identical decoration to the small round splint box which he also made. The unpainted top of the lid was originally inlaid with diamond motifs, which have long since disappeared.

Structure: The lid is made from a single plank of softwood. The strap hinges are still intact.

163 Oval Storage Box

Halifax County
Birchbark storage container decorated with carved circle and star motifs
Artist unknown
Circa 1790 1820
Dimensions: 25.5 × 11.0 × 15.2 cm (10 1/16 × 4 5/16 × 6 inches)
Private collection

This is one of the finest examples of Micmac work in birchbark. The base is made by overlapping four layers of bark, the inner layer acting as the liner for the box, the next two layers forming part of the ornamentation with sawtooth borders, top and bottom. The outer layer is pierced with various circle and star motifs which use the third layer of birchbark as a background for the designs. The lid is constructed in a similar manner of four layers of bark which are then applied to pine, forming the underside of the lid.

There is no doubt as to the Micmac origin of this box. Birchbark was used to make various types of objects for storage, including bowls and lidded containers. Bark was also used as the base for quillwork. The designs on this container are exactly like the compass-work motifs found on Micmac quillwork.[1] The maker employed three variations of this design by piercing the six-pointed stars, by carving the bark between the points of the star, and by using both techniques to create a four-pointed "open" compass motif.

Structure: Bentwood construction made by overlapping birchbark and pegging the layers together. There is no evidence of sewing. The inside bottom of the base has a liner of pine laid over a birchbark bottom. Although the lid no longer recesses into the base, the box is completely original and was never painted. The outer layers of bark have a medium to dark brown patina.

1. Ruth Holmes Whitehead, *Micmac Quillwork,* (Halifax: The Nova Scotia Museum, 1982), p. 138, pp. 181-185.

164 Small Birchbark Container

South Shore of Nova Scotia
Original decorated birchbark
Artist unknown
Circa 1860-1880
Dimensions: height with lid 5.7 cm (2 1/4 inches), diameter 9.0 cm (3 9/16 inches)
Private collection

This small round birchbark storage box is an excellent example of birchbark work practised by the Micmac Indians for their own domestic use and for sale and trade. The entire box is made from bark and decorated with small semicircle motifs on the sides and a more intricate design on the lid.

Structure: Made from birchbark, the box is held together with natural fibre, probably spruce root. A wooden rim on the interior lip of the base adds strength and rigidity to the box.

165 Whalebone Ditty Box with Heart

Lunenburg County

Whalebone with applied heart and softwood top and bottom

Artist unknown

Circa 1883

Dimensions: height with lid 11.1 cm (4⅜ inches), diameter 16.2 cm (6⅜ inches)

Collection of Mr and Mrs Francis Coutellier, Moncton, New Brunswick

According to an inscription on the inside of the lid, this box was presented to H. Maria Murray by her grandmother Harriet Hamilton Fraser in July, 1883. The whalebone heart inset into the softwood lid suggests that this was a presentation gift given by grandmother Fraser to her granddaughter, perhaps as a birthday or coming of age present.

Structure: The sides of the base and lid are made from whalebone bent into a circular form, lapped and tied with wire on the base, and copper nails on the top. The lid and base are made from softwood secured to the whalebone with small copper brads. There is some minor damage to the upper lip of the base with loss of whalebone.

166 Knife Box

Lunenburg County

Unpainted and carved hardwood

Artist unknown

Circa 1800-1820

Dimensions: 31.5 × 9.0 × 15.2 cm (12⅜ × 3$^{11}/_{16}$ × 6 inches)

Collection of Leslie J. Langille, Lunenburg, Nova Scotia

This knife box appears never to have been painted. Unpainted accessories and furnishings are found within the Lunenburg Germanic decorative tradition. The designs carved into either end of this box are both different, but reflect similar motifs found on Lunenburg-German utilitarian objects. This box probably dates from the first quarter of the nineteenth century based on construction and hardware details, a suggestion indicating just how early some of these geometric motifs actually date, and just how long the tradition of carving and painting abstract designs on furniture and accessories in Lunenburg has been an accepted part of the ethnic heritage of that county.

Structure: Plank construction with rabbet joints secured with both wooden pegs and forged nails. The centre divider is open mortised through the end pieces.

167 Knife Box

Liverpool, Queens County
Carved and incised hardwood
Artist unknown
Circa 1800-1830
Dimensions: 33.0 × 13.0 × 17.2 cm (13 × 5⅛ × 6¾ inches)
Collection of Joseph Schneider House, Kitchener, Ontario

This hardwood cutlery tray is incised with concentric hearts on the sides and geometric designs on the ends. The centre divider has been pierced with a heart shape for carrying purposes.

Structure: Plank construction with rabbet joints that are entirely pegged with small wooden pins. The bottom is also pegged as is the centre board to the ends. There is no evidence that the box was ever painted.

Published: Michael Bird and Terry Kobayashi, *A Splendid Harvest: Germanic Folk and Decorative Arts in Canada,* (Toronto: Van Nostrand Reinhold Ltd., 1981), p. 37.

168 Knife Box*

Queens County
Carved and painted softwood
Artist unknown
Circa 1820-1890
Dimensions: 31.8 × 30.5 × 24.2 cm (12½ × 12 × 9½ inches)
Collection of Richard Henning Field and Deborah Field, Halifax, Nova Scotia

Although very simply made and decorated, this particular knife box has a lot of folk appeal. The box is chip-carved along the top edges of the sides and on the curved carrying handle, and the sides are incised with a series of hearts and "stick" star motifs resembling snow flakes.

Structure: Plank construction with butt corners held together with rose-head nails. The base board is chamfered with extended edge. The box is in the original coat of dark brown paint.

*This piece will be on view in Halifax only

169 Knife Box

Found in Birchtown, Shelburne County

Original red painted softwood with carved decorative motifs painted in white

Artist unknown

Circa 1840-1860

Dimensions: 44.3 (at the top) × 12.0 (at the front) × 14.3 cm (17 7/16 × 4 11/16 × 5 5/8 inches)

Private collection

This knife box is only painted red on three sides, with carved six pointed star and compass star motifs on the front, and carved five pointed star motifs on the sides. These geometric designs are accentuated because they are painted in white. The scalloping of the front adds a further decorative dimension to the box, each scallop containing a carved six pointed star painted in white.

Structure: Plank construction with splayed sides and front but vertical backboard. Square nailed butt joints and corners.

Exhibited: Decorated Nova Scotia Furnishings, Dalhousie University Art Gallery, Halifax, Nova Scotia, July 5-August 6, 1978.

Published: Tom Lackey, *Decorated Nova Scotia Furnishings,* (Halifax: Dalhousie University Art Gallery, 1978), pp. 6, 32.

170 Candle Box

Walden, Lunenburg County

Original green painted softwood

Artist unknown

Circa 1840-1860

Dimensions: 44.0 × 14.5 × 13.7 cm (17 5/16 × 5 3/16 × 5 1/8 inches)

Private collection

Candles were one of the earliest forms of household illumination. They are listed in inventories in rural New England dating as early as 1676.[1] In order to prevent discolouration, cracking and accidental damage, tallow candles were stored in long narrow wooden boxes sometimes divided into two compartments.[2] Usually such boxes had sliding lids; today it is common practice to call any box with a sliding lid a candle box. This particular example is typical of this form, but has the addition of a lollipop handle carved out of the solid piece of softwood forming the sliding lid, and decorated with incised lines.

Structure: Plank construction with butt joints which are square nailed. The lid is chamfered to allow it to slide smoothly into the groove along the top inside of the box.

1. Abbott Lowell Cummings (Ed), *Rural Household Inventories, 1675-1775,* (Boston: The Society for the Preservation of New England Antiquities, 1964), pp. 11, 26, 132.
2. Nina Fletcher Little, *Neat and Tidy: Boxes and Their Contents Used in Early American Households,* (New York: E. P. Dutton, 1980), pp. 147-148.
The best candles were fashioned from beeswax, bayberry wax and spermaceti — a substance found in the head of the sperm whale (Nina Fletcher Little, *Ibid,* p. 148).

171 Candle Box

Halifax or Colchester County
Original painted and decorated softwood
Artist unknown
Circa 1850-1870
Dimensions: 28.0 × 15.2 × 23.0 cm (11 × 6 × 9$^{1}/_{16}$ inches)
Collection of Leslie J. Langille, Lunenburg, Nova Scotia

A very fine example of a candle box with sliding lid. The decoration is painted in yellow-ochre and orange, over what appears to be the original red ground pigment.

Structure: Plank softwood construction with square nailed butt joints. The chamfered lid slides into the grooves along the top inside of the box. The interior is undivided and painted green. There is a finger pull carved at one end of the lid.

172 Candle Box

Lunenburg County
Original green painted and decorated softwood
Artist unknown
Circa 1890-1910
Dimensions: 30.0 × 10.0 × 20.0 cm (11$^{13}/_{16}$ × 3$^{15}/_{16}$ × 7$^{7}/_{8}$ inches)
Collection of Leslie J. Langille, Lunenburg, Nova Scotia

A good example of a candle box with sliding lid, decorated with a five pointed star and pinwheel. The natural wood and original green colour create a two-tone motif.

Structure: Plank construction with butt joints that are held in place with round nails. The lid slides smoothly into a groove along the top inside of the box. The interior is divided into two compartments. The initials PR are carved on the underside of the lid. The box is made from softwood and is in the original green colour. The lid has a finger pull carved at one end to make it easier to slide the lid.

173 Double Wall Box

North Range Corner, Digby County

Overpainted softwood

Artist unknown

Circa 1850-1870

Dimensions: 28.0 × 38.1 × 12.7 cm (11 × 15 × 5 inches)

Collection of Paul Killawee and Judy Aymar, Queensland, Nova Scotia

An example of a simple utilitarian wall box with double scalloped backboard used for storage, probably in the hearth room or workshop. The two holes hidden by the front of the top tier were used for hanging the box on a wall.

Structure: Plank construction with butt joints that are square nailed. The front of each tier is angled outward. The present cream-yellow paint is over the original green-black.

174 Double Wall Box

Lunenburg County

Original red painted softwood and oak backboard with black paint decoration

Artist unknown

Circa 1860-1880

Dimensions: 33.0 × 48.5 × 11.4 cm (13 × 19$\frac{1}{8}$ × 4$\frac{1}{2}$ inches)

Private collection

Wall boxes were often used in the kitchen/hearth rooms of eighteenth and nineteenth century households to hold various utensils and accessories. This particular example was decorated by the maker with the words "spoons" and "knives & forks" which leaves little doubt as to what objects were to be stored in the box.

Structure: Plank construction with simple butt joints which are square nailed. The backboard is oak and the rest softwood. It is not unusual to find oak as either a primary or secondary wood used in furniture construction in port towns, or ship building centres such as Lunenburg or Halifax, where such hardwood was used in ship construction.

175 Hanging Wall Box

Chezzetcook, Halifax County
Overpainted softwood with incised hearts
Artist unknown
Circa 1850-1870
Dimensions: 27.5 × 18.5 × 18.5 cm (10 13/16 × 7 1/4 × 7 1/4 inches)
Collection of Chris Cooper, Dartmouth, Nova Scotia

This wall box was originally painted a blueberry colour and is now overpainted a mustard yellow. There are three incised hearts along the front of the box, one on the backboard, and two on the sides. The interior is divided into two compartments. The wire hanging apparatus is recent and perhaps added when the box was repainted. It was originally hung on the wall through a small hole in the backboard.

Structure: Plank construction with butt joints. The entire box is square nailed.

176 Hanging Wall Box

Cumberland County
Unpainted softwood
Artist unknown
Circa 1850-1870
Dimensions: 28.6 × 19.0 × 14.0 cm (11 1/4 × 7 7/16 × 5 1/2 inches)
Collection of Jerry and Debbie Vidito, Kentville, Nova Scotia

Another example of a hanging wall box, this time including drawer. The front is formed by the wood used for the molding. The lid is hinged with two external strips of leather and the case is dovetailed. The box has never been painted, the wood having turned a dark colour from age and "airburn".

Structure: Plank construction with dovetailed joints that are nailed with small square brads and pinned with wooden pegs. The drawer is dovetailed front and back with the remains of a small brass loop pull. The drawer front is lapped and formed from the molding. Two interior compartments in the box, none in the drawer. The back extends into a shaped hanging support.

177 Hanging Wall Box

Hants County
Original painted softwood
Artist unknown
Circa 1860-1870
Dimensions: 33.7 × 41.0 × 21.5 cm (13¼ × 16⅛ × 8$\frac{7}{16}$ inches)
Collection of Jerry and Debbie Vidito, Kentville, Nova Scotia

A wall box with the lid hinged with pegs, in the manner of lids on tills in blanket boxes. The plank backboard is shaped into a triptych form creating a very decorative as well as functional utilitarian object.

Structure: Plank construction with square nailed butt joints. The backboard extends into shaped hanging support. The interior is one large compartment. The box is painted a deep red-brown.

178 Hanging Wall Box

Terrence Bay, Halifax County
Original carved and painted softwood
Artist unknown
Circa 1890-1920
Dimensions: 30.0 × 20.3 × 14.0 cm (13 × 8 × 5½ inches)
Collection of Patricia and Tom Lackey, Toronto, Ontario

This ornately carved wallbox is decorated with a series of incised and painted diamond motifs along the front sides, while the chamfered molding is incised with a crosshatch design, and the back of the box with a semi-circle motif. Although the box is constructed completely of round nails, its decorative treatment suggests an earlier tradition and date.

Structure: Plank construction with rabbet joints, the bottom board is butted and nailed to the sides. Paint combination was originally red, black and white. Hung on wall with single hole through curved backboard.

Exhibited: Decorated Nova Scotia Furnishings, Dalhousie University Art Gallery, Halifax, Nova Scotia, July 5-August 6, 1978.

Published: Tom Lackey, *Decorated Nova Scotia Furnishings,* (Halifax: Dalhousie University Art Gallery, 1978), pp. 7, 32.

179 Wall Box with Mirror and Towel Rack

Lunenburg County
Original painted softwood with applied and inset mirrors
Artist unknown
Circa 1890-1910
Dimensions: 29.3 × 66.0 × 10.0 cm (11⁹⁄₁₆ × 26.0 × 3¹⁵⁄₁₆ inches)
Private collection

Although the decoration of this piece is typical for Lunenburg County, the combination of a wall box, mirror, towel rack and comb box is common to homes at the turn of the century as an object used in the bed or bathroom area, and in some cases near an outside door.

It is for this reason that some of these types of boxes and small individual mirrors are referred to as "last look", implying that one could check his/her appearance before going out in public.

Structure: Plank construction with a combination of round and square nails. The decorations are painted in a series of brown, red and gold colours and the small mirror is inset directly into the front panel of the comb box. The mirror is nailed to the back board.

180 Wall Box with Mirror and Towel Rack

Blockhouse, Lunenburg County
Original painted, carved and shaped softwood
Made by Niran Begin
Circa 1890-1910
Dimensions: 29.5 × 66.0 × 11.0 cm (11⅝ × 26 × 4⁵⁄₁₆ inches)
Private collection

Another very fine example of a wall box with last look mirror and a series of cut out hearts and diamond in the panel immediately below the top shelf. The mirror is chip-carved with diamonds, a design repeated along with a star motif on the front panel of the wall box, which is also outlined in a double row of chip-carving. This wall piece has a strong decorative statement reflecting the Lunenburg-German heritage of its maker.

Structure: The piece is in the original dark brown-black paint over what appears to be an original primer coat of varnish.

Exhibited: Decorated Nova Scotia Furnishings, Dalhousie University Art Gallery, Halifax, Nova Scotia, July 5-August 6, 1978.

Published: Tom Lackey, *Decorated Nova Scotia Furnishings,* (Halifax: Dalhousie University Art Gallery, 1978), p. 29, 32.

181 Wall Shelf with Mirror

Lunenburg County
Original varnished and carved ash (?)
Artist unknown
Circa 1890-1910
Dimensions: 26.5 × 62.5 × 11.5 cm (10$\frac{7}{16}$ × 24$\frac{5}{8}$ × 4$\frac{1}{2}$ inches)
Private collection

A very ornate example of a wall shelf with mirror and a complex series of cutouts including a heart in the centre panel below the lower shelf. The varnish originally used on the surface has turned a medium brown tone.

Structure: Plank construction with butt joints. Screws and glue are used on all joints.

182 Comb Box with Mirror

Lunenburg County
Original painted and carved softwood
Artist unknown
Circa 1900-1920
Dimensions: 51.0 × 49.0 × 14.0 cm (20$\frac{1}{16}$ × 19$\frac{5}{16}$ × 5$\frac{1}{2}$ inches)
Private collection

Another example of a mirror/comb box combination, this one with the mirror set into a carved maple leaf with applied sail boat. The paint is a combination of gold and silver. Two hearts are set on either side of the mirror.

Structure: Plank construction and round nails. Two finials are missing on either side of the mirror.

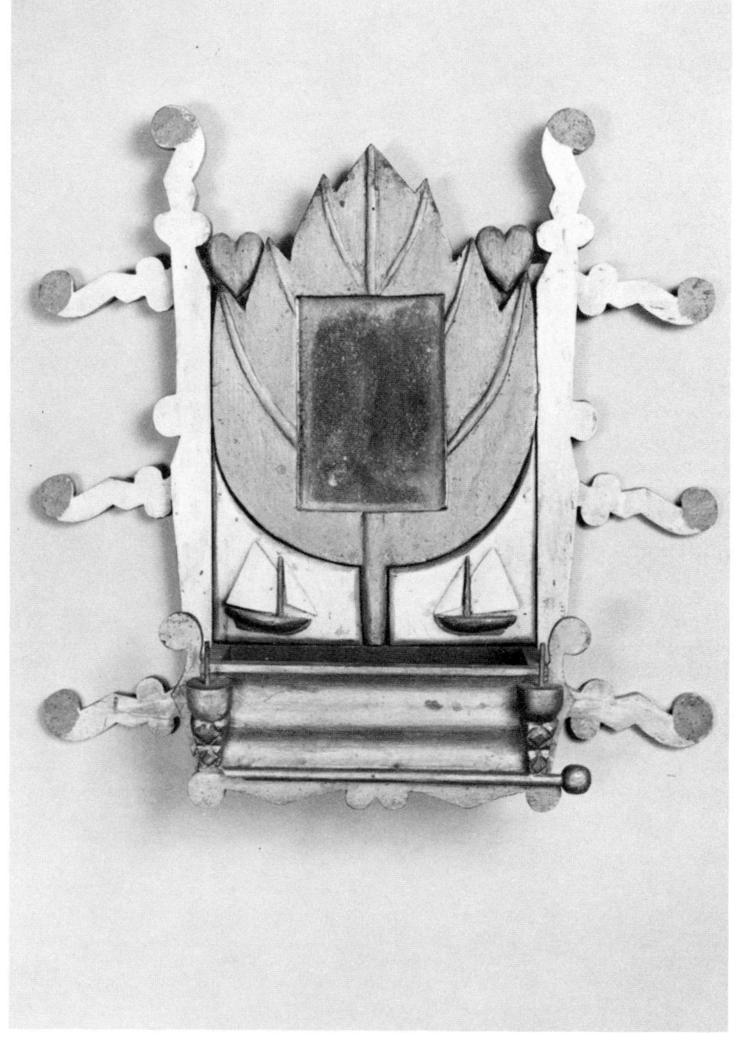

183 Sail-Cloth Wall Hanging

Oyster Pond, Halifax County

Original painted sail-cloth of three masted ship fringed with knotted twine and having two storage pouches

Artist unknown, but it is attributed to a member of the Myers family of Oyster Pond

Circa 1870-1890

Dimensions: 55.4 × 41 cm (21¾ × 15¾ inches)

Collection of the Dartmouth Heritage Museum, Dartmouth, Nova Scotia

This is a fine example of a sail-cloth wall hanging used for storage purposes, probably in the kitchen, workshop or on board ship. This particular hanging has two storage pouches fringed with knotted twine in an open lattice weave pattern. Knotting was a typical sailor's craft required of any good seaman, and was often used to embellish small utilitarian items such as ditty bags and needle cases, and sometimes the borders of sail-cloth mats. This is one of two examples known to this author. The other hanging was found in New Brunswick and is presently in the National Museum of Man Folk Art Collection in Ottawa. This example also has storage pouches and a ship painted in the centre of the cloth.[1]

Members of the Myers family, from whom the hanging was obtained by the Dartmouth Heritage Museum, indicate that the piece has always been in the family, with tradition suggesting that it was made in the last quarter of the nineteenth century when the Myers owned a small fishing schooner. Perhaps the wall hanging was used on board that vessel.

History: The hanging was donated to the Dartmouth Heritage Museum in 1977.

Structure: The pouches are simply formed by folding the bottom of the sail-cloth upwards and spot sewing them in place by hand. The rim of the pockets and the edges of the cloth are painted a mustard-yellow brown, creating a border or frame around the painting of the ship. Twine was then knotted in an open lattice weave pattern and sewn to the edges of the pockets and along the top of the cloth, creating a scalloped shaped fringe.

Exhibited: At the Quaker House in Dartmouth, Nova Scotia during the Summer of 1984.

1. Both of these wall hangings reflect the tradition of painted sail-cloth used for floor and sea chest coverings in the provinces of Nova Scotia and New Brunswick.

Refer to colour plate XXII, page 25

184 Document Box

First South, Lunenburg County

Painted softwood

On the inside of the lid is the pencil inscription, "Abraham Hirtle, First South, Lunenburg, N.S."

Circa 1830-1850

Dimensions: 23.2 × 18.8 × 16.0 cm (9⅛ × 7⅜ × 6$\frac{5}{16}$ inches)

Collection of Joseph Schneider House, Kitchener, Ontario

This small box exhibits typical Germanic colour and design with its compass stars in red, yellow and black. The corners of the lid, sides and ends are painted with black semi-circles often found on other examples of decorative folk art in Lunenburg County, including gameboards and table tops. The inscription inside the lid could be the name of the owner or maker.

Structure: Plank construction with dovetailed joints. The box opens using only one hinge which is set in the centre. There is a small brass loop to help lift the lid. The bottom is nailed with a series of small forged nails. Two pieces of molding have been replaced on the front and left bottom

Published: Michael Bird and Terry Kobayashi, *A Splendid Harvest: Germanic Folk and Decorative Arts in Canada,* (Toronto: Van Nostrand Reinhold Ltd., 1981), p. 37.

Refer to colour plate XX, page 24

185 Document Box

Crousetown, Lunenburg County
Original green painted softwood with stencilled floral decorations
Made by a member of the Stewart family
Circa 1840-1860
Dimensions: 50.5 × 19.5 × 24.0 cm ($19\frac{7}{8} \times 7\frac{11}{16} \times 9\frac{7}{16}$ inches)
Collection of Judy and Earle Rhodenizer, Pleasantville, Nova Scotia

This box is earlier than its companion piece (following illustration) but made by a member of the same family. This box has the identical stencilled floral decoration on the front and sides as the other box.

Structure: Plank construction with dovetailed joints front and back. The hinges and lock are brass, and there is an interior till on the right side with a lid.

186 Document Box

Crousetown, Lunenburg County
Original red painted softwood with stencilled decorations and initials
Made by a member of the Stewart family
Circa 1860
Dimensions: 38.5 × 17.5 × 19.0 cm ($15\frac{3}{16} \times 6\frac{7}{8} \times 7\frac{1}{2}$ inches)
Collection of Judy and Earle Rhodenizer, Pleasantville, Nova Scotia

This is a very fine document box with the initials of the maker (S.S.) painted on the lid, and hand stencilled floral decorations painted on the front and sides of the box. The overall paint is original red. The multiple molding around the lid and base adds to the refinement of this piece.

Structure: Plank construction with rabbet joints that are square nailed. Brass lock and hinges. There is no interior till.

187 Painted Storage Box

Lunenburg County
Original painted and decorated softwood
Artist unknown
Circa 1840-1860
Dimensions: 17.3 × 8.8 × 10.2 cm (6 13/16 × 3 7/16 × 4 inches)
Collection of Mr and Mrs Francis Coutellier, Moncton, New Brunswick

An exceptional example of a painted and decorated storage box from Lunenburg County, combining white, red, green and black paint, in a complex abstract design of diamonds. The two sides of the box are identical in painted decoration, as are the front and back. The lid has a variation on the theme.

Structure: Plank construction with butt joints held together with small square nails. There is no lock or lock clasp. The hinges are brass attached with square nails.

188 Document Box

Lunenburg, Lunenburg County
Carved and painted softwood
Artist unknown
Circa 1845-1865
Dimensions: 45.5 × 17.3 × 24.0 cm (17 15/16 × 6 13/16 × 9 7/16 inches)
Collection of Leslie J. Langille, Lunenburg, Nova Scotia

There are three boxes of this same type known with painted decorations and a diamond pattern carved out of the solid plank sides. Two of these boxes were found in the Riverport area of Lunenburg County, with this one purchased from the Rhuland family[1] of Lunenburg. All are presumed to be by the same maker based on similarities of construction detail, and painted and carved decoration. They all have domed lids with no carving, but various painted decorations.

Structure: Plank construction with rabbet joints that are square nailed. The diamonds are carved from the solid planks of wood. Outside hinges, lock and lock clasp original. The box is painted in alternating red and black squares. There is no division of the interior.

1. Builders of the "Bluenose I" and "Bluenose II."

189 Document Box

Probably Colchester County
Original grained painted softwood with applied star motifs
Artist unknown
Circa 1860-1880
Dimensions: 34.5 × 13.5 × 22.0 cm ($11\frac{5}{8} \times 5\frac{5}{16} \times 8\frac{11}{16}$ inches)
Collection of Mr and Mrs Francis Coutellier, Moncton, New Brunswick

A good example of a document box in original paint with two applied star motifs on the lid.

Structure: Plank construction with rabbet joints. The interior is divided into three compartments. The hinges, lock clasp, and lock are brass. The paint is an original dark brown combed over a red underpaint.

190 Document Box

Probably Lunenburg County
Original painted softwood
Artist unknown
Circa 1870-1890
Dimensions: 47.0 × 19.5 × 22.5 cm ($18\frac{1}{2} \times 7\frac{11}{16} \times 8\frac{7}{8}$ inches)
Collection of Patricia and Tom Lackey, Toronto, Ontario

An excellent example of a document box with a painted compass star motif on the lid. This is a classic storage box probably used on board a fishing vessel. The maker painted the sides of the box while keeping the molding a natural colour, creating an attractive two-tone decorative scheme. The star motif is painted red and dark yellow-gold in a grey diamond, surrounded by a field of green. The box has a lock and brass carrying pulls on both ends. There is a small till on the left side of the interior. The hinges are brass and the escutcheon is cut from copper.

Structure: The box is in excellent condition with one small break in the molding along the top edge near the front. Plank construction with rabbet joints that are nailed.

191 Dome-Topped Document Box

Lunenburg County
Original inlaid and varnished softwood
Made by the Wambolt brothers, LaHave Islands, Lunenburg County
Circa 1880-1900
Dimensions: 26.7 × 12.0 × 14.5 cm ($10\frac{1}{2} \times 4\frac{3}{4} \times 5\frac{11}{16}$ inches)
Collection of Jerry and Debbie Vidito, Kentville, Nova Scotia

This is one of the finest examples of an inlaid box from Nova Scotia. Made by the Wambolt brothers who also made the sewing box shown in this exhibition, it is inlaid with the full complement of Lunenburg-German decorative motifs including heart, star, diamond and tulip. The latter was cleverly made on the sides of the domed lid from the combination of a tulip and heart design. The interior of the box has a lift-out till which is divided into three compartments (a sliding lid is missing from the centre compartment), and like the interior of the case, is lined with red cotton. It is likely that this box was used to store valuables such as jewellery (it has a lock) or was used on a desk to secure important documents.

Structure: Plank construction with blind butt joints hidden by applied molding that is attached with small metal pins. The box is inlaid with mahogany and oak. The brass handle is original as are the brass hinges and lock.

192 Three Document Boxes

Lunenburg County

Carved and painted softwood

Artist unknown

Circa 1880-1910

Dimensions: top — 31.0 × 11.0 × 15.0 cm ($12\frac{3}{16} \times 4\frac{5}{16} \times 5\frac{3}{4}$ inches)
middle — 31.5 × 11.0 × 16.0 cm ($12\frac{1}{4} \times 4\frac{5}{16} \times 6\frac{5}{16}$ inches)
bottom — 28.0 × 13.0 × 13.5 cm ($12 \times 5\frac{1}{8} \times 5\frac{5}{16}$ inches)

Private collection

All three of these document boxes are excellent examples of small utilitarian objects decorated with designs and motifs commonly found in Lunenburg County Germanic decorative folk art. It is possible that the top and middle boxes are by the same maker based on similarity of decoration, construction technique, and dimensions. The first two pieces have painted decorations, while the third example has designs that are both painted and lightly carved into the surface of the sides and front only.

Structure: The top and middle boxes have plank construction with butt joints and molding attached with square and round nails. The top example has a lock and clasp and small brass hinges. The middle example has no lock or clasp, but similar hinges. There are no divisions in the interior of either box. The box on the bottom is also of plank construction but with dovetailed joints. The molding is attached with square nails. There was a small lock (now missing) with clasp. There is a small interior till on the bottom side which had a lid that is now missing. This box probably dates earlier than the other two examples.

193 Document Box

Yarmouth County

Carved and unpainted hardwood with applied hardwood and softwood decorations

Artist unknown

Circa 1890-1910

Dimensions: 30.0 × 12.0 × 15.2 cm (11 13/16 × 4 3/4 × 6 inches)

Collection of George Christie, Bear River, Nova Scotia

This box is ornately decorated with a series of complex compass rose and circular motifs made of individual heart designs. The maker has alternately used light and dark hardwood and softwood to help emphasize these shapes and add colour to this unpainted piece. The box is decorated on all sides.

Structure: Plank construction with mitered joints that are nailed with small brads. The decorations are applied and glued in place. The box sits on small square feet and has a shaped skirt on all four sides.

194 Table Chest

Pictou County

Painted softwood, early dark brown over original red paint

Artist unknown

Circa 1850-1870

Dimensions: 43.0 × 22.5 × 30.5 cm (16 7/8 × 8 7/8 × 12 inches)

Collection of Pascal and Angela Dinaut, Great Village, Nova Scotia

During the mid-seventeenth century "cases of boxes" began to appear in the estate inventories of Massachusetts. These references include mention of "chest of boxes", "cabinet of boxes" and a "box of drawers". Certainly these designations could refer to small chests of multiple drawers built within a plain outer casing.[1] This nineteenth century example was either used on the top of a chest of drawers or a table, perhaps in the bedroom or kitchen, to hold personal or domestic accessories. The shaped base and crudely carved drawer pulls add a folk quality to the chest.

Structure: Plank construction of softwood with dovetailed dust shelf between drawers and lap joints in the case. Drawers are dovetailed front and back and nailed in front on top drawer. Hand carved pulls held in place with replaced screws (modern). The skirt in front is lapped to the case and shaped, while the ends are shaped from the solid side boards of the case. The dark brown is over the original red paint, which could be a ground pigment. There is some slight damage to the front skirt and to the bottom of the back board.

1. Nina Fletcher Little, *Neat and Tidy: Boxes and Their Contents Used in Early American Households,* (New York: E.P. Dutton, 1980), pp. 183-84.

195 Miniature Lift-Top Blanket Chest

Somerset, Kings County
Original grained painted decoration on softwood
Artist unknown
Circa 1850-1860
Dimensions: 35.5 × 40.5 × 16.0 cm (13 15/16 × 15 15/16 × 6 5/16 inches)
Collection of Jerry and Debbie Vidito, Kentville, Nova Scotia

An excellent example of a miniature four drawer, lift-top blanket chest with original paint. Chests of this size could either be a cabinetmaker's sample or a child's chest for play. The quality of this piece suggests the former, with such chests also being used for the storage of personal objects in the manner of document boxes.

Structure: Plank construction with butt and mitered joints on the case, and butt and lapped joints on the drawers. Drawer molding is out of the solid of the case while the base and lid molding is applied with small square nails. The drawer knobs are attached with small square brads through the shaft extending into the interior of each drawer compartment, while the turned feet are pegged into the bottom board of the case and nailed. The present leather hinges on the lid are replacements for the originals which were probably small metal butt hinges.

196 Blanket Chest

Bridgewater, Lunenburg County
Original painted and decorated softwood
Artist unknown
Circa 1840-1860
Dimensions: 115.0 × 42.5 × 47.0 cm (41 5/16 × 16 3/4 × 18 1/2 inches)
Collection of Barbara Doiron, Black Point, Nova Scotia

This very ornately decorated blanket chest was found in Bridgewater where examples of painted furniture with similar decoration are known, probably by the same artist. The stylized "rope" pattern is in yellow and combined with a series of red patches, all painted over the original red/brown ground paint. A label on the right side of the box indicates that the piece was at one time shipped to a Mrs Colp on Spring Garden Road in Halifax. Colp, or its other variations, Culp and Kolb, are Lunenburg County names.

Structure: Six-board plank construction with dovetail corners. Molded base flat to the floor. Strap hinges, box lock and clasp all original. Till on right side of interior, with three small compartments on left side across bottom. The interior was later painted green. The top board overhangs at the back of the box so that when it is pushed against a wall nothing can fall off the lid and down behind the chest.

197 Blanket Chest

Lunenburg County

Original black sponged painted decoration on softwood

Artist unknown

Circa 1860-1880

Dimensions: 110.6 × 39.4 × 50.8 cm (40 × 15½ × 20 inches)

Private collection

An excellent example of a decorated chest from Lunenburg County. The sponge decoration is painted in black over the original green ground. Other examples of this type of decoration have been found along the South Shore.

Structure: Six-board plank construction with dovetail corners. Molded base flat to the floor. Strap hinges, box lock and clasp all original. Till on right of interior with lid molded from solid on front edge.

Exhibited: Decorated Nova Scotia Furnishings, Dalhousie University Art Gallery, Halifax: Nova Scotia, July 5-August 6, 1978.

Published: Tom Lackey, *Decorated Nova Scotia Furnishings,* (Halifax: Dalhousie University Art Gallery, 1978), pp. 17, 34.

198 Spruce Gum Boxes

"The Lumberman's Secret" — Upper Cornwall, Lunenburg County

"The Lumberman's Book" — Lunenburg County

Softwood inlaid with wood and wax and chip-carved with various geometric motifs

Artist unknown, but both boxes are attributed to the same craftsman

Circa 1880-1900

Dimensions: "The Lumberman's Secret" — 10.2 × 15.0 × 5.1 cm (4 × 5⅞ × 2 inches)
"The Lumberman's Book" — 10.7 × 15.0 × 5.0 cm (4¼ × 5⅞ × 1¹⁵⁄₁₆ inches)

Private collection

Both of these spruce gum boxes are ornately decorated with playing card motifs, compass stars and various abstract designs created by first carving the motifs, then inlaying them with various coloured wax or contrasting woods. These inlaid designs are accentuated by various complementary chip-carved motifs. Although the inlaid material has not undergone chemical analysis, microscopic examination and oral tradition support the suggestion that the inlaid substance is sealing or bees wax coloured with pigments (in this case red and green), and inlaid into the carved areas while in a melted or semi-hard state. This suggestion, however, must eventually be supported by chemical analysis, based on recent research into Pennsylvania-German inlaid furnishings which has revealed that sulfur and not wax was used, to create the decoration within that decorative folk tradition.[1] Objects simulating the appearance of bound books provide a fascinating element in Canadian/American folk art. Pieces in this form have been found in wood, stone and pottery.[2] Eighteenth century book boxes were probably used to hold various prayer books and small Bibles[3], but in the late nineteenth and early twentieth centuries these boxes are categorized as containers for spruce gum, a substance which as the name implies, was the sap or pitch which would bleed from cuts or bruises in the bark of the spruce tree. Although usually in a semi-hard or hard state, the gum softened to a pink chewing-gum consistency when in contact with the warmth of the mouth.[4] As a result it is often assumed that these spruce gum boxes were made during leisure time by the loggers in the lumber camps of Nova Scotia, New Brunswick and Maine, and were made to hold more than spruce gum, frequently being given to wives and sweethearts as tokens of love and friendship to hold personal trinkets or other domestic keepsakes.[5]

Structure: Both boxes are carved and hollowed out from a single block of softwood with sliding lids grooved into the top and bottom. Red and green wax and wood is inlaid into the various decorative motifs which are then outlined with various chip-carved designs. In addition, both boxes have wooden "clasps" carved to simulate brass clasps to secure the book when closed. There is some minor loss of inlay.

1. Benno M. Forman, "German Influences in Pennsylvania Furniture", In Catherine E. Hutchins (Ed), *Arts of the Pennsylvania Germans,* (New York: W.W. Norton & Company, Inc., 1983,) p. 162.
2. Nina Fletcher Little, *Neat and Tidy: Boxes and Their Contents Used in Early American Households,* (New York: E.P. Dutton, 1980), pp. 51-52.
3. Nina Fletcher Little, *Ibid,* pp. 52-54.
4. Nina Fletcher Little, *Ibid,* p. 54.
5. Nina Fletcher Little, *Ibid,* p. 54.

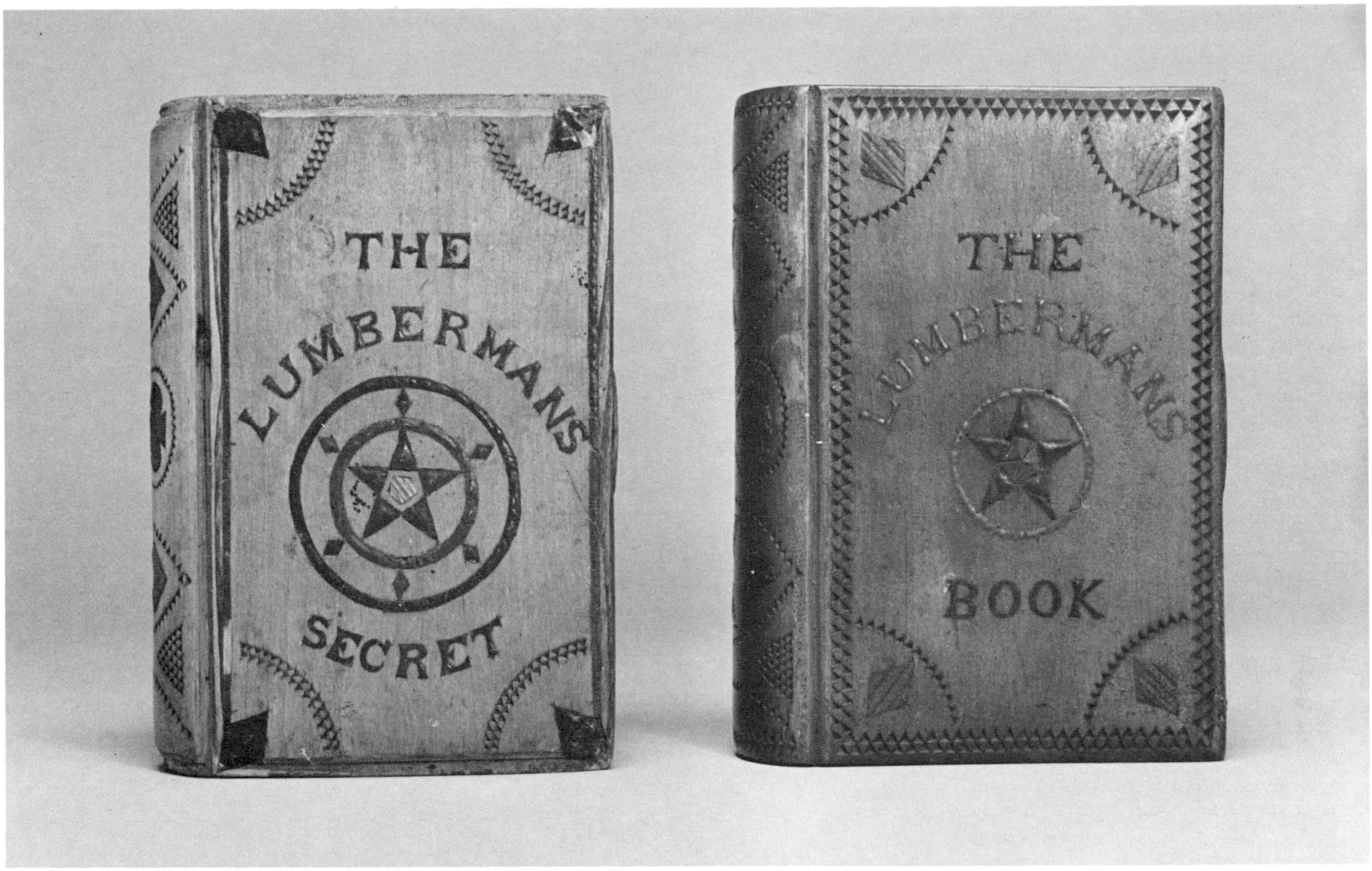

THE
LUMBERMANS
SECRET
THE
LUMBERMANS
BOOK

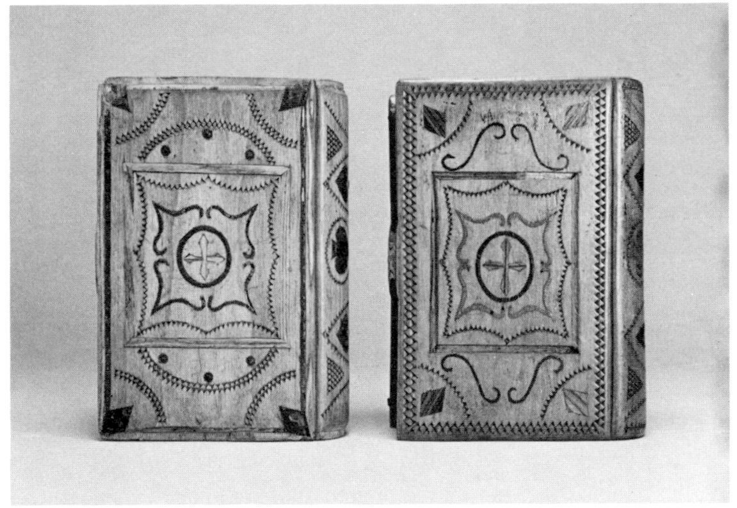

Refer to colour plate XXIV, page 26

199 Spruce Gum Boxes

"Remember Me" — Five Islands, Pictou County

"Friendship and Love" — Lunenburg County

Softwood inlaid with wood and wax and chip-carved with various decorative motifs

Artist unknown, but both boxes are attributed to the same craftsman even though one was found in Five Islands and the other in Lunenburg County. The mobile nature of personal accessories is obviously a problem in establishing firm provenance on any article, and particularly difficult in suggesting attribution to a specific maker whether known or anonymous. However, on the basis of design and execution of the inlaid motifs, there seems little doubt that both of these spruce gum boxes were made by the same craftsman.

"Remember Me" is dated 1917[1] on the back

"Friendship and Love" circa 1910-1920

Dimensions: "Remember Me" — 11.0 × 17.5 × 4.0 cm ($4\frac{5}{16} \times 6\frac{7}{8} \times 1\frac{9}{16}$ inches)

"Friendship and Love" — 9.5 × 20.5 × 4.0 cm ($3\frac{3}{4} \times 6\frac{11}{16} \times 1\frac{9}{16}$ inches)

Private collection

Both of these spruce gum boxes are inlaid with decorative motifs using various coloured waxes, and in the case of the "Friendship and Love" box, wood inlay as well. The similarity in design and workmanship between the two boxes is remarkable — both have almost identical motifs on the spines including the chip-carving, and both have diamond borders on the front surrounding the central motifs, with almost identical chip-carved semi-circles. Although the central motifs on the front and back are different, there is little doubt that they were made by the same hand, and are two very fine Nova Scotia examples of the spruce gum box form.

Structure: Both boxes are carved and hollowed from a single block of softwood with sliding lids grooved into the top and bottom. Red, green and pink wax along with wood has been used for inlay. Both boxes are also chip-carved with various motifs which complement the inlaid designs. The clasps are missing from both boxes, and "Remember Me" has been painted gold to simulate bronze-edged pages.

Exhibited: Decorated Nova Scotia Furnishings, Dalhousie University Art Gallery, Halifax, Nova Scotia, July 5-August 6, 1978. ("Remember Me" only)

1. This box could have been made as a token of love and friendship perhaps by a soldier leaving overseas to fight in World War I (1914-1918).

200 Spruce Gum Box

Blandford, Lunenburg County
Hardwood inlaid with various coloured wax with inset mirror
Artist unknown
Dated 1895
Dimensions: 10.8 × 15.0 × 5.1 cm (4¼ × 5⅞ × 2 inches)
Private collection

This is one of the more philosophical pieces in the exhibition. In keeping with the other examples of spruce gum boxes in the show, the maker of this particular example created a poignant statement by placing a mirror in the centre of the front of the box, then carving and inlaying with red wax the words "This is True" around the mirror.

Probably the most interesting motif carved and inlaid into this box is the "flower-in-pot" design on the back. This particular motif has been found recently on several other items from Lunenburg County, and in some respects can be considered a benchmark image of Lunenburg-German decoration, similar to the tulip in Pennsylvania-German folk art.

Structure: The box is carved and hollowed out from a single block of softwood with sliding lids grooved into the top and bottom. Red, green and black wax has been inlaid into the carved designs and words including the date 1895 on the spine. The box is in the condition in which it was found, with the mirror unfortunately broken.

201 Spruce Gum Box

Wileville, Lunenburg County
Softwood inlaid with red wax
Artist unknown
Dated 1899
Dimensions: 9.5 × 14.5 × 4.0 cm ($3\frac{3}{4} \times 5\frac{11}{16} \times 1\frac{9}{16}$ inches)
Private collection

Although this particular gum box is not as ornately inlaid and chip-carved as some examples, the designs which are limited to the front and back (and not the spine) are effectively executed. The inlaid chip-carved diamonds form frames around the "title" of the book and the back cover motif.

The word "Mari" might refer to a girl's name (Mary or Maria), however, in French the word translates as bridegroom or husband suggesting that the box was made by a bride as a gift to her husband on their wedding day with the date 1899 the year they were married.

Structure: The box is carved and hollowed out from a solid block of softwood. Red wax is inlaid into the various carved motifs, words and date. The box has the standard wooden "clasp". Except for some minor loss of wax inlay it is in original condition.

202 Spruce Gum Barrel

Blandford, Lunenburg County
Original carved and stained softwood
Artist unknown
Circa 1860
Dimensions: 11.0 × 5.5 cm ($4\frac{5}{16} \times 2\frac{1}{8}$ inches)
Private collection

Although this barrel has sustained some unfortunate damage over the years, it is still a dramatic example of woodcarving with five-pointed star, chevron and gothic arch decorative motifs. The barrel staves are also carved in relief, helping to create a complex geometric effect.

Structure: The barrel is carved and hollowed out from a solid block of softwood. It is missing both top and bottom lids and is cracked from warpage. The softwood is stained a dark brown-black colour.

203 Spruce Gum Barrel

Lunenburg County

Softwood inlaid with wax

Artist unknown, with possible attribution to the same craftsman that made the "This Is True" spruce gum box

Circa 1870-1890

Dimensions: 10.0 × 5.8 cm ($3\frac{15}{16}$ × $2\frac{5}{16}$ inches)

Private collection

Spruce gum barrels are not as commonly found as the spruce gum boxes, and this is one of the very few known to exist with wax inlay. Similar to the boxes, the barrels are a late nineteenth and early twentieth century product of the lumbercamps of Nova Scotia, made in leisure time to hold spruce gum and other trinkets.

This particular barrel is inlaid with red and black wax in a series of diamonds, five-pointed stars and semi-circle motifs on the sides of the barrel, and a five-pointed star on the top and bottom. In addition, barrel staves are carved out of the solid, helping to create a very realistic article in miniature.

Structure: The barrel is carved and hollowed out from a single block of softwood in the same fashion as the spruce gum boxes. Red and black wax has been used for the inlay with the remainder of the barrel unpainted.

204 Carved Barrel With Dice and Stick Game

Lunenburg County

Original carved and painted softwood with softwood dice and stick game

Artist unknown

Circa 1860-1880

Dimensions: 8.5 × 9.0 cm, diameter at top- 6.0 cm ($3\frac{3}{8}$ × $3\frac{9}{16}$ inches, diameter at top- $2\frac{3}{8}$ inches)

Private collection

When this barrel was found it contained a carved dice and stick game, composed of two dice with the dots marked in pencil, and eleven carved sticks. Also included were two dried beans which may have a connection to the rest of the game pieces. Although the name and rules of this game have yet to be determined, the barrel might have been made to hold these pieces. The outside of the barrel is painted in a series of open black squares on the red ground.

Structure: The barrel is carved and hollowed from a solid block of softwood. The lid is carved with a rim to fit inside the barrel, and has a small hole to make it easier to remove, breaking any "airlock" that might be created.

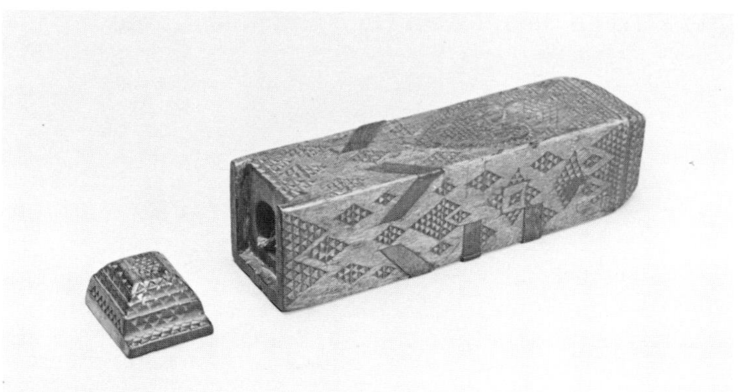

205 Needle Case with Carved Heart

Lunenburg County
Original chip-carved and decorated hardwood
Artist unknown
Circa 1840-1860
Dimensions: 17.0 × 4.0 × 4.0 cm (6 $^{11}/_{16}$ × 1 $^{9}/_{16}$ × 1 $^{9}/_{16}$ inches)
Private collection

This is one of the most ornate cases known from Nova Scotia. It is made from a solid block of hardwood which has been hollowed out to hold sailor's needles used to repair nets and sailcloth. Both ends and all four sides are chip-carved with various geometric motifs, mostly in the form of diamonds and triangles. On one side there is a chip-carved heart. In addition, darker pieces of wood have been inlaid into the case, forming a series of arrow shapes and abstract designs. The case still contains various sized steel needles.

Structure: Carved from a solid block of hardwood with sliding lid. The case has never been painted.

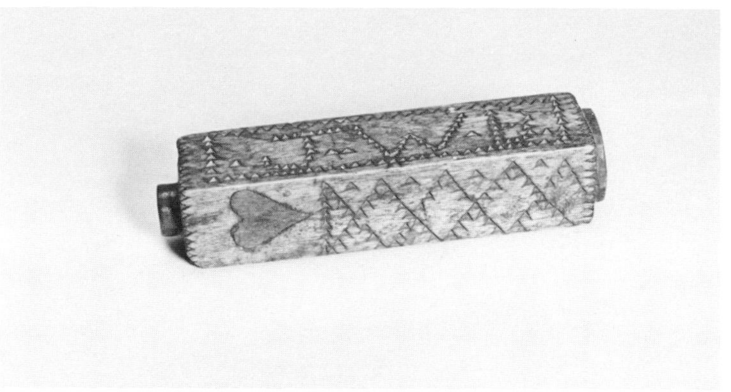

206 Sailor's Needle Case*

Lunenburg County
Chip-carved and inlaid hardwood
Artist unknown, but the initials J.W.B. are carved into one side of the case
Circa 1870-1890
Dimensions: 15.2 × 3.8 × 3.8 cm (6 × 1½ × 1½ inches)
Collection of Richard Henning Field and Deborah Field, Halifax, Nova Scotia

Similar to the previous example, and possibly by the same maker, this needle case has a series of chip-carved abstract motifs on two of the sides, the initials J.W.B. on a third side, and an inlaid wooden heart and abstract motif on the fourth.

Structure: Carved from a solid block of hardwood with sliding lid that fits into a groove at one end. This case has never been painted.

*This piece will be on view in Halifax only

207 Needle Case

Lunenburg County
Original carved and stained softwood
Artist unknown
Circa 1860-1880
Dimensions: 13.0 (overall length) × 3.0 (diameter) cm ($5\frac{1}{8}$ × $1\frac{3}{16}$ inches)
Collection of Pascal and Angela Dinaut, Great Village, Nova Scotia

A fine needle case carved with heart and diamond motifs, typical of the decorative traditions found in Lunenburg County, reflecting the Germanic heritage of that region of the province.

Structure: The needle case is probably lathe turned from two pieces of softwood. The lid fits flush. The designs are incised by hand and irregular in outline.

208 Needle Case

Lunenburg County
Original carved softwood wrapped with fine twine and painted
Artist unknown
Circa 1860-1880
Dimensions: 18.5 × 4.4 cm ($7\frac{1}{4}$ × $1\frac{3}{4}$ inches)
Private collection

An example of a more common form of needle case. A wooden cylinder with stopper is wrapped with fine twine, usually in several layers, which creates fancy designs. The cylinder is then painted in one or several colours. This particular case has a shaped wooden stopper, and the twine is painted in shades of red, brown and black.

Structure: The needlecase is original throughout.

209 Squid Jigger Case and String Winder*

Lunenburg County
Chip-carved and inlaid hardwood
Artist unknown, but the initials J.Z.C. are carved on one side of the string winder
Circa 1870-1890
Dimensions: 15.5 × 8.9 × 4.6 cm ($6\frac{1}{8}$ × $3\frac{1}{2}$ × $1\frac{13}{16}$ inches)
Collection of Richard Henning Field and Deborah Field, Halifax, Nova Scotia

This combination squid jigger case and string winder is one of the more interesting nautical items in the exhibition. The squid jigger was kept in the case (the lid is missing) with one end attached to string which was wrapped around the winder-handle inlaid on one side with a boot. The other side is carved with the initials J.Z.C. The case is chip-carved with compass star motifs and inlaid with diamonds, a heart, club and spade.

Structure: Carved from a solid block of hardwood. The missing lid was grooved into the case. The inlaid spade is a replacement. The case was never painted.

*This piece will be on view in Halifax only

210 Fish String Winder

Lunenburg County

Carved and incised softwood

Artist unknown

Circa 1870-1890

Dimensions: 15.2 × 1.2 × 8.4 cm (6 × ½ × 3⁵⁄₁₆ inches)

Collection of Terry Kobayashi and Michael Bird, Kitchener-Waterloo, Ontario

This fish string winder features chip-carved hearts and floral elements, the handle ending in two heart motifs.

Structure: Carved from a solid piece of softwood, the piece is unpainted except for some of the designs which are outlined in pencil.

Published: Michael Bird and Terry Kobayashi, *A Splendid Harvest: Germanic Folk and Decorative Arts in Canada,* (Toronto: Van Nostrand Reinhold, Ltd., 1981), p. 39.

211 Hatchel*

Rose Bay, Lunenburg County

Carved and incised hardwood with inset iron spikes

Artist unknown

Circa 1790-182

Dimensions: 17.5 × 58.4 × 15.2 cm (6⅞ × 23 × 6 inches)

Collection of Richard Henning Field and Deborah Field, Halifax, Nova Scotia

This particular hatchel is one of three known from Lunenburg County, all by the same maker with almost identical pierced hearts and incised flower-in-pot decoration. This particular example is unpainted, while the other two are painted, and is from the Zinck house in Rose Bay, a Cape Cod dating circa 1780.

A hatchel was used to clean the flax of any shive remaining after swingling and to separate the fibre to give the fine fibre the characteristics of linen. Flax was usually processed on a course hatchel first and then on a finer one. For the finest quality linen, a third hatchel with smaller, more closely set teeth was used. Handfuls of swingled straw are grasped at one end and drawn repeatedly through the teeth of the hatchel until it is clean and the bast bundles have been separated into individual fibers. As well as being the final cleaning operation, hatcheling removes the remaining short fibres, which form the second grade of tow.[1]

It should be noted that the two incised motifs of flowers-in-pot are other examples of this recurring decorative design, which might be considered a benchmark ornamentation of late eighteenth to mid-nineteenth century Lunenburg-German material folk culture.

Structure: Hardwood plank fitted with inset hardwood board set with a series of iron spikes. The ends of the hatchel have pierced hearts, one of which is damaged. The flower-in-pot motifs are complemented with a series of chevron designs around the border of the inset board holding the spikes. Since this hatchel is unpainted, and the other two similar examples are, it is possible that this example was never finished by the maker.

1. Harold B. Burnham and Dorothy K. Burnham *"Keep Me Warm One Night": Early Handweaving in Eastern Canada,* (Toronto: University of Toronto Press, 1972), p. 29.

*This piece will be on view in Halifax only

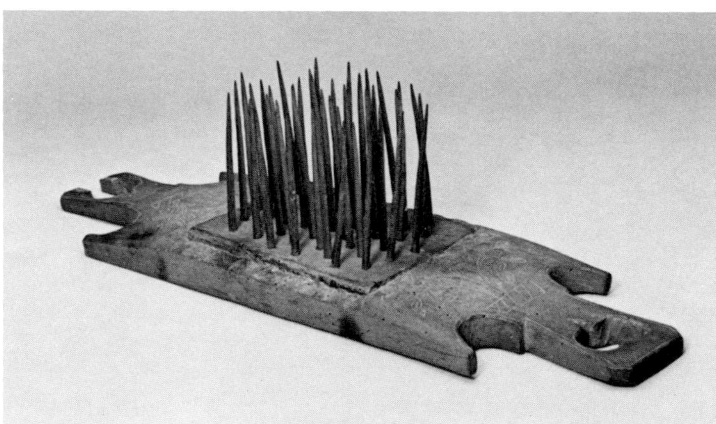

212 Niddy-Noddy

Probably Soldier's Cove, Cape Breton County
Carved, incised, painted and in-laid hardwood
Artist unknown, but the name G. Hunson and the initials M.F. are carved into the piece.
Circa 1840-1860
Dimensions: 49.5 × 36.5 cm (19½ × 14¾ inches)
Collection of Terry Kobayashi and Michael Bird, Kitchener-Waterloo, Ontario

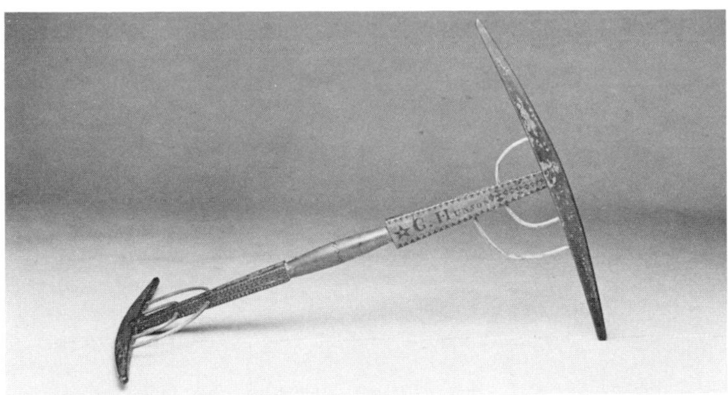

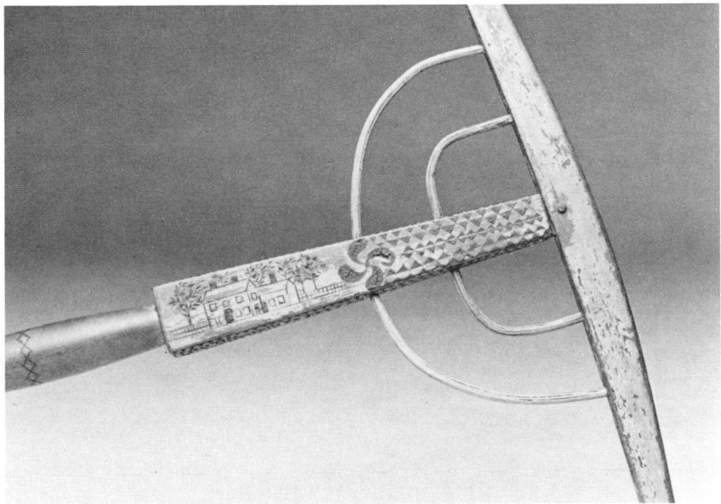

When wool has been spun, it is usually taken from the bobbin and skeined. One of the earliest and simplest devices for carrying out this operation is accomplished with this oddly shaped tool. When in use, the name for this device is obvious, as the yarn is guided over the ends of the arms, it first nods one way then the other. They were used extensively throughout the Maritime Provinces.[1]

This particularly example is one of the most elaborate known. Found in Cape Breton, it could be of American origin. The square shank posts on either side of the hand grip are incised, and chip-carved with various motifs including a "flying" swastika, a house, hearts, stars and the name and initials of two individuals. Most of these designs have been in-laid with red wax. On one shank there are two flower-in-pot motifs similar to those found in Lunenburg County.

Structure: The ends are pegged into the shaped and carved shaft which is made from one piece of hardwood.

1. Harold B. Burnham and Dorothy K. Burnham, *"Keep Me Warm One Night": Early Handweaving in Eastern Canada*, (Toronto: University of Toronto Press, 1972), p. 38.

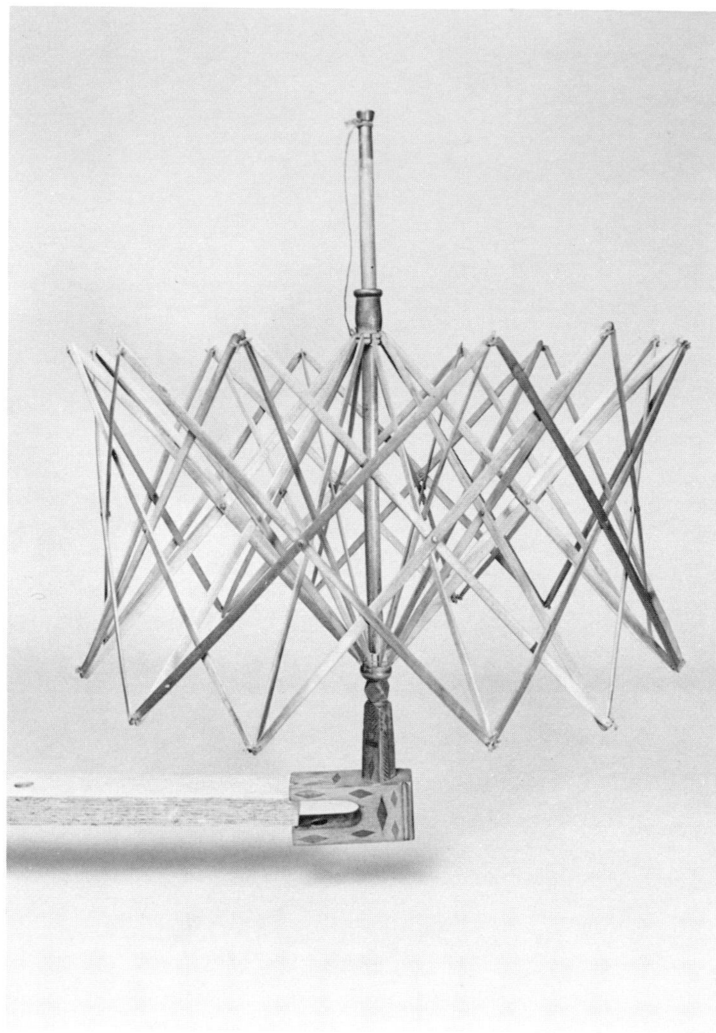

213 Table Umbrella Swift*

Shelburne County

Hardwood with carved and inlaid table clamp and stock

Artist unknown

Circa 1860-1880

Dimensions: length when closed — 57.2 cm (27½ inches)

Collection of Richard Henning Field and Deborah Field, Halifax, Nova Scotia

Swifts are used for unwinding skeins of yarn, the opposite of reels or wool winders, which are used for making skeins of yarn. This type of swift takes its name from the fact that the hub on the axel may be raised or lowered to adjust the size of the cage on which the skein is held, an action which is identical to the opening and closing of an umbrella.[1]

This particular example is mounted onto a table with a clamp and stock inlaid with wood, red wax and pewter geometric and floral decorations, and has a pewter top fineal. The motifs include diamonds and a shield in the clamp, and on the stock a series of tree and flower-in-pot motifs inlaid with red wax. Although found in Shelburne County, it is possible that this swift is of Lunenburg origin, or perhaps made by someone of German descent from that county, suggested by the presence of the flower-in-pot motif.

Structure: Made of hardwood, the stock is set into the clamp, a tightening screw is probably missing. The arms are tied with twine at the ends to permit the umbrella action, and square nailed at the centre to allow them to "scissor" when the swift is opened and closed. A small carved polyhedron "washer" is set above the stock on the shaft to allow smooth rotation when the swift is in operation. The pewter fineal is "dovetailed" onto the top of the shaft.

1. Harold B. Burnham and Dorothy K. Burnham, *"Keep Me Warm One Night": Early Hand weaving in Eastern Canada*, (Toronto: University of Toronto Press, 1972), p. 40.

*This piece will be on view in Halifax only

214 Miniature Wool Winder

Queens County

Original green painted softwood and hardwood

Artist unknown, but pencilled on the bottom of the base is "from Zacharias Veinot"

Circa 1890-1910

Dimensions: 23.0 × 20.3 cm (9$\frac{1}{16}$ × 8 inches), radius 14.5 cm (5¾ inches)

Collection of Murray E. Stewart, Berwick, Nova Scotia

This miniature wool winder was probably made as a late nineteenth century "educational" toy for a little girl, or perhaps was simply meant to be a miniature of a large scale example. The name pencilled on the bottom is probably the owner's name.

Structure: The base is shaped from a solid block of hardwood while the rest of the winder is made from softwood. The wheel is tenoned but not pinned to the verticle post, which in turn is tenoned and wedged into the base. The wheel arms are tenoned but not pegged to the crossbars, the wheel rotating around a round nail shaft. The green paint is original.

215 Sewing Box

Kentville, Kings County
Original softwood box with applied decorations and cushioned lid
Artist unknown
Circa 1880-1890
Dimensions: 33.0 × 15.1 × 19.0 cm (11 × 5$^{15}/_{16}$ × 7½ inches)
Collection of Mr and Mrs Francis Coutellier, Moncton, New Brunswick

An interesting example of a sewing box with a cushioned lid that could be used for pins and needles. The sides of the box are decorated with applied diamond motifs while the front of the piece has a combination of diamond and heart designs.

Structure: The box is missing one small diamond from the lower right corner of the front, and a piece of molding from the right side. The soft wood is stained a dark brown with traces of a flat varnish. Plank construction with butt joints and brass hinges. It never had a lock or lock clasp. The interior is undivided. The interior of the lid is sealed with a single plank of softwood, presumably the hollow space that is created holding the stuffing material under the cushion top. The material used for the cushion is probably not original.

216 Sewing Box

Lunenburg County
Original inlaid and varnished softwood
Made by the Wambolt brothers, LaHave Islands, Lunenburg County
Circa 1890-1910
Dimensions: 15.2 × 37.5 × 15.5 cm (6 × 14¾ × 6¼ inches)
Collection of Jerry and Debbie Vidito, Kentville, Nova Scotia

This sewing box with spool tree topped by a pincushion is ornately inlaid with various decorative motifs common to the Lunenbürg-German tradition in Nova Scotia. These motifs include the three most commonly found designs, the heart, diamond and star or compass star. They are inlaid with various types of woods such as mahogany and oak that contrast against the lighter wood background. The box contains a drawer with opposing false drawer front, both set with small porcelain pulls. The base has an intricate cutout pattern on all four sides. The spool tree is set into the top of the case and made of two circles set with metal pins suitable for holding 12 spools of thread. A pincushion covered with tartan fabric finishes off the top of the tree.

Structure: Plank construction with butt joints on the case and drawer. The tree is mortised into the top of the case. There is some damage to the base cutout.

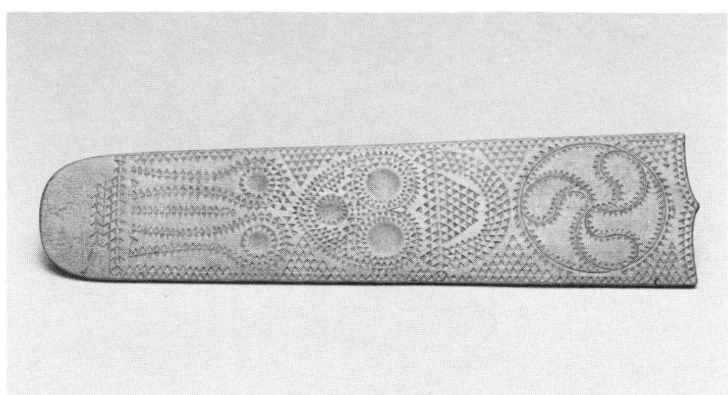

217 Busk

Lunenburg County
Carved and incised hardwood
Artist unknown
Circa 1840-1860
Dimensions: 29.0 × 7.0 (widest point) cm (11 7/16 × 2 3/4 inches)
Collection of Terry Kobayashi and Michael Bird, Kitchener-Waterloo, Ontario

This hardwood corset stay has a chip-carved heart and "flying" swastika. The overall pattern is very ornate and finely executed.

Structure: Made from a single piece of hardwood. On the reverse side the name Cecile Duion (Duiron?) is crudely carved, perhaps by a child. This could be the family name of the individual for whom the busk was originally made.

Published: Michael Bird and Terry Kobayashi, *A Splendid Harvest: Germanic Folk and Decorative Arts in Canada*, (Toronto: Van Nostrand Reinhold, Ltd. 1981), p. 39.

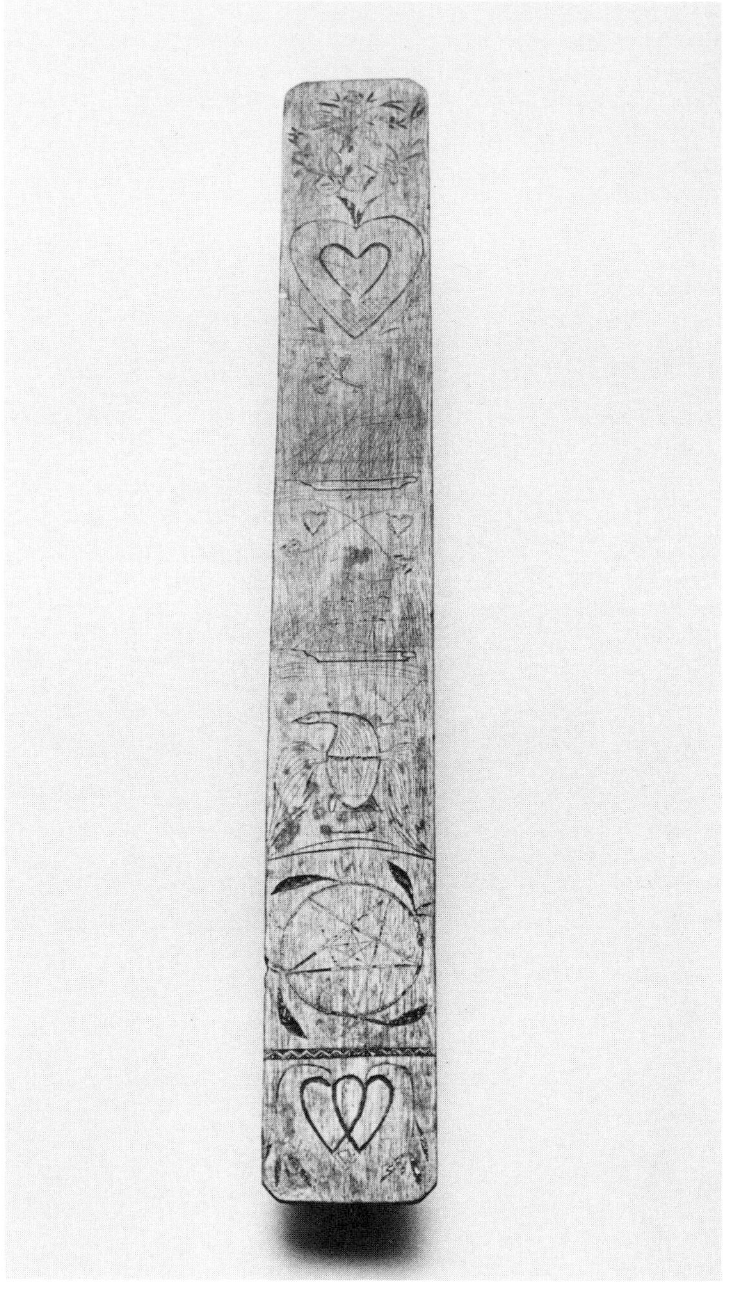

218 Busk*

Soldier's Cove, Cape Breton County
Hardwood with incised and inlaid decoration
Artist unknown
Circa 1860-1880
Dimensions: 4.2 × 33.0 cm (1 5/8 × 13 inches)
Collection of Richard Henning Field and Deborah Field, Halifax, Nova Scotia

A busk was used in a woman's corset to deepen the cleavage and support posture. This particular example is one of the few found in this province,[1] and is incised and inlaid with red and black wax decorations including: five sailing vessels; hearts; crossed swords; a compass star; floral decortion; and an American eagle. Although the presence of the eagle suggests a New England origin, this is difficult to determine because the person who made this busk may have lived in, or sailed from, ports along the East Coast, and it perhaps seemed natural to include it along with other motifs reflecting his life experiences and occupation. It should also be noted that the wax inlay technique is very similar to other decorated objects found in the same region of Cape Breton, and along the South Shore, which supports the Nova Scotia provenance.

Structure: The busk is made from a single piece of hardwood, probably birch, and is decorated on both sides. The corners have been rounded, and there is a slight curve in the wood, probably from its function in the corset.

1. Many of the examples of New England busks are made from whalebone. For examples in both wood and bone see Beatrice Garven, *The Pennsylvania German Collection*, (Philadelphia: Philadelphia Museum of Art, 1982), p. 58. Michael Bird and Terry Kobayashi, *A Splendid Harvest: Germanic Folk and Decorative Arts in Canada*, (Toronto: Van Nostrand Reinhold Ltd., 1981), p. 39. Cynthia V.A. Schaffner and Susan Klein, *Folk Hearts: A Celebration of the Heart Motif in American Folk Art*, (New York: Alfred A. Knopf, 1984), p. 90.

*This piece will be on view in Halifax only

219 Reliquary Shelf

Conquerall Bank, Lunenburg County
Original painted, carved and incised softwood
Artist unknown
Circa 1870-1890
Dimensions: 20.0 × 39.0 × 11.0 cm (7⅞ × 15⅜ × 4$\frac{5}{16}$ inches)
Collection of Jerry and Debbie Vidito, Kentville, Nova Scotia

At least six of these reliquary shelves have been found in Lunenburg County. This is the most ornately carved piece found to date, but still resembles the other shelf in this exhibition. It is impossible to identify the carver, but based on the form and style of those found thus far and examined by this author, there were at least two makers, one working around the Bridgewater-LaHave area, the other around the Blockhouse-Mahone Bay region.

This particular example was used like all reliquary shelves as a means to show the mementos of departed loved ones. Based on Catholic tradition where sacred relics of various Saints or other church objects were displayed, these shelves combine religious and secular meaning for the families. A photograph of the deceased was placed in the arched opening cut in the backboard (examples with two such openings are known), and the platform shelf itself was used to place personal items of the deceased or loved one, who may not be dead but just away for a long time at war or sea. These objects could include hair or jewellery, items which would allow the living to remember the departed, and if not deceased, hope and pray for their safe return.

Structure: The reliquary has one break near the top finial. Made of plank construction with butt joints that are nailed with small square brads, the shelf is ornately carved with a series of heart and fleur-de-lis designs.

The shelf can either be hung on the wall or set on a table or chest. The front legs have been carved in the form of human feet with boots. The entire piece has been carved with a serrated edge, is incised with various cross-hatched designs, and is painted in a later yellow-cream ochre paint.

220 Reliquary Shelf

Probably Lunenburg County
Carved and overpainted softwood
Artist unknown
Circa 1870-1890
Dimensions: 23.5 × 50.3 × 9.2 cm (9¼ × 19$^{13}/_{16}$ × 3⅝ inches)
Collection of George Christie, Bear River, Nova Scotia

An ornate overpainted example of a reliquary shelf with pierced hearts and other geometric motifs. Several examples with very similar designs have been found in Lunenburg County, mostly around Mahone Bay, suggesting they were made by the same individual or manufacturer. This example can hold two photographs of loved ones or deceased family members.

Structure: The top finial has been repaired and the entire shelf has been overpainted a deep red colour. Plank construction with butt joints and small square-headed brads. The original colour was probably a dark green-black colour.

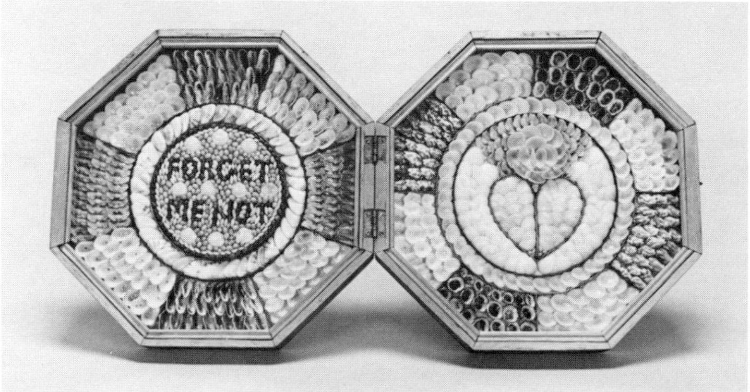

221 Sailor's Valentine*

Probably Bridgewater, Lunenburg County
Hinged octagonal refinished softwood case opening into two identical glass cases containing a "valentine" made from a pattern of various shells.
Artist unknown
Circa 1890-1910
Dimensions: 23.0 × 23.0 (closed) × 7.0 cm (9$^{1}/_{16}$ × 9$^{1}/_{16}$ × 2¾ inches)
Collection of the DesBrisay Museum, Bridgewater, Nova Scotia.

This is a typical sailor's valentine, which although not made here, nonetheless reflects the Spirit of Nova Scotia. These valentines were made by craftsmen and women of various Caribbean Islands and purchased by seamen as souvenirs for wives and sweethearts. Most of these valentines usually depict some sentiment concerning love, such as this example which has "Forget Me Not" worked in small brown shells in the left-hand case.

History: This valentine was donated to the DesBrisay Museum in 1966 by Maggy and Emma Gow of Bridgewater, Nova Scotia.

Structure: As one can appreciate, these shells often become loose over the years. This example is no exception, having undergone some replacement of shells. The case, which is made from softwood, has unfortunately been refinished, but traces of the original red paint can still be seen. The various inlaid shells are indigenous to the waters of the Caribbean. The glass is held in place with small sections of molded softwood.

*This piece will be on view in Halifax only

A

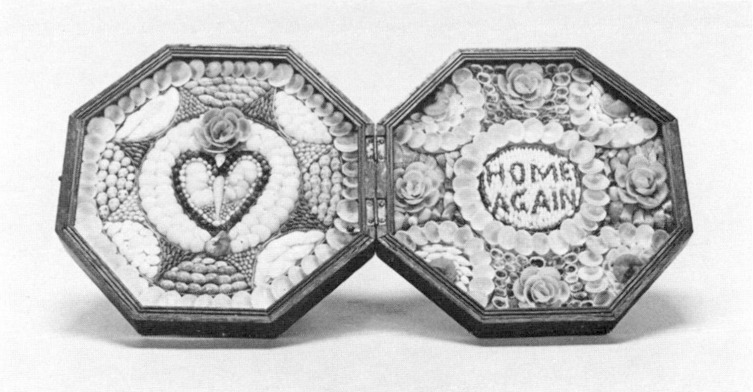

B

222 Sailor's Valentines*

South Shore or Lunenburg County

Made from hinged octagonal boxes opening into two identical glass cases containing various shells arranged to form abstract designs and decorative motifs

Artists unknown

Circa 1890-1910

Dimensions:
A — 23.0 × 23.0 (closed) × 6.5 cm ($9\frac{1}{16} \times 9\frac{1}{16} \times 2\frac{9}{16}$ inches),
B — 23.0 × 23.0 (closed) × 7.0 cm ($9\frac{1}{16} \times 9\frac{1}{16} \times 2\frac{3}{4}$ inches),
C — 23.0 × 23.0 (closed) × 7.0 cm ($9\frac{1}{16} \times 9\frac{1}{16} \times 2\frac{3}{4}$ inches),
D — 22.0 × 22.0 × 6.0 cm ($8\frac{5}{8} \times 8\frac{5}{8} \times 2\frac{3}{8}$ inches),
E — 23.0 × 23.0 (closed) × 7.0 cm ($9\frac{1}{16} \times 9\frac{1}{16} \times 2\frac{3}{4}$ inches)

Collection of Mr and Mrs Francis Coutellier, Moncton, New Brunswick

These examples of sailor's valentines are among the finest known, with two supporting the origin of these boxes as the Caribbean Islands, in this case Barbados. All five examples reflect the sailor's preoccupation with home and loved ones while at sea. Two combine the well used phrase, "HOME AGAIN", with various motifs particularly the heart, while one takes this sentiment a bit further with the phrase "HOME AGAIN LOV" (sic). Probably one reason why so many of these valentines are found along the South Shore of Nova Scotia (Lunenburg, Shelburne and Yarmouth Counties) is because of the active trade between the ports of Lunenburg, Liverpool, Shelburne, and Yarmouth, and the Caribbean, particularly the islands of Bermuda and Barbados.

Structure: The condition of all five of these valentines is good, but as can be expected with objects so fragile, some of the shells have become loose and are missing.

*These pieces will be on view in Halifax only

Refer to colour plate XXI, page 24

C

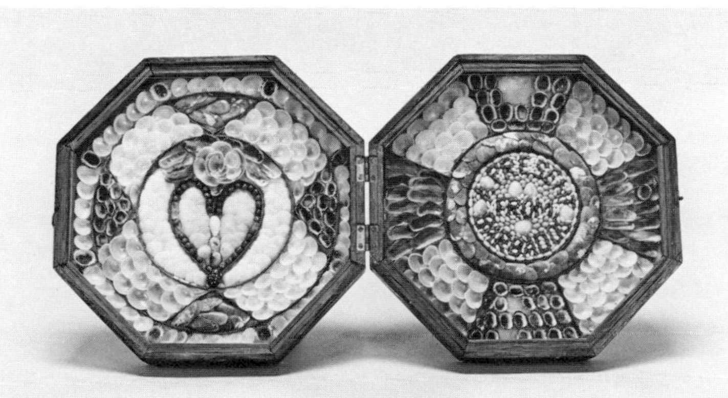

D

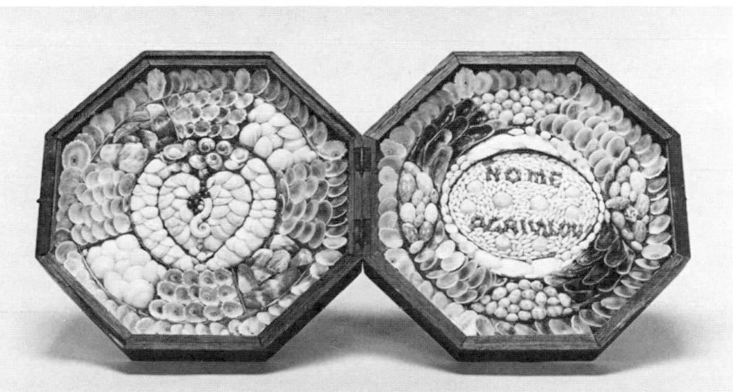

E

223 Powderhorn

Probably Lunenburg County
Carved horn
Probably made by George Freil whose name is carved into the horn
Circa 1810-1830
Dimensions: 27.5 × 6.5 cm ($10^{13}/_{16} \times 2^{9}/_{16}$ inches)
Collection of the DesBrisay Museum, Bridgewater, Nova Scotia

Decorated powder horns have usually been considered as historical objects valued for the people, places and dates often carved into the designs, or through association with specific individuals. However, the art of scrimshaw — decorative carving in horn, ivory, shell or bone — was a traditional pastime of seamen sailing from the ports of the Atlantic Provinces and New England throughout the nineteenth century. It was also an art form practised by various carvers, particularly during the French and Indian War (1755-1763) in the United States, connected with the militia of the time.[2] This tradition was continued throughout the nineteenth century by many men involved with hunting, the frontier and woodsmanship in both Canada and the Eastern United States.

A powderhorn carried black powder used to load, prime and fire shots from the musket rifles of the day,[3] but it is assumed that many of these elaborately decorated horns were actually intended as souvenirs or gifts.[4] As most carved horns are unsigned, it is speculation as to whether the name George Freil is that of the owner or maker. In either case the maker of this particular horn incorporated typical Lunenburg County motifs into the decoration including: six-pointed star/flower motifs, a series of three compass-rose designs, and the intriguing figure of an Indian with the faint outline of a headdress, holding a spear in his right hand, and wearing what appears to be a long coat with large military-like buttons.

It is difficult to say whether George Freil was a sailor or frontiersman, perhaps involved in campaigns in the United States, but judging by the figure of the Indian the suggestion that Freil was a woodsman or farmer seems likely. In addition, the traces of a minute amount of black powder inside the horn strongly indicates that this particular example was not made as a gift or souvenir, but was actually used.

Structure: Carved and decorated cow horn with a wooden pull-out stopper at one end and an inset wood plug (softwood) carved with a star motif at the opposite end.

Published: Michael Bird, *Canadian Folk Art: Old Ways in a New Land,* (Toronto: Oxford University Press, 1983), p. 103.

1. William H. Guthman, "Powder Horns of the French and Indian War, 1755-1763", In *The Magazine Antiques*, Volume CXIV, No. 2 (August, 1978), p. 312.
2. William H. Guthman, *Ibid*, p. 320.
3. Many muskets, black powder, and shot are mentioned in the estate inventories of Lunenburg County between 1769 and 1849, along with occasional mention of powderhorns. (Thesis notes, Richard Henning Field, Dalhousie University, January, 1985.)
4. William H. Guthman, *Ibid*, p. 317.

224 Powderhorn with Tulip and Compass-Star Motifs

Lunenburg County

Carved horn

Artist unknown, the initials A.I.D. are carved in the wooden cap at the large end

Circa 1820-1840

Dimensions: 20.3 × 7.7 cm (8 × 3 inches)

Collection of Chris Huntington, Hamm's Hill, Nova Scotia

This is truly one of the masterpieces of this exhibition. The horn is deeply carved with various motifs, including a compass-star, tulip-in-pot motif, flowers that resemble sunflowers, and a series of overlapping fan designs. The maker of this powderhorn obviously had some training in carving and decorating objects. The wooden end at the widest portion of the horn is initialed A.I.D. Again the tulip-in-pot motif reflects the Lunenburg-German origins of this piece.

Structure: Carved and incised from a solid horn. The butt plug is missing.

225 Powderhorn

Eastern Shore, probably Halifax County

Carved horn

Artist unknown

Circa 1850-1860

Dimensions: 51.0 × 10.0 cm ($20\frac{1}{16} \times 3\frac{15}{16}$ inches)

Collection of Pascal and Angela Dinaut, Great Village, Nova Scotia

This powderhorn with turned stopper and butt plug with finial, is an early example incised with various decorative motifs, including a ship, house, a fish that looks like a flounder, bird, seal, horse, (?) and an eagle-like bird. These designs are all executed near the butt end of the horn in a manner which suggests that they were drawn by someone not very proficient in carving, but who had a sense of design. These images probably represent objects, animals and scenes from the artists everyday experiences.

Structure: Carved and decorated cow horn with wooden stopper and plug. The plug is missing one piece along the edge.

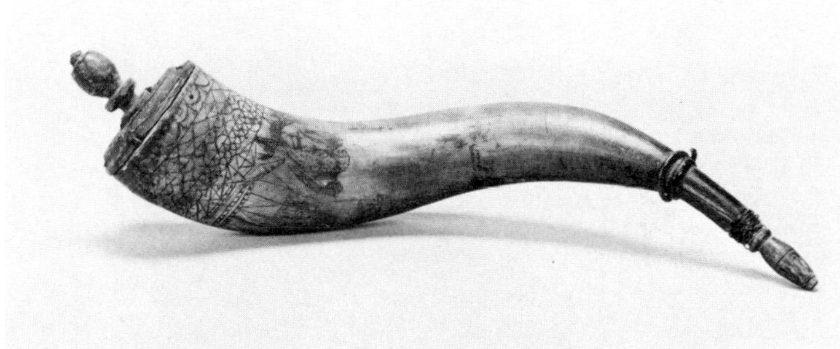

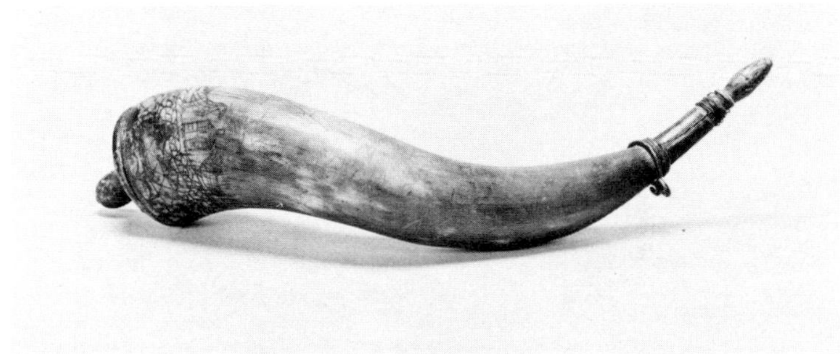

226 Crooked Knife

Caledonia, Queens County
Carved and stained burl
Artist unknown
Circa 1860-1880
Dimensions: 29.5 × 7.5 × 11.5 cm ($11\frac{5}{8} \times 2\frac{15}{16} \times 4\frac{9}{16}$ inches)
Private collection

This is one of the most dramatically carved examples of a crooked knife from Nova Scotia. The snake is wrapped around the bear in fierce battle with open jaws locked into the bear's neck. The carving is exquisitely detailed, including the bear fur and snake scales. In addition, the blade is not hafted and secured to the handle by the common method of wrapped brass wire, but is similar to a knife, using a metal socket into which the end of the handle is fitted.

Crooked knives are used by pulling toward the user, unlike the ordinary knife which is used in an outward motion. Considered to be of Indian origin, crooked knives were made by both native peoples and non-natives alike, particularly lumbermen, as tools for making basket splints and carving and decorating other objects.[1] The blade is used by placing the thumb in the outer curve of the handle which allows the user to pull with a controlled motion toward the body, and efficiently use the angle of the blade which is generally set at about 45 degrees. Blades were often made from straight razors or other metal objects such as files.[2]

Structure: The blade is hafted into the carved handle using a socket of metal.

1. According to Douglas Sellen, born in Halifax in October 1909, there were three types of crooked knives each with different blades used for varying functions: (1) A large wide blade used for splitting the staves used for making baskets, and for carving the rough shape out of a solid block, (2) a medium blade used for finer carving, making basket splints and finishing work, and for incising decorative motifs on flat surfaces, and (3) a finer pointed or curved blade, particularly near the end, used for detailed incising and chip-carving, and for carving and finishing pieces in corners and curved sections. Mr. Sellen also stated that as a boy he knew of ". . .several men from Lunenburg County who made crooked knives for the Indians". He also indicated that crooked knives were made for right and left handed people, and that this could be determined by the curve of the handle, and angle of the thumb rest. (This information was recorded in conversation with Mr. Sellon on July 9, 1985 at the Art Gallery of Nova Scotia).
2. Wesley Mattie (et al.), *From the Heart,* (Toronto: McClelland and Stewart Limited in cooperation with the National Museum of Man, Ottawa, 1983), p. 24.

227 Crooked Knife

Annapolis County
Carved hardwood
Artist unknown
Circa 1860-1880
Dimensions: 26.3 × 4.0 × 6.5 cm ($10\frac{3}{8} \times 1\frac{9}{16} \times 2\frac{9}{16}$ inches)
Private collection

Although this knife was found in Annapolis County it could just as easily come from Lunenburg County and been described as a product of Germanic folk art. Establishing provenance for any object is difficult because of the mobile nature of most items which makes them easily transportable as personal possessions, and because of the activity of antique dealers and collectors. However, it is also important to understand that certain motifs are universal in their appeal and application. The tree of life motif, the heart, and the bird all appear as decorative designs in their own right and are often used in combination with other motifs. The carving on the handle of this crooked knife combines all three of these elements in a decoration which is compelling in its symbolism.

After creating a spiral handle, the maker carved a tree of life in a small flower pot, topped with a central heart with three small hearts carved inside, and ending with a tulip or perhaps thistle design. Sitting on top of this decoration is a bird perched at an angle, almost as if singing. On the sides of the handle are a series of chip-carved and incised motifs which complement the overall design. Although it is impossible to determine what meaning the carver intended when he created this knife, it is clear from the way it was made that the design was well planned, or copied from another source. It is reminiscent of the decoration found on Pennsylvania and Ontario-German fraktur[1], and appears on other examples of decorative folk art from Lunenburg County.

Structure: Unlike most crooked knives, the blade is hafted and secured to the handle not by brass wire but with twine which appears original.

1. Michael Bird, *Ontario Fraktur: A Pennsylvania-German Folk Tradition in Early Canada,* (Toronto: M.F. Feheley Publishers Limited, 1977), p. 61, illustration 56.

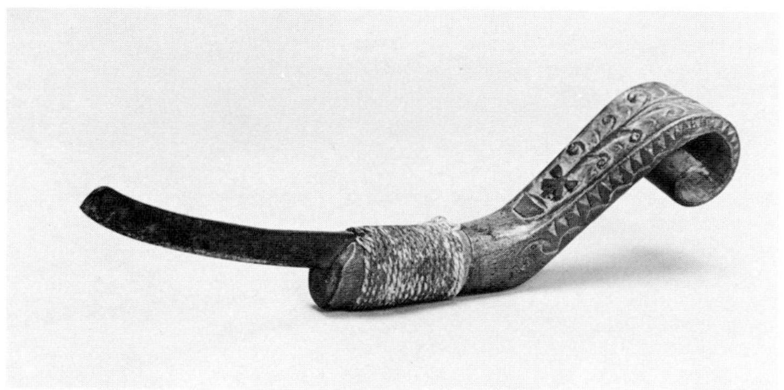

228 Crooked Knives

South Shore or Lunenburg County
Original stained and carved hardwood
Artists unknown
Circa 1860-1880
Dimensions: left — 23.5 × 7.0 × 3.5 cm ($9\frac{1}{4} \times 2\frac{3}{4} \times 1\frac{3}{8}$ inches),
right — 27.0 × 7.5 × 3.0 cm ($10\frac{5}{8} \times 2\frac{15}{16} \times 1\frac{3}{16}$ inches)
Collection of Mr and Mrs Francis Coutellier, Moncton, New Brunswick

These are two of the finest crooked knives known in terms of their carving and overall decorative folk appeal. The knife on the left has one of the most interesting handles encountered. The entire spiral of wood is carved from one piece and forms the handle. Thinning the wood and slowly bending the handle into this spiral shape, probably through the use of low heat, took patience and control on the part of the maker.

The other knife handle is intricately carved with a stylized snake head motif. The diamonds and minute cross-hatching may have been created to suggest serpent scales.

Structure: The handles of both knives are made from solid blocks of hardwood, with the knife blade hafted to the handle and held in place with brass wire. The knife on the left has had the wire replaced with black electrical tape, but remains of the original wire are still intact under this wrapping.

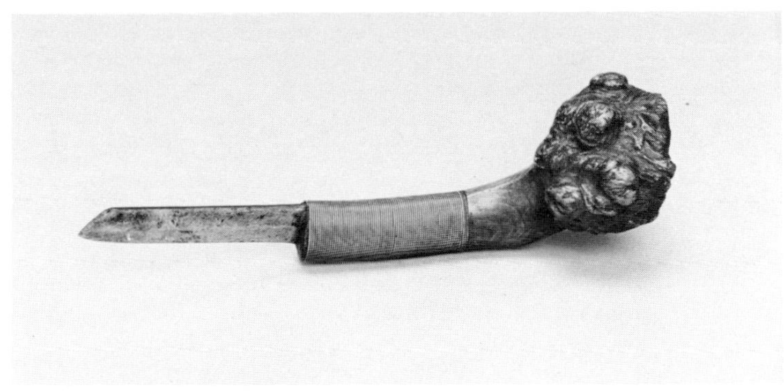

229 Crooked Knife

Annapolis County
Original red painted burl
Artist unknown
Circa 1870-1880
Dimensions: 22.5 × 7.0 × 7.5 cm ($8\frac{7}{8} \times 2\frac{3}{4} \times 2\frac{15}{16}$ inches)
Private collection

The handle of this crooked knife is made by carving a natural burl knot, creating an efficient thumb rest by which to hold and use the knife. The handle was then painted red. It is possible that this particular knife is Micmac in origin.

Structure: The blade is hafted and secured by a light wrapping of brass wire.

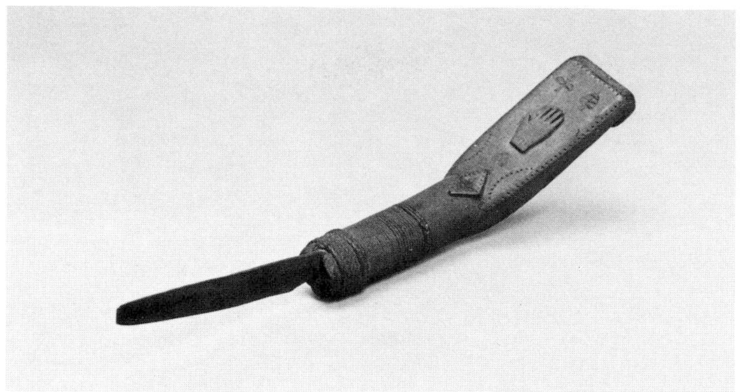

230 Crooked Knife

Blockhouse, Lunenburg County

Original carved and decorated hardwood

Artist unknown

Circa 1870-1880

Dimensions: 25.0 × 6.0 × 3.0 cm (9 13/16 × 2 3/8 × 1 3/16 inches)

Collection of Judy and Earle Rhodenizer, Pleasantville, Nova Scotia

An interesting example of a crooked knife with a carved diamond and open hand motif on the handle. A spade and club motif are inset in wax into the end of the handle. This knife was found in a car body shop and the paint is not original.

Structure: The blade is hafted into the carved handle and held in place with a wrapping of brass wire.

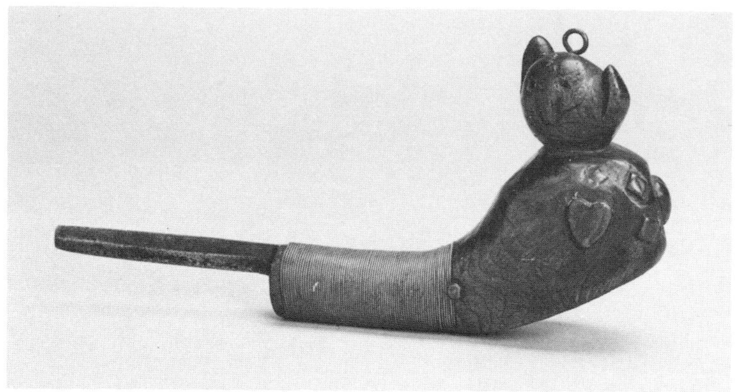

231 Crooked Knife

Lunenburg County

Carved burl

Artist unknown

Circa 1880-1890

Dimensions: 23.0 × 4.0 × 11.0 cm (9 1/16 × 1 1/16 × 4 5/16 inches)

Private collection

Animals are often incorporated into the geometric designs of crooked knives, or the handle is carved in the form of a particular species of wild or domesticated beast. This particular example is in the form of a cat with whiskers and lopsided ears. Two diamonds and two hearts are carved in relief on the "chest" of the cat just above the thumb rest. Although somewhat crudely made, probably using the natural form of the burl to suggest the shape and contours of the handle, the cat's face gives the knife a whimsical appearance.

Structure: The knife is in excellent condition with the blade hafted and secured into the handle with brass wire. At a later date an eye hook was added on the top of the cat's head probably for hanging from a wall or shelf.

232 Crooked Knife

Lunenburg County
Carved and varnished hardwood with carved softwood lunch box
Artist unknown
Circa 1890-1920
Dimensions: 24.8 × 4.0 × 9.8 cm ($9^{13}/_{16}$ × $1^{9}/_{16}$ × $3^{7}/_{8}$ inches)
Private collection

This particular knife handle is carved in the form of a dog carrying a lunch box in his mouth. The subject matter makes this one of the more humorous examples illustrating the imagination used to create these very personal utilitarian objects.

Structure: The blade is hafted and secured into the handle with brass wire. A recent saw cut has been made into the handle near the end of the coil of wire. The wood was originally varnished.

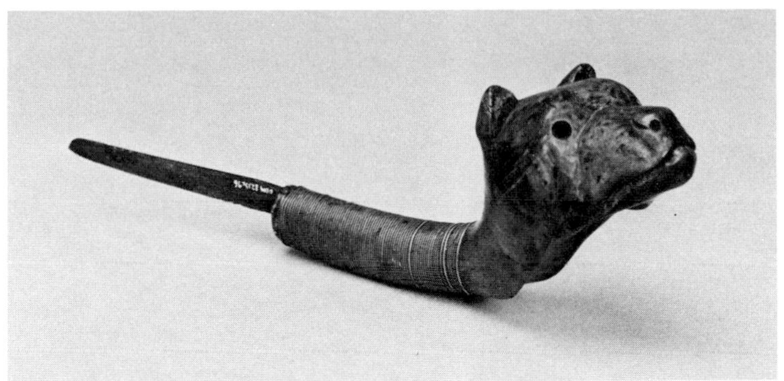

233 Crooked Knife

Probably Lunenburg County
Carved burl
Artist unknown
Circa 1880-1890
Dimensions: 24.0 × 4.5 cm ($9^{7}/_{16}$ × $1^{3}/_{4}$ inches)
Collection of the DesBrisay Museum, Bridgewater, Nova Scotia

Another example of a crooked knife handle carved in the form of an animal, in this instance a dog. The carving is particularly fine and life-like.

Structure: The blade is hafted into the handle and secured with fine brass wire.

234 Crooked Knife

Lunenburg County
Original carved burl
Artist unknown
Circa 1870-1890
Dimensions: 23.0 × 2.5 × 5.8 cm ($9^1/_{16}$ × 1 × $2^1/_4$ inches)
Private collection

Another example of a crooked knife carved in the form of an animal, in this case a dog.

Structure: The knife is carved from a single piece of burl which has never been painted or stained. The blade is hafted to the handle and secured with brass wire.

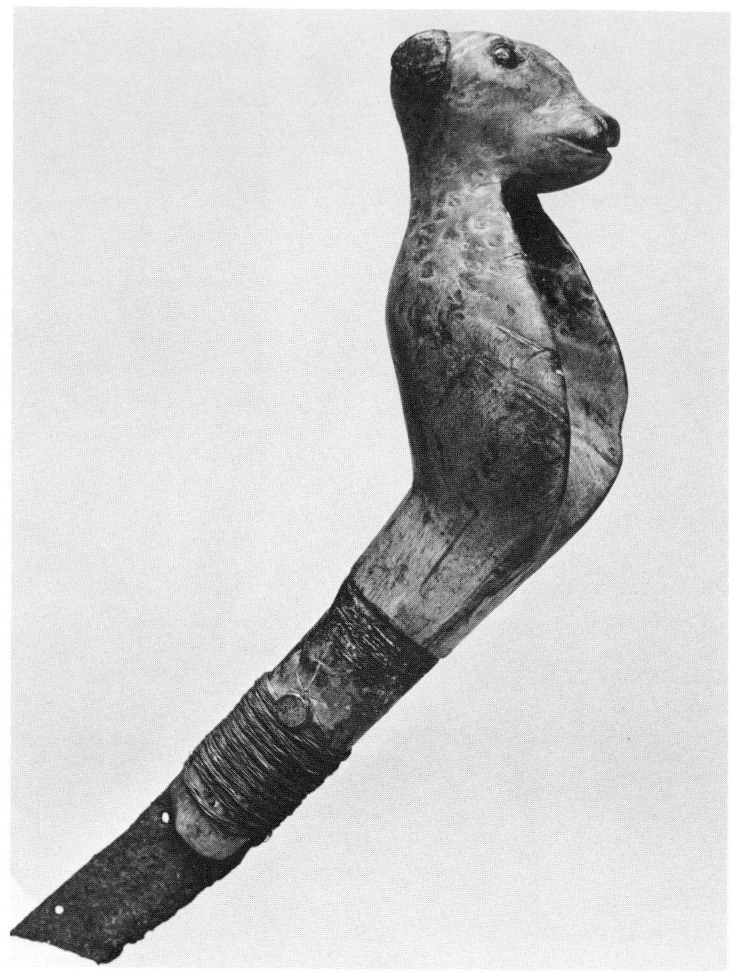

235 Crooked Knife

Lunenburg County
Carved burl/bird's eye maple
Artist unknown
Circa 1870-1890
Dimensions: 21.2 × 4.4 × 8.5 cm ($8^5/_{16}$ × $1^3/_4$ × $3^3/_8$ inches)
Private collection

Another example of a knife carved in the form of a dog with inlaid glass eyes, one of which is missing.

Structure: The knife was carved from a solid piece of burl/bird's eye maple and was stained or painted dark brown or black at one time. One of the glass inlaid eyes is missing and the brass wire helping to secure the blade to the handle is a later replacement.

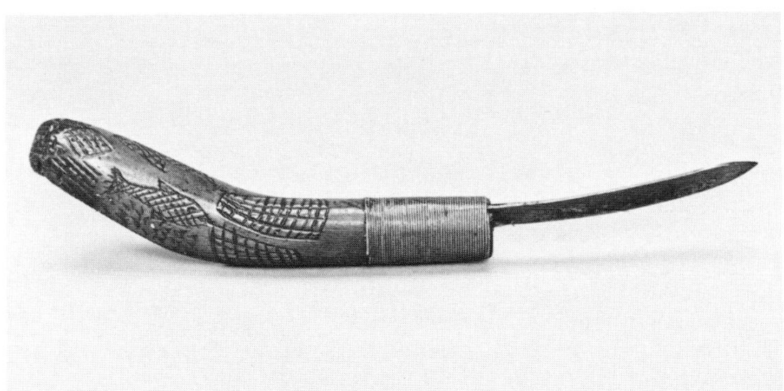

236 Crooked Knife

Lunenburg County
Carved and varnished hardwood
Artist unknown
Circa 1880-1890
Dimensions: 25.9 × 3.0 × 5.5 cm (10$\frac{3}{16}$ × 1$\frac{3}{16}$ × 2$\frac{3}{16}$ inches)
Private collection

This knife is incised with a series of abstract geometric motifs and two fish, complete with fins and scales. The decoration is simple and the form of the handle follows the natural angle of the piece of wood from which it was made. The entire handle has been treated with a coat of glossy varnish.

Structure: The blade is hafted and secured into the handle with brass wire.

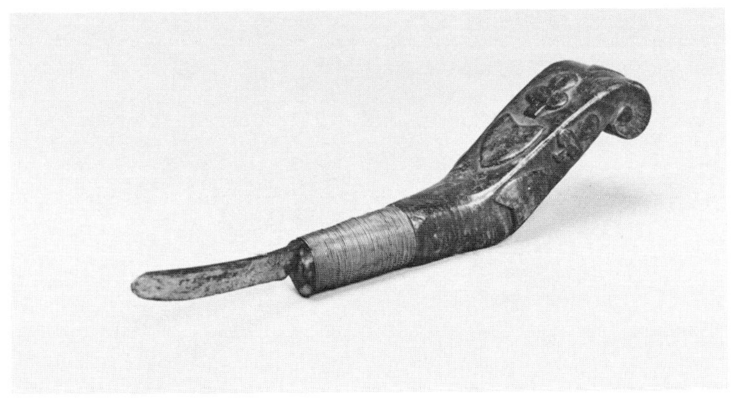

237 Crooked Knife

Lunenburg County
Carved bird's eye maple
Artist unknown
Circa 1880-1890
Dimensions: 25.5 × 4.0 × 6.0 cm (9$\frac{5}{8}$ × 1$\frac{9}{16}$ × 2$\frac{3}{8}$ inches)
Private collection

The use of playing card motifs — heart, diamond, club and spade — are some of the most common designs carved into the handles of crooked knives, and usually appear together. Knives with only carved hearts or diamonds, for example, can be interpreted as having other meanings. But the combination of card motifs cannot, and certainly reflect the most common leisure time activity among companions in the lumbercamps and by friends and family at home.

Structure: The knife is carved from a solid piece of bird's eye maple. The blade is hafted and secured with brass wire.

238 Three Crooked Knives

left — Cumberland County
centre — Annapolis Valley region
right — Cumberland County
Carved and decorated hardwood
Artists unknown
Circa 1870-1890
Dimensions: left — 23.5 × 3.5 × 11.0 cm (9$\frac{1}{4}$ × 1$\frac{3}{8}$ × 4$\frac{5}{16}$ inches)
centre — 25.0 × 5.1 × 6.0 cm (9$\frac{7}{8}$ × 2 × 2$\frac{3}{8}$ inches)
right — 24.5 × 3.5 × 8.0 cm (9$\frac{5}{8}$ × 1$\frac{3}{8}$ × 3$\frac{1}{8}$ inches)
Collection of Pascal and Angela Dinaut, Great Village, Nova Scotia

These three crooked knives are excellent examples of this form with the one on the left and the one in the centre having typical playing card motifs carved into the handles. The centre knife only has diamond, heart and spade with no club, while the other two have all four motifs. The knife on the right has an ornately chip-carved handle.

Structure: All three knives are carved from solid pieces of hardwood with the blade hafted into the handle and secured with brass wire. This wire is missing in the centre example. The knife handle on the right is missing a small piece of wood near the end, which judging by the smooth wear, has been lost for some time.

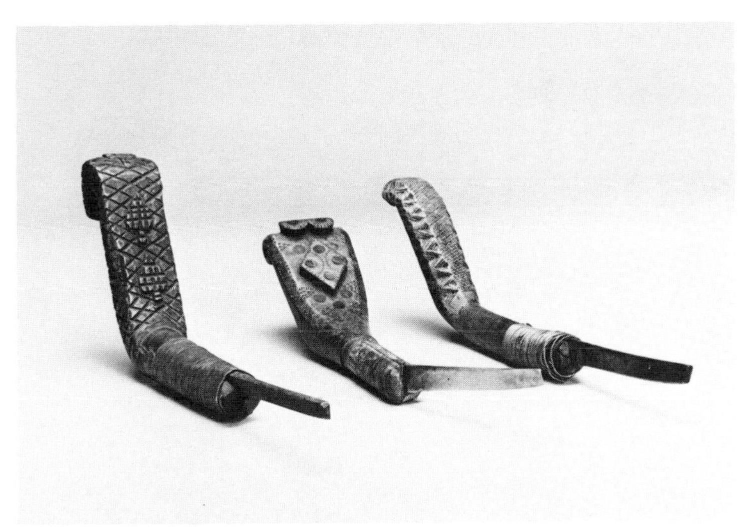

239 Crooked Knife

South Shore of Nova Scotia
Painted and carved hardwood
Artist unknown
Circa 1880-1890
Dimensions: 28.0 × 5.0 × 7.0 cm (11 × 1$^{15}/_{16}$ × 2$^{3}/_{4}$ inches)
Private collection

The handle of this knife is carved with graduated hearts and diamonds painted various colours, with chip-carved edges. Further decoration on the handle consists of painted heart motifs in red.

Structure: The wire used to secure the blade into the handle is loose.

240 Crooked Knife

Cape Breton County
Carved and stained burl
Artist unknown
Dated 1893
Dimensions: 19.5 × 3.5 × 6.0 cm (7$^{11}/_{16}$ × 1$^{3}/_{8}$ × 2$^{3}/_{8}$ inches)
Private collection

The handle of this knife is carved in the form of five graduated hearts which follow the sweeping curve of the thumb rest. The hearts are carved from the solid wood and decorated with chip-carved designs. The date 1893 is neatly incised into the top of the handle near the point of the large heart.

Structure: Traces of dark brown stain or paint remain on the handle. A portion of the large heart is missing. The blade is well worn from use and is hafted into the handle and secured with brass wire.

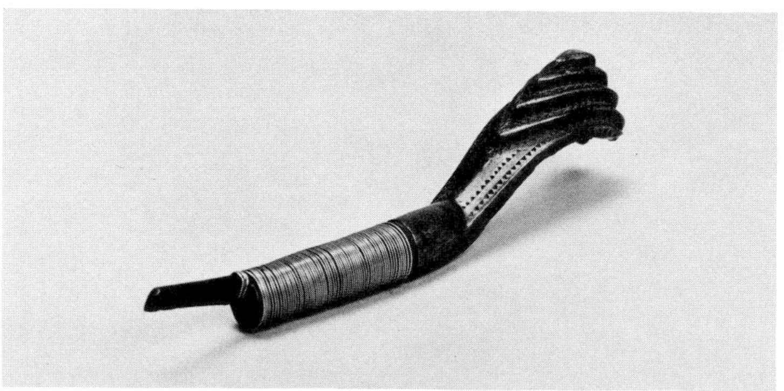

241 Crooked Knife

Lunenburg County
Carved hardwood
Artist unknown
Circa 1880-1900
Dimensions: 24.5 × 3.5 × 8.0 cm (9$^{5}/_{8}$ × 1$^{3}/_{8}$ × 3$^{1}/_{8}$ inches)
Collection of Terry Kobayashi and Michael Bird, Kitchener-Waterloo, Ontario

The crooked knife has six hearts carved in relief on the handle.

Structure: The blade is hafted and secured into the handle with copper wire. The ends of the wire are held in place with square nails.

Published: Michael Bird and Terry Kobayashi, *A Splendid Harvest: Germanic Folk and Decorative Arts in Canada,* (Toronto: Van Nostrand Reinhold, Ltd., 1981), p. 38.

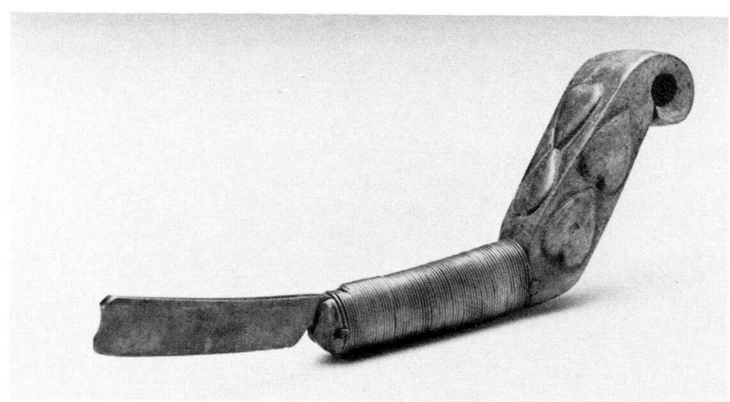

242 Crooked Knife

Cumberland County

Carved and incised burl with pewter inlay

Artist unknown, the initials GWD are incised into the handle

Circa 1870-1890

Dimensions: 25.7 × 4.5 × 8.0 cm (10⅛ × 1¾ × 3⅛ inches)

Private collection

The handle of this knife is incised with a tree motif and carved in a series of graduated designs, including two semi-circles and a heart. The blade is set into the handle with an elaborate inlay of pewter locked into the wood through an intricate series of "teeth" which act as dovetails to secure the two sections together. Just above the tree are the incised initials GWD which might refer to the maker or the owner of the knife.

Structure: The handle may have been stained or painted dark brown or black at some time in the past. The knife is hafted and secured into the handle with pewter inlay.

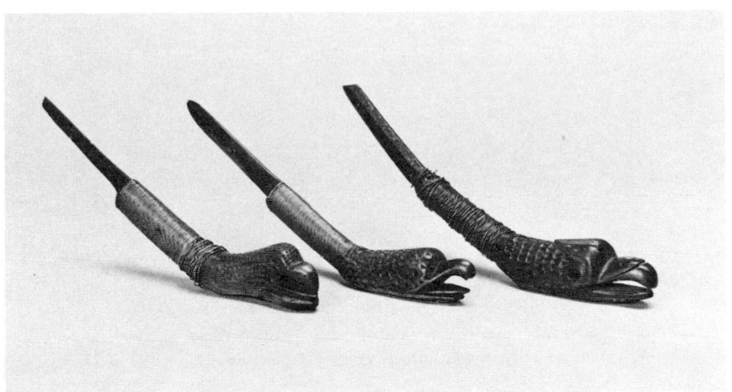

243 Crooked Knives

All Lunenburg County

left — natural wood, middle — red paint and stain,
right — dark stain. All are made from hardwood.

All three knives made by Eli Croft (1860-1935?)

Circa 1890-1920

Dimensions: left — 25.5 × 2.3 × 6.5 cm (10$\frac{1}{16}$ × ¾ × 2$\frac{9}{16}$ inches)
middle — 25. 0 × 2.5 × 6.0 cm (9$\frac{13}{16}$ × 1 × 2⅜ inches).
right — 25.5 × 2.8 × 5.5 cm (10$\frac{1}{16}$ × 1⅛ × 2$\frac{3}{16}$ inches)

Private collection

Eli Croft was born in Camperdown, Lunenburg County and as a young man worked as a gold prospector and blacksmith. He was a prolific carver making a wide range of objects including canes, full-standing figures, and chests of drawers decorated with various wooden details.[1] These three crooked knives are fine examples of his work and represent three distinct stages in his style ranging from the early period (left) through the middle to late periods (middle and right).

Carved in the form of eagles, these knives show a developing style, beginning with the left knife which is simple and has a less developed form than the middle piece. In the last version (right) the form is a fully developed eagle design with flattened crest and inlaid eyes, the inlay unfortunately missing. This last knife exhibits a bold forceful style of carving which gives the eagle head more life and vibrancy.

Crooked knives were tools used for making basket splints and other utilitarian objects and were made usually by hafting straight razor blades to ornately carved handles.

Structure: All three knives are in good condition with blades and handles showing wear from use. Once the handle is carved, the razor is mounted into the haft and secured using a tight wrapping of brass wire, which in the left and right examples has come undone. In addition, the inlaid eyes are missing from the right example.

Exhibited: Decorated Nova Scotia Furnishings, Dalhousie University Art Gallery, Halifax, Nova Scotia, July 5-August 6, 1978.

1. *Folk Art of Nova Scotia,* (Halfiax: Art Gallery of Nova Scotia, 1976), p. 28. This exhibition catalogue includes a biographical profile of Croft.

244 Ball in Cage Cane

Antigonish County
Original stained hardwood
Artist unknown
Circa 1860-1880
Dimensions: 92.0 × 3.5 × 3.5 cm ($36\frac{3}{16}$ × $1\frac{3}{8}$ × $1\frac{3}{8}$ inches)
Private collection

Canes are one of the objects that woodcarvers are likely to spend a lot of time and attention on. They are very personal and individual articles which were highly fashionable, the more ornate examples acting as show-pieces for a carver's art and skill, and probably used on special occasions.[1] This particular cane is an excellent example of one of the more popular ball in cage motifs.

Structure: The cane is carved from a solid piece of maple or birch. The exact identity of the wood is difficult to determine because of the dark stain applied to the wood. Each ball in cage is carved individually, the entire cane tapering from top to bottom.

1. Wesley Mattie (et al), *From the Heart,* (Toronto: McClelland and Stewart Limited in cooperation with the National Museum of Man, Ottawa, 1983), p. 37.

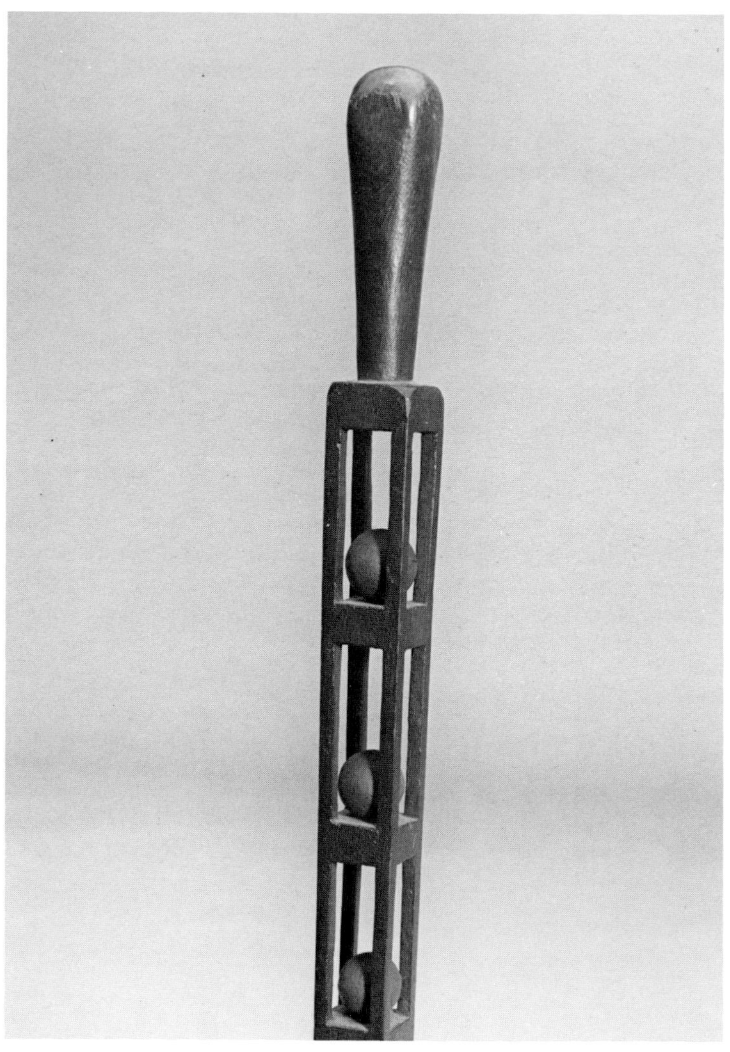

245 Cane with Woman's Face

Probably Annapolis Valley region
Original carved and painted hardwood
Artist unknown
Circa 1860-1890
Dimensions: 7.6 (head) × 77.0 cm (3 × $30\frac{5}{16}$ inches)
Collection of Jerry and Debbie Vidito, Kentville, Nova Scotia

The handle of this cane is carved from a piece of burl in the form of a woman's face. It is difficult to determine the origin of this piece, although the face does suggest Micmac carving. The back of the head and the shaft is painted a light blue.

Structure: The cane is carved from a single piece of hardwood with a burl knot at one end from which the face is carved.

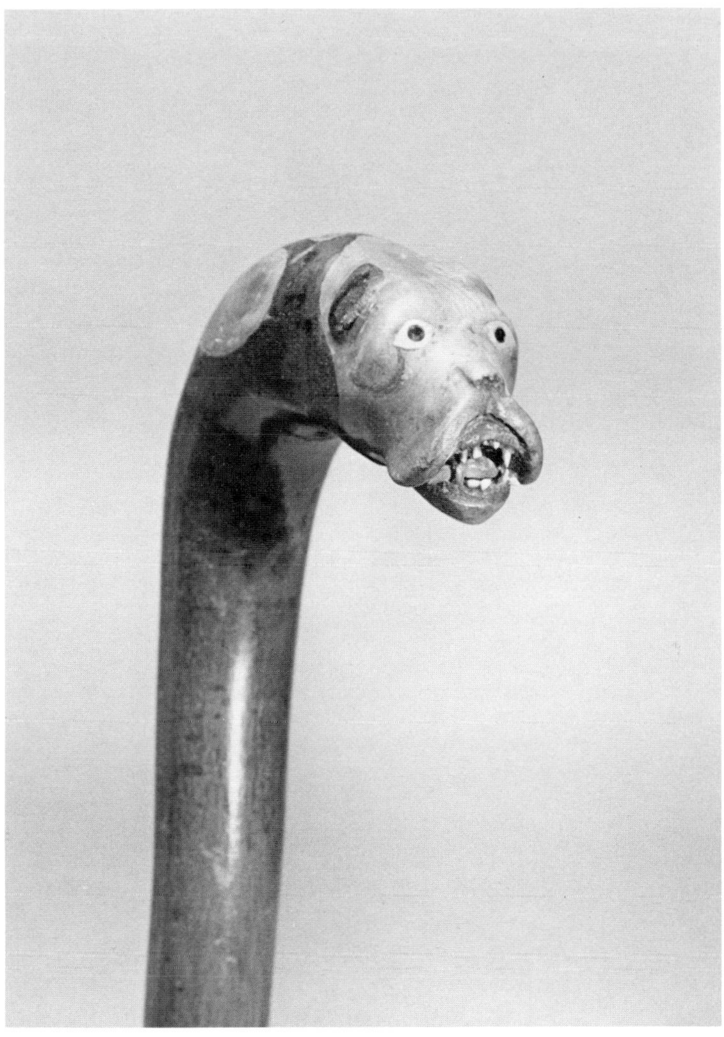

246 Carved Cane with Dog-Head Handle

Digby County
Carved and varnished hardwood with inset animal teeth, and inlaid mother-of-pearl.
Artist unknown
Circa 1870-1890
Dimensions: length — 91.5 cm (36 inches)
Collection of Gerald Ferguson, Halifax, Nova Scotia

A superb example of a cane carved with a dog-head handle inlaid with real animal teeth.

Structure: The two-tone colour of the dog head is accomplished by revealing the lighter underlayer of wood. The teeth appear to be from a domestic cat. The end of the cane is tipped with a brass and iron point. The cane has a highly polished varnished finish.

247 Snake and Hand Cane

Musquodoboit Harbour, Halifax County
Original black painted softwood
Artist unknown
Circa 1880-1890
Dimensions: 2.5 × 79.5 cm (1 × $31\frac{5}{16}$ inches)
Collection of Jerry and Debbie Vidito, Kentville, Nova Scotia

This cane has a carved snake wrapped around the shaft with an arm and hand grasping its head near the bent handle at the top. The coiled serpent is one of the most common decorative motifs found on canes.

Structure: The cane is carved from a single piece of softwood, and painted black. There is a lot of paint loss from use around the handle area.

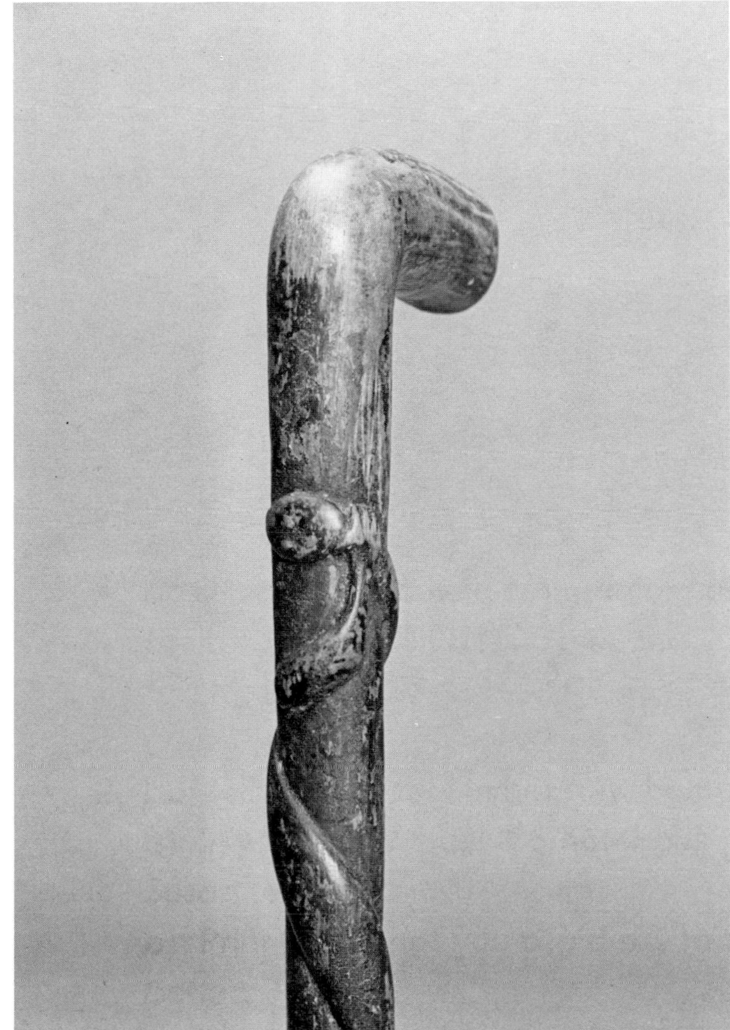

248 Snake Cane

Stellarton, Pictou County
Carved and painted softwood
Made by John Forbes
Circa 1930-1940
Dimensions: length — 94.0 cm (37 inches)
Private collection

A very fine example of a cane with snake entwined. The snake is attached to the shaft of the cane and painted with yellow and red polka dots. The head of the cane is carved into the shape of a four-pronged talon, or claw, holding an egg-shaped object. Although a late example of a snake cane, this is a very dramatic rendition of this form.

Structure: Carved and painted softwood. There is an original brass sleeve just beneath the carved and unpainted top of the cane.

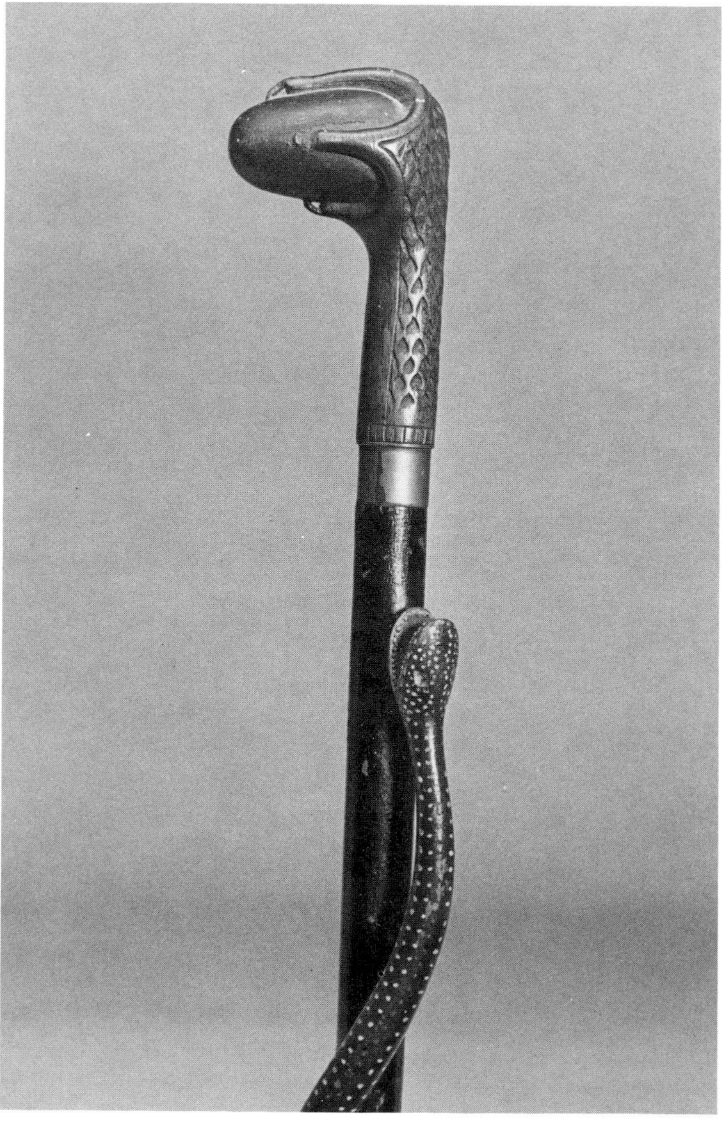

249 Butterprint

Lunenburg County
Carved and incised hardwood
Artist unknown
Circa 1830-1850
Dimensions: 12.7 × 3.8 cm (5 × 1½ inches)
Collection of Joseph Schneider House, Kitchener, Ontario

This is one of the most outstanding butterprints known from Nova Scotia. It is a superb example of decorative folk art in the Germanic tradition from Lunenburg County. The central motif of a six pointed compass star is composed of a hexagon and geometric arcs. This entire design is surrounded by six hearts carved in deep relief with the background areas between the hearts incised and cross-hatched, creating a low key contrast against the complex overall design.

Structure: Carved from a single block of hardwood. A handle is attached on the reverse side with a single screw and two forged nails.

Published: Michael Bird and Terry Kobayashi, *A Splendid Harvest: Germanic Folk and Decorative Arts in Canada,* (Toronto: Van Nostrand Reinhold, Ltd., 1981), p. 44.

250 Butterprints

top, Cow; middle, 3 Fish on String; bottom, Sheep
Probably Annapolis Valley region
Carved and turned hardwood
Artist unknown
Circa 1870-1890
Dimensions: Cow — 11.5 × 8.0 cm ($4\frac{1}{2} \times 3\frac{1}{8}$ inches),
3 Fish — 9.3 × 7.5 cm ($3\frac{5}{8} \times 2\frac{15}{16}$ inches),
Sheep — 9.5 × 13.5 cm ($3\frac{3}{4} \times 5\frac{5}{16}$ inches).
Collection of Jerry and Debbie Vidito, Kentville, Nova Scotia

Butter, which was made in the home, was usually shaped with cylindrical or square moulds, sometimes being formed into bricks and simply marked with the producer's seal. The stamps usually displayed geometric motifs, plants, flowers or animals.[1] These three examples illustrate the typical animal motifs found on butterprints.

Structure: The prints are carved and turned from one piece of hardwood. The cylinder on the sheep print is lathe turned.

1. Wesley Mattie (et al), *From the Heart,* (Toronto: McClelland and Stewart Limited in cooperation with the National Museum of Man, Ottawa, 1983), pp. 30-31

251 Butterprint

New Glasgow, Pictou County
Original carved hardwood
Artist unknown
Circa 1840-1860
Dimensions: 3.5 (diameter of print) × 20.5 (including handle) × 1.5 cm ($3\frac{3}{8} \times 8\frac{1}{16} \times \frac{5}{8}$ inches)
Collection of Chris Cooper, Dartmouth, Nova Scotia

The handle of this butterprint is carved out of the solid wood and not attached to the print. Butterprints of this type are often called "lollipops", the name an obvious adaption from the popular candy on a stick. This example has a six-pointed star motif with what can only be called random carving on the reverse, much in the manner of a pencil doodler. Included on the reverse is the incised name Katie, a small carved heart, a diamond and a very stylized pine tree with roots. Although this carving is probably done by a child, the actual print itself was carved by someone with some previous experience. It is interesting to note that the edges of the design are almost rounded from use.

Structure: The butterprint is carved from a solid block of maple.

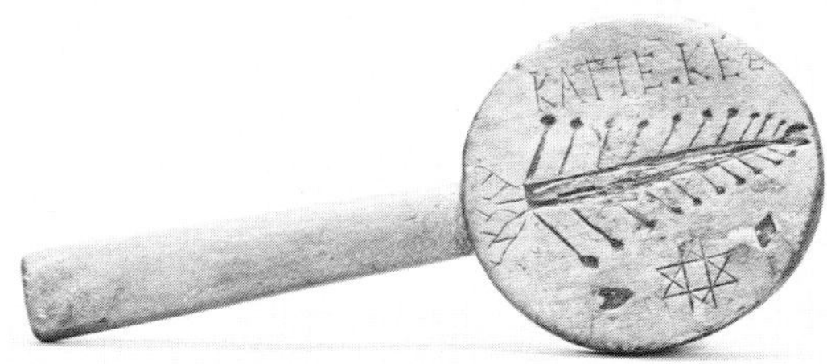

252 Butterprint

Guysborough County
Unpainted carved hardwood
Artist unknown
Circa 1840-1860
Dimensions: 11.0 × 21.0 × 2.0 cm ($4\frac{5}{16} \times 8\frac{1}{4} \times \frac{3}{4}$ inches)
Collection of Pascal and Angela Dinaut, Great Village, Nova Scotia

A very fine example of a two-sided lollipop butterprint ornately carved with an intricate star on one side, and abstract heart motifs on the other.

Structure: The butterprint handle is carved from the solid piece of wood used to make the lollipop. A small hole in the end of the handle was used to hang the print when not in use.

253 A Pair of Square Butterprint/Butter Paddles

Cape George, Richmond County
Both double-sided carved and decorated softwood
Artist unknown
Circa 1840-1860
Dimensions: left — 10.2 × 18.1 cm (4 × 7⅛ inches)
right — 9.5 × 19.7 cm (3¾ × 7¾ inches)
Collection of Paul Killowee and Judy Aymar, Queensland, Nova Scotia

This pair of butterprints were found in the same house, and according to family tradition, have been a part of the domestic utensils of the household for generations. The presence of a carved thistle on the left hand print certainly supports the Scottish roots of the family from whom they were purchased. The carved star on the right hand print is in keeping with similar motifs found in the region. The reverse of both prints are reeded and served as paddles to work the butter. When finished, the print sides were used to impress the butter with these carved designs.

A question, however, still remains as to their origin. Similar square butterprints are unknown to this author from Nova Scotia, however, butter paddles with the same reeding and shape are very common. It is quite possible that the maker of these utensils simply adopted this form in creating a double-sided tool used in the manufacturing of butter. It is entirely possible, however, that they were brought as settler's effects from Scotland, or perhaps purchased at a later date by a family member travelling abroad.

Structure: Both prints are made from softwood, and carved and decorated with two central motifs on one side, surrounded by incised cross-hatching, and reeded on the reverse side. Both handles end in carved hearts.

254 Butterprint

Middle Musquodoboit, Halifax County
Original carved hardwood
Artist unknown
Circa 1850-1870
Dimensions: 9.0 × 2.5 cm ($3^{9}/_{16}$ × 1 inch)
Collection of Chris Cooper, Dartmouth, Nova Scotia

A rather crude example of a butterprint with a swirling geometric pattern around a central star motif. This print never had a handle and is very thick, allowing one to grasp the print firmly while pressing the pattern into the butter.

Structure: The print is carved from a solid block of hardwood.

255 Butterprints

South Shore of Nova Scotia

Carved hardwood

Artist unknown

Circa 1850-1870

Dimensions: left — 12.0 × 7.0 cm ($4^{11}/_{16}$ × $2^{3}/_{4}$ inches)
right — 11.0 × 13.5 cm ($4^{5}/_{16}$ × $5^{5}/_{16}$ inches)

Collection of Shelburne County Museum (Ross-Thomson House), Shelburne, Nova Scotia

Both butterprints are early examples of this form. The designs are deeply carved to leave bold decorations when pressed into freshly made butter. The print on the left is carved with four heart motifs, while the one on the right has stylized heart/floral designs.

Structure: Both prints are carved from solid blocks of hardwood with the handle on the left part of the print, while the handle on the one on the right is removable, and fits into a square opening protruding through to the decorated side.

256 Lollipop Butterprint with Swirl Design

River John, Pictou County

Carved softwood

Artist unknown

Circa 1860-1880

Dimensions: 11.4 × 22.2 × 1.3 cm ($4\frac{1}{2} \times 8\frac{3}{4} \times \frac{1}{2}$ inches)

Collection of Pauline and Jowe Creighton, Jordon, Ontario

This two-sided butterprint is one of the best examples of this form to be found in the province. A swirl pattern on one side, and a six pointed star pattern on the reverse, indicate that the maker of this print had an excellent sense of design and carving skill. The edges of both sides are also chip-carved.

Structure: Carved from a single block of softwood, the butterprint shows signs of use on the handle. The wood is highly patined along the edges of the print and the handle.

257 Butterprints

All Kentville area, Kings County

The three lollipop prints are made of hardwood, the stamp print is made of softwood. All are carved and unpainted.

Artists unknown

Circa 1840-1860

Dimensions: A — diameter 10.0 × length 26.5 cm ($3\frac{15}{16} \times 10\frac{7}{16}$ inches)
B — diameter 10.0 × length 26.0 cm ($3\frac{15}{16} \times 10\frac{5}{16}$ inches)
C — diameter 8.5 × length 24.0 cm ($3\frac{5}{16} \times 9\frac{7}{16}$ inches)
D — diameter 9.5 × length 25.0 cm ($3\frac{3}{4} \times 9\frac{7}{8}$ inches)

Collection of Mr and Mrs Francis Coutellier, Moncton, New Brunswick

All four of these butterprints are excellent examples of just how complex geometric designs could be on these utilitarian objects. Two have heart motifs, and two have stylized star designs. They were all purchased in the Kentville area of Nova Scotia, from dealer/collectors who bought them locally.

Structure: The lollipop prints have the handles carved from the solid piece of wood. All are unpainted and deeply carved.

258 Gameboard *Checker/Chess*
Bridgewater, Lunenburg County
Original red and black paint on single softwood plank
Artist unknown
Circa 1860-1880
Dimensions: 34.7 × 35.6 × 2.0 cm (13½ × 14 × ¾ inches)
Private collection

This gameboard is probably by the same maker that produced two tables, one a drop-leaf tapered-leg table found in Dartmouth, Nova Scotia but no doubt originally from Lunenburg County, and the other a tapered-leg work table found in Mahone Bay, Nova Scotia. Both tables are without drawers, the drop-leaf is decorated with a series of semi-circles along the edges of the top and leaves, while the work table has semi-circles only in the four corners of the top. There is little doubt that this gameboard was made or decorated by the same individual.[1]

The board is the standard 8 × 8 square variety which could be used to play checkers or chess. The playing field is created by alternating red and black squares while the semi-circle decoration is black.

Structure: The board is made from a single softwood plank with pit-saw marks on the reverse. The board never had moldings. The painted decoration continues from the playing surface around the edges of the board.

Exhibited: An Exhibition of Canadian Gameboards of the 19th and 20th centuries from Ontario, Quebec and Nova Scotia. Organized and circulated by the Art Gallery of Nova Scotia, October 23, 1981-February 15, 1983.

Published: Richard Field (Ed.), *Gameboards: Canadian Gameboards of the 19th and 20th Centuries From Ontario, Quebec and Nova Scotia,* (Halifax: Art Gallery of Nova Scotia, 1981). The board is illustrated with description on page 51.

1. For illustrations of these two tables see Tom Lackey, *Decorated Nova Scotia Furnishings,* (Halifax: Dalhousie University Art Gallery, 1978), p. 11 (catalogue numbers 59 and 65).

259 Gameboard *Parcheesi and Checker/Chess*
Crousetown, Lunenburg County
Painted and decorated softwood
Artist unknown
Circa 1860-1880
Dimensions: 70.3 × 70.5 cm (27¹¹⁄₁₆ × 27¾ inches)
Collection of Judy and Earle Rhodenizer, Pleasantville, Nova Scotia

This is a fine gameboard from Lunenburg County exhibiting traditional design and decorative motifs. It is a double-sided board with parcheesi and checker/chess.

Structure: The board is made from a single plank of softwood with molding attached with square nails.

Refer to colour plate XIX, page 23

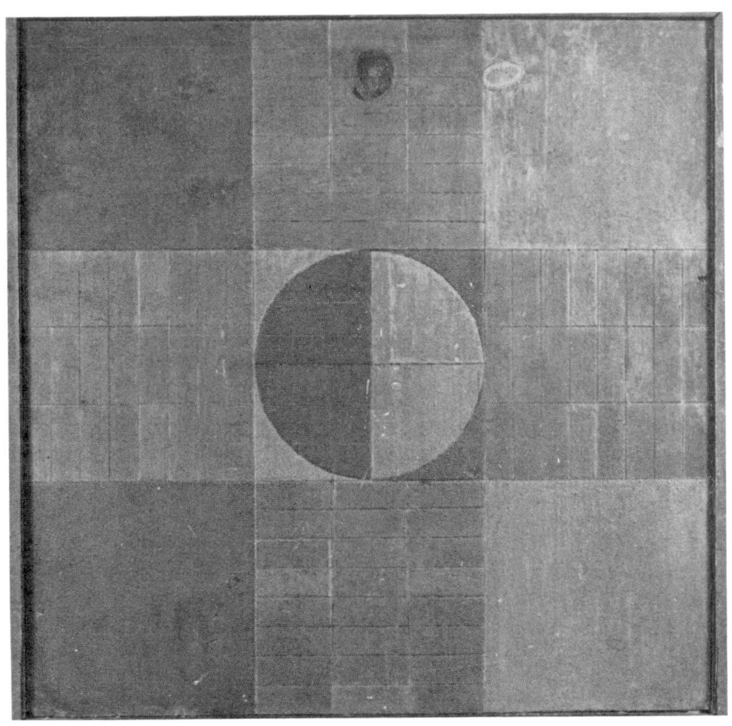

260 Gameboard *Parcheesi*
Lunenburg County
Painted softwood with attached moldings
Artist unknown
Circa 1860-1880
Dimensions: 38.4 × 38.4 × 3.0 cm (15 1/16 × 15 1/16 × 1 1/8 inches)
Collection of the Art Gallery of Nova Scotia, Halifax, Nova Scotia

An excellent example of a parcheesi board from Lunenburg County painted in very muted colours of dark brown, light brown and black.

Structure: Plank construction from a single piece of softwood. The molding is attached with small square nails. The reverse of the board was used to keep score for a three handed card game.

Exhibited: An Exhibition of Canadian Gameboards of the 19th and 20th centuries from Ontario, Quebec and Nova Scotia. Organized and circulated by the Art Gallery of Nova Scotia, October 23, 1981-February 15, 1983.

Published: Richard Field (Ed.), *Gameboards: Canadian Gameboards of the 19th and 20th Centuries From Ontario, Quebec and Nova Scotia,* (Halifax: Art Gallery of Nova Scotia, 1981). The board is illustrated with description on page 62.

261 Gameboard *Parcheesi and Checker/Chess*
Scotts Bay, Kings County
Painted softwood with hardwood moldings
Artist unknown
Circa 1870-1890
Dimensions: 47.5 × 46.5 × 2.0 cm (18 11/16 × 18 5/16 × 13/16 inches)
Collection of Jerry and Debbie Vidito, Kentville, Nova Scotia

An excellent example of a painted two-sided gameboard decorated with a series of circles, six-pointed pinwheels and eight-pointed compass roses on the parcheesi side, and alternately decorated squares on the reverse checker/chess side. This board is similar to others found in Nova Scotia, particularly Lunenburg County, with similar painted details and decorative motifs, specifically on the parcheesi board.[1]

Structure: A single softwood plank forms the playing board which in turn is painted to form the games on both sides with red, black, green and yellow colours. The unpainted molding is made of hardwood and attached with small square brads and butt jointed.

1. For similar examples and further information on gameboards see Richard Field (Ed.), *Canadian Gameboards of the Nineteenth and Twentieth Centuries From Ontario, Quebec and Nova Scotia,* (Halifax: Art Gallery of Nova Scotia, 1981), pp. 58-60. This exhibition catalogue also includes an introduction into "The History and Rules of the Game" by Dr. Elliott Avedon, Curator of the Museum and Archive of Games at the University of Waterloo, Waterloo, Ontario.

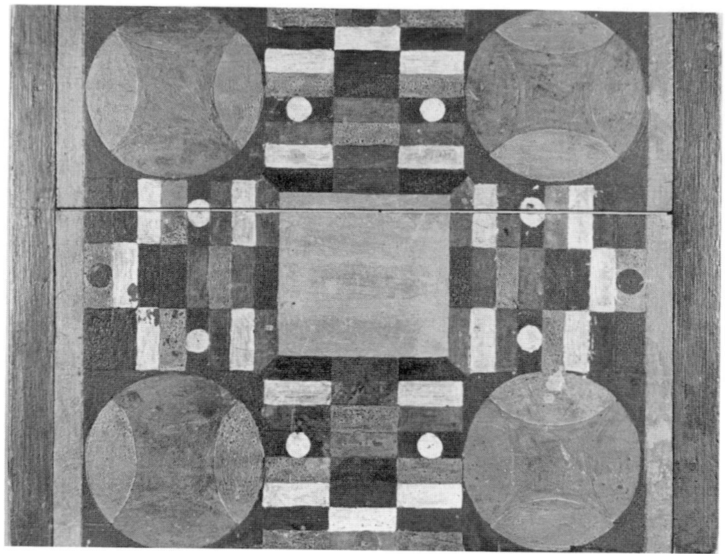

262 Gameboard *Parcheesi*

Annapolis County
Original painted softwood with painted softwood molding
Artist unknown
Circa 1880-1900
Dimensions: 48.5 × 37.5 × 2.0 cm ($19\frac{1}{8} \times 15\frac{3}{4} \times \frac{3}{4}$ inches)
Collection of Jerry and Debbie Vidito, Kentville, Nova Scotia

An example of a one-sided parchessi board made from two pieces of softwood with bread-board type moldings. The semi-circle decorations in the four corners of the board are similar to other examples found in Nova Scotia.[1] The board is painted in various colours of green, red, white, yellow and grey.

Structure: The playing surface is made from two softwood planks, one which is stamped on the reverse Java-Mocha, probably from an advertisement on the side of a wooden packing crate. The planks are held together by two pieces of molding attached at either end of the board with square nails.

1. Richard Field (Ed.), *Canadian Gameboards of the Nineteenth and Twentieth Centuries From Ontario, Quebec and Nova Scotia,* (Halifax: Art Gallery of Nova Scotia, 1981), p. 57.

263 Gameboard *Checker/Chess*

Port Lorne, Annapolis County
Original painted softwood
Artist unknown
Circa 1890-1910
Dimensions: 35.7 × 34.5 × 2.0 cm ($14\frac{1}{16} \times 13\frac{1}{16} \times \frac{3}{4}$ inches)
Collection of Jerry and Debbie Vidito, Kentville, Nova Scotia

On one side of this board is a painted 8 × 8 checker/chess game with alternating black and white squares, bordered by a red frame. On the reverse is the painting of a ship under sail which appears to be named CVIOO. Rigged as a schooner, the vessel is flying three flags all of which could be imaginary, although the flag flying from the main gaff where the ensign is usually flown appears to be a house flag (Williams ?), as does the flag flying from the fore trunk. The third flag has not been identified.

It is not that unusual to find gameboards with paintings on the reverse side which could be displayed as decorative objects when not in use.[1]

Structure: The board is made from a single plank of softwood with no moldings or hardware to help in identifying the age of this object. The edges of the board have been painted white, and someone has written the initials GY and G in some of the white squares which may be a clue as to the identity of the owner or maker of this board.

1. Richard Field (Ed.), *Canadian Gameboards of the Nineteenth and Twentieth Centuries From Ontario, Quebec and Nova Scotia,* (Halifax: Art Gallery of Nova Scotia, 1981), p. 32.

264 Gameboard *Parcheesi and Checker/Chess*
Upper LeHave, Lunenburg County
Painted softwood with attached moldings
Artist unknown
Circa 1900-1910
Dimensions: 45.2 × 45.2 × 2.9 cm (18¾ × 18¾ × 1⅛ inches)
Collection of the Art Gallery of Nova Scotia, Halifax, Nova Scotia

A gameboard with parcheesi on one side and checker/chess on the reverse. The parcheesi side has an elaborate use of semi-circle motifs, a form of decoration also found on the corners of tables from Lunenburg County.

Structure: Plank construction from a single piece of softwood. The moldings are attached with round nails.

Exhibited: An Exhibition of Canadian Gameboards of the 19th and 20th centuries from Ontario, Quebec and Nova Scotia. Organized and circulated by the Art Gallery of Nova Scotia, October 23, 1981-February 15, 1983.

Published: Richard Field (Ed.), *Gameboards: Canadian Gameboards of the 19th and 20th Centuries From Ontario, Quebec and Nova Scotia,* (Halifax: Art Gallery of Nova Scotia, 1981). The board is illustrated with description on pages 56-57.

265 Gameboard *Checker/Chess*
Probably Colchester County
Original painted softwood
Artist unknown
Circa 1900-1910
Dimensions: 32.0 × 32.0 × 2.5 cm (12⅝ × 12⅝ × 1 inch)
Collection of Pascal and Angela Dinaut, Great Village, Nova Scotia

A simple example of a gameboard with squares painted red and white. At one time paper numbers were pasted in the corners of the red squares only, perhaps to help teach children the game.

Structure: The board is made from a single plank of softwood. The molding is attached with round nails and unpainted. The reverse side of the board is also unpainted.

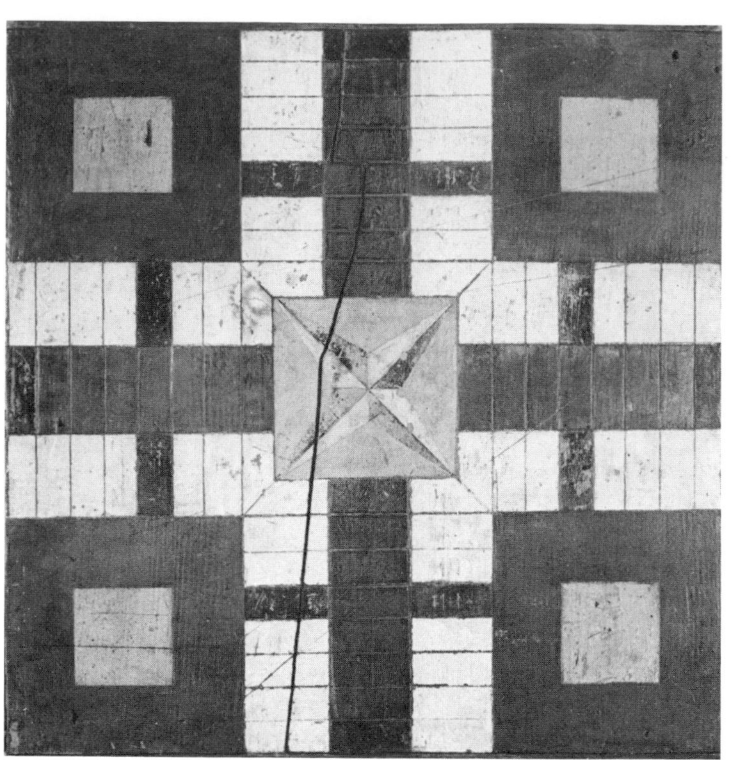

266 Gameboard *Parcheesi*
South Shore of Nova Scotia
Painted softwood with attached molding
Artist unknown
Circa 1900-1920
Dimensions: 41.5 × 43.0 × 1.3 cm ($16\frac{5}{16}$ × $16\frac{15}{16}$ × $\frac{1}{2}$ inches)
Collection of Carl Boswick, Chester, Nova Scotia

A one-sided parcheesi board with moldings attached to only two sides of the board. The central four-pointed star is "home", while simple square motifs that decorate the four corners are painted the same yellow colour as the background for the star.

Structure: Plank construction from a single piece of softwood. The board has two age cracks. The molding is attached with round nails, and is covered on the reverse with a piece of cheese cloth.

267 Gameboard *Parcheesi*
Lunenburg, Lunenburg County
Painted softwood with applied softwood molding
Made by a member of the Mason family
Circa 1925
Dimensions: 56.0 × 55.5 × 3.2 cm ($22\frac{1}{16}$ × 22 × $1\frac{1}{4}$ inches)
Collection of Terry Kobayashi and Michael Bird, Kitchener-Waterloo, Ontario

This parcheesi board is one of the outstanding objects of decorative folk art from Lunenburg County. Although dating circa 1925, rather late in terms of some of the objects in this exhibition, it is an example of just how persistent and enduring the folk decorative tradition was in Lunenburg County specifically, and Nova Scotia generally. The colour scheme is common to the area, and the painted house which acts as "home" for the parcheesi game is a wonderful touch.

Structure: Plank construction with round nails and brass hinges and screws. The board can be folded image in, for carrying and storage purposes.

Published: Michael Bird and Terry Kobayashi, *A Splendid Harvest: Germanic Folk and Decorative Arts in Canada,* (Toronto: Van Nostrand Reinhold, Ltd., 1981), p. 43.

Richard Field, *Gameboards: An Exhibition of Canadian Gameboards of the 19th and 20th Centuries From Ontario, Quebec and Nova Scotia,* (Halifax: Art Gallery of Nova Scotia, 1981), p. 60.

268 Courting Mirror*

Margaree Forks, Inverness County
Original carved and painted softwood with inset mirror
Artist unknown
Circa 1780-1800
Dimensions: 15.2 × 38.9 × 2.1 cm (6 × 15$\frac{5}{16}$ × $\frac{13}{16}$ inches)
Collection of Leslie J. Langille, Lunenburg, Nova Scotia

This is one of the most important objects in this exhibition. Found in Cape Breton, this mirror reflects the best in eighteenth century decorative folk art. Purchased from a member of the MacDonald family, it is possible that the pierced design, which resembles the letter M, stands for the initial of the name of a previous owner. The upper portion of the frame is also shaped and incised with a series of semi-circle and chevron motifs, probably reflecting the Irish or Scottish decorative origins of this piece.

As usual, mirrors of this type, size, and period, are often referred to as courting mirrors, presumably based on the fact that such a mirror was made by a prospective suitor of an intended bride. This type of mirror is more commonly found in the Eastern United States. This is one of the very few examples known to this writer from the Maritime Provinces with impeccable Canadian/Nova Scotia provenance.

Structure: The mirror frame is carved from a solid plank of softwood. The glass inset into a hollowed out recess and held in place with border molding attached with brass and wooden pins. It is painted a dark red/black which is well worn in places from use. It is difficult to determine if the mirror glass is original.

*This piece will be on view in Halifax only

269 Last-Look Mirror

Hants County
Original painted softwood with inlaid mirror fragment
Artist unknown
Circa 1840-1860
Dimensions: 11.0 × 21.5 × 2.0 cm (4⁵⁄₁₆ × 8⁷⁄₁₆ × ¾ inches)
Collection of Jerry and Debbie Vidito, Kentville, Nova Scotia

Mirrors or looking-glasses were always very important objects, often expensive and difficult to replace. Their value can be appreciated by considering this example which utilizes a broken mirror piece for which a special frame has been made out of a solid piece of softwood.[1] The mirror is inlaid into the frame, the maker following the broken shape of the glass, and held in place with three wooden pegs. A hole in one end suggests it was not only used as a hand-mirror, but hung on the wall as well. These small types of mirrors have often been referred to as last-look mirrors because of the suggestion that they often hung by a door and were used to check one's appearance before going out in public.

Structure: The mirror is set into a solid piece of softwood which has been painted a dark brown. It is held in place with three wooden pins. The mirror shows wear probably from being held in the hand.

1. For a remarkably similar example see Russell Hawes Kettle, *The Pine Furniture of Early New England,* (New York: Dover Publications, Inc., 1949), pp. 168-171 (figure 168).

270 Mirror or Picture Frame on Stand

South Shore of Nova Scotia
Original carved and unpainted softwood
Artist unknown
Circa 1870-1890
Dimensions: 12.5 × 10.4 × 4.5 cm (4¹⁵⁄₁₆ × 4⅛ × 1¾ inches)
Collection of George Christie, Bear River, Nova Scotia

This small frame pivots on two carved and decorated posts, and was probably used on a night table or chest of drawers to hold either a small mirror (for a child?), or the photograph of a loved one. The frame and stand are both carved and incised, and decorated with three five-pointed star motifs.

Structure: The frame and stand is made from softwood and varnished. The posts are open mortised through the base, and the back of the frame is nailed with small round brads forming a recess for the mirror or photograph and glass.

271 Footstool

Clearland, Lunenburg County
Dark brown painted softwood with scallop-shaped skirts
Artist unknown
Circa 1840-1860
Dimensions: 60.0 × 32.0 × 14.0 cm (11⅝ × 12⅝ × 5½ inches)
Private collection

Benches and footstools are common items listed in the household inventories of the late eighteenth and early nineteenth centuries in Lunenburg County, sometimes replacing chairs as the predominent form of seating.[1] Benches were a common seating form in Pennsylvania-German households as well, although many were built into the walls[2] and not free standing as in Lunenburg County.

This particular example has scallop-shaped skirts with incised reeding along the underedge of each apron. In addition, the ends of the top are also shaped. The shaped plank legs are splayed for stability and end in four small feet which give a sense of lightness to the stool. Footstools of this size were probably also used by small children as seating, romantic tradition suggesting they were set by the open hearth on a cold winter's night thereby giving them other names such as "cricket stool" or "hearth stool".

Structure: Plank construction with butt joints that are square nailed. The wood is softwood and the existing paint is an early overpaint close in colour to the original medium/dark brown. Except for two missing scallops, one on each skirt, the stool is in original "as found" condition.

1. Richard Henning Field, "Proxemic Patterns: Eighteenth Century Lunenburg-German Domestic Furnishings and Interiors", Paper presented at the Atlantic Canada Eighteenth Century Society meetings at Dalhousie University in March, 1985.
2. Benno M. Forman, "German Influences in Pennsylvania Furniture", In Catherine E. Hutchins (Ed), *Arts of the Pennsylvania Germans,* (New York: W. W. Norton & Company, Inc., 1983), pp. 112-115.

272 Footstool

Lunenburg County
Red painted softwood
Artist unknown
Circa 1860-1880
Dimensions: 39.0 × 19.0 × 17.5 cm (15⅜ × 7$\frac{7}{16}$ × 6⅞ inches)
Collection of June E. Miller and Murray E. Stewart, Berwick, Nova Scotia

A small footstool with shaped ends on the top board, and modified boot-jack cutouts on the plank legs. The red paint is original with a later application of varnish.

Structure: Plank construction with butt joints that are square nailed. The edge of the top is shaped and cut out. The plank legs have both cracked, and repairs have been carried out using square nails to secure strips of wood to the inside of the legs to retard further splitting.

273 Footstool

Lunenburg County

Original painted and decorated softwood

Artist unknown

Circa 1860-1870

Dimensions: 42.6 × 20.0 × 25.0 cm (16¾ × 7⅞ × 9⅞ inches)

Collection of Pascal and Angela Dinaut, Great Village, Nova Scotia

An excellent example of a footstool with a painted six-pointed star motif on the centre top. The ground paint is the original red.

Structure: Plank construction with butt joints that are square nailed. There are two cracks in the plank legs, one with an early square nail repair using a leather splint to hold the piece together.

274 Rigid Heddle or Tape Loom

Probably Church Point or Comeauville, Digby County

Unpainted softwood

Maker uncertain, but the initials 'SD' and the date 1820 are scratched into one side of the loom

Circa 1820

Dimensions: 63.6 × 26.8 × 1.2 cm (25 × 10½ × ½ inches). The heddle is measured at its widest point, the thickness of the plank varies from 1.9 cm (¾ inch) to 1.0 cm (⅜ inch).

Collection of Fort Anne National Historic Park, Annapolis Royal, Nova Scotia

This paddle-shaped tool was used to weave narrow bands and tapes for various domestic purposes. It was used by resting it on a hard surface, held between the legs, or secured to a wall or fixed object with strings through the two drilled holes opposite the heddle reed. It could also be suspended over a peg or hook. The warp threads passed alternately through the slits and corresponding holes. By raising and lowering the threads, sheds were formed. The threads through the holes remained stationary while those in the slits moved above and below them; the weft was passed through and beaten into place.[1]

Information attached on a small piece of paper glued to the heddle identifys the 'SD' as Seraphim Doucette (Doucet) who was either the maker or the owner of the loom. The date 1820, which is scratched next to the initials, is in keeping with the expected date of this piece.

History: The heddle was donated by S. F. Comeau to Fort Anne in 1924. Although it is not known how it came into Mr. Comeau's possession, the heddle has been on permanent display at Fort Anne since that time.

Structure: The heddle is made from one piece of softwood which has never been painted, but is now highly patinaed and dark brown-black in colour. The grain of the wood runs the length of the loom. Two small splits have been repaired by drilling two holes on either side of the split and then binding together with twine in a manner similar to the way cracks in china are often repaired. The heddle is in excellent and original "as found" condition with the remains of contemporary weaving materials attached to the holes and slits.

1. Harold B. Burnham and Dorothy K. Burnham, *"Keep Me Warm One Night": Early Handweaving in Eastern Canada,* (Toronto: University of Toronto Press, 1972), p. 49. Beatrice Garvan, *The Pennsylvania German Collection,* (Philadelphia: Philadelphia Museum of Art, 1982), pp. 60-61.

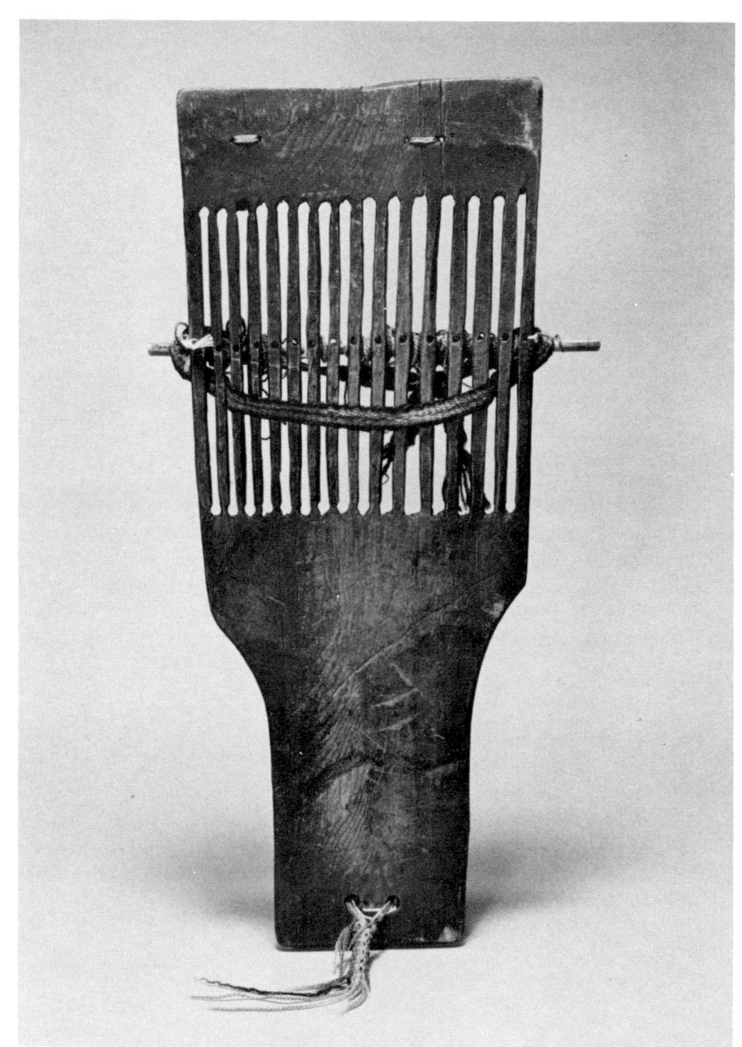

275 Bandloom with Rigid Heddle

Hamm's Hill, Lunenburg County
Decorated and painted softwood and hardwood
Artist unknown
Circa 1820-1840
Dimensions: 50.8 × 33.0 × 17.8 cm (20 × 13 × 7 inches)
Collection of Chris Huntington, Hamm's Hill, Nova Scotia

This is perhaps one of the most important Lunenburg County objects in the exhibition. What makes this bandloom so significant is the decoration on the outer side of the rigid heddle, and the tulip shaping on both the support posts for the reel and the top of the rigid heddle. The incised motifs include three pinwheels, a band of cross-hatching, and a series of cross-hatched ovals along the end of the base-board. All of these motifs are very Germanic, but the presence of the tulip on a piece this early suggests that this motif may have been more popular than previously thought in Lunenburg County.

Structure: The bandloom dates very early, made entirely with forged (rose-head) nails. Plank construction with butt joints, the reel supports are mortised through the baseboard. The reel is made of hardwood, the rest of the loom from softwood. The gear and the ratchet are early replacements with the ratchet square nailed in position.

276 Bandloom with Rigid Heddle

Blandford, Lunenburg County
Softwood with incised decoration
Artist unknown
Circa 1830-1850
Dimensions: 41.2 × 30.5 × 14.0 cm ($16\frac{1}{4}$ × 12 × $5\frac{1}{2}$ inches)
Collection of the Nova Scotia Museum, Halifax, Nova Scotia

This decorated tape loom has a series of freehand designs typical of the work found in Lunenburg County. This loom was possibly used by Mrs. Seboya (Seaboyer ?) of Blandford, and is known to have been taken by her daughter, Elizabeth, to Oak Island when she married, circa 1840. Mr. Anthony Graves of Oak Island then passed the loom to his daughter Sophia Graves (1844 ?-1930 ?) who married Henry Peter Sellers of Chester Basin.

Structure: Plank construction with mitered joints that are pegged. The rigged heddle and warp beams supporting the reel are mortised through the base and pegged and nailed.

277 Bandloom with Rigid Heddle

Kings County
Original red and green painted softwood
Artist unknown
Circa 1840-1860
Dimensions: 47.0 × 48.2 × 22.2 cm (18½ × 19 × 8¾ inches)
Collection of Jerry and Debbie Vidito, Kentville, Nova Scotia

An excellent example of a bandloom with rigid heddle used for weaving tapes and narrow bands for garters, men's suspenders, laces and ties for clothing, suspension loops for towels and many other purposes.[1] This particular loom has a lot of "country" appeal because of its red decoration and its construction.

Structure: Plank pine construction with butt and mortise and tenon construction joined with square nails.

1. Harold B. Burnham and Dorothy K. Burnham, *"Keep Me Warm One Night": Early Handweaving in Eastern Canada,* (Toronto: University of Toronto Press, 1972), pp. 50-51.

278 Footstool/Bandloom with Rigid Heddle

Probably Lunenburg County
Original dark brown painted softwood
Artist unknown
Circa 1850-1870
Dimensions: 48.5 × 21.0 × 15.0 cm (19⅛ × 8¼ × 5⅞ inches)
Private collection

This is perhaps a unique example of a footstool that can be converted to a bandloom. The idea certainly has merit, as most looms of this type resemble stools or benches turned upside down. This particular example uses one of the plank legs as the rigid heddle which is mounted into the frame of the stool, while simple wrap beams (dowels) have been set between two posts at the back, which also act as legs. Although you could not wind off as much warp as on the bandlooms with hand cranked reels, this particular loom was essentially operated in the same manner with the weft beaten into place either with the fingers or with a knife beater. The tapes and narrow bands woven with these tools were used for garters, men's suspenders, laces and ties for clothing, suspension loops for towels, and for many other purposes.[1]

Structure: Plank construction with butt joints that are square nailed. The plank and post legs are open mortised and nailed into place. The brown paint is original.

1. Harold B. Burnham and Dorothy K. Burnham, *"Keep Me Warm One Night": Early Handweaving in Eastern Canada,* (Toronto: University of Toronto Press, 1972), p. 50.

279 Mortar and Pestle

Probably Barrington, Shelburne County
Original red painted hardwood for both mortar and pestle
Artist unknown
Circa 1810-1830
Dimensions: 32.7 × 17 cm ($12\frac{7}{8} \times 6\frac{5}{8}$ inches) for the mortar, 29.2 × 8.0 cm ($11\frac{1}{2} \times 3\frac{1}{4}$ inches) for the pestle with the width measured at the widest point of the head.
Collection of the Cape Sable Historical Society, Barrington, Nova Scotia

Mortars were employed from antiquity onward to crush food, herbs and spices for domestic use. The first mortars were probably hollow stumps or logs, sometimes massive in size to contain large quantities of food and grain. Smaller ones were used by apothecaries (and alchemists in the medieval period) to pulverize herbs, drugs or other chemicals.[1] This particular mortar still has its original pestle and was probably used in the preparation of food grains, herbs and spices in the kitchen. Mortars were essential tools in the transformation of raw materials from the natural to the artificial and usable, a process that usually took place in the kitchen/hearth room of most late eighteenth and early nineteenth century households. With the use of the hearth and such tools as mortars and pestles, this unbroken food/fiber was turned into broken food/fiber (such as grain into meal or flour) and then changed into improved food/fiber through preparation and cooking (such as bread).[2]

This mortar is carved from a single block of hardwood, and has a wide base equal to its top diameter, which combined with the weight of the wood, insures stability while in use. The mortar is decorated with deep chip-carving around the outer rim of the base, and in the centre of the block, which helps delineate the upper portion of the mortar with its hollowed-out container and the solid portion underneath which serves as a pedestal.

History: The mortar and pestle was donated to the Cape Sable Historical Society prior to 1960 by a member of the Watson family of Barrington.

Structure: Both the mortar and pestle are carved from solid blocks of hardwood and retain their original coat of red paint, now much worn, on the inside of the mortar and on the working end of the pestle. The pestle has a minor age crack and there is evidence of dormant wood worm activity in both the mortar and pestle.

1. Metropolitan Museum of Art, *The Secular Spirit: Life and Art and the End of the Middle Ages,* (New York: The Metropolitan Museum of Art, 1975), p. 114.
2. Robert Blair St. George, " 'Set Thine House in Order': The Domestication of the Yeomany in Seventeenth-Century New England", In *New England Begins: The Seventeenth Century* (Boston: Museum of Fine Arts, 1982, 3 Volumes), p. 161, pp. 168-170 (Volume 2).

280 Watch Hutch

Lunenburg County, possibly Rose Bay
Carved and varnished hardwood (mahogany?)
Artist unknown
Circa 1850-1860
Dimensions: 8.0 × 16.5 × 4.0 cm (3⅛ × 6½ × 1$^{9}/_{16}$ inches)
Private collection

Watch holders were used to secure pocket watches, which were placed inside the hutch so the face was visible, and then hung on the wall or placed on a table. Not only did this help to protect the pocketwatch, but it also allowed a time piece to have greater use when the owner was not carrying it on his person. Generally a watch hutch would be used at the end of the day's business and probably placed in a bedroom. The watch hutch usually has the overall design of a long case clock. This example could be of American origin, perhaps brought to the province in the personal effects of new arrivals migrating from the United States.

Structure: Plank construction with butt joints. The outer sides and back board are attached with nails to the solid block of mahogany from which the inner sides and front are carved.

281 Ladle

South Shore or Annapolis Valley Region
Original green-black painted hardwood
Artist unknown
Circa 1850-1870
Dimensions: 42.0 × 11.4 cm (16½ × 4½ inches)
Collection of Leslie J. Langille, Lunenburg, Nova Scotia

Although the exact provenance of this piece is unclear, it was definitely found in Nova Scotia, and is a good example of a plain utilitarian object used for domestic purposes.

Structure: The ladle is carved from a solid block of hardwood and painted a green-black colour. There is an age-crack on one end of the ladle cup.

282 Knife Sheath

South Shore or Lunenburg County
Birchbark with traces of black paint
Artist unknown
Circa 1850-1870
Dimensions: 4.2 × 19.1 × 2.0 cm (1⅝ × 7½ × ¾ inches)
Private collection

Probably of Micmac origin, this birchbark sheath was made to carry a small knife and attached to the belt by the means of several loops.

Structure: The sheath is made by folding one single strip of bark in a U shape which is then cross-wrapped with a continuous narrow band of bark in a manner similar to a basket weave. There are traces of black paint remaining on the sheath.

283 Church Collection Box

Chester, Lunenburg County
Painted hardwood
Artist unknown
Circa 1860-1880
Dimensions: 10.5 × 134.0 × 7.6 cm (4⅛ × 52¾ × 3 inches)
Collection of Paul Killawee and Judy Aymar, Queensland, Nova Scotia

The long handle on this church collection box allowed contributions to be collected from members of the congregation sitting in the middle of the church pews without having to pass a collection plate from hand to hand. This particular example is in the original red paint. The bottom inside of the box is lined with cloth to deaden the sound of the money being collected.

Structure: Plank construction with butt joints that are nailed with small square-headed brads. The bottom of the box is shaped and extends into the handle.

284 The Flying Man on the High Bar

Probably Colchester County

Original carved and painted softwood with twine

Artist unknown

Circa 1870-1890

Dimensions: 17.8 × 44.6 cm (7 × 11$^{9}/_{16}$ inches)

Collection of Mr. and Mrs. Francis Coutellier, Moncton, New Brunswick

This is certainly one of the more appealing children's toys to be found in Nova Scotia. When the two unpainted portions of the side supports are gently pushed and released, the man is set in motion flying around the string, and because of his articulated joints, he performs various acrobatic acts. The lever on the right side also generates this same operation.

Structure: Softwood held together with metal braces and square nails. The figure is carved in profile with fully articulated joints.

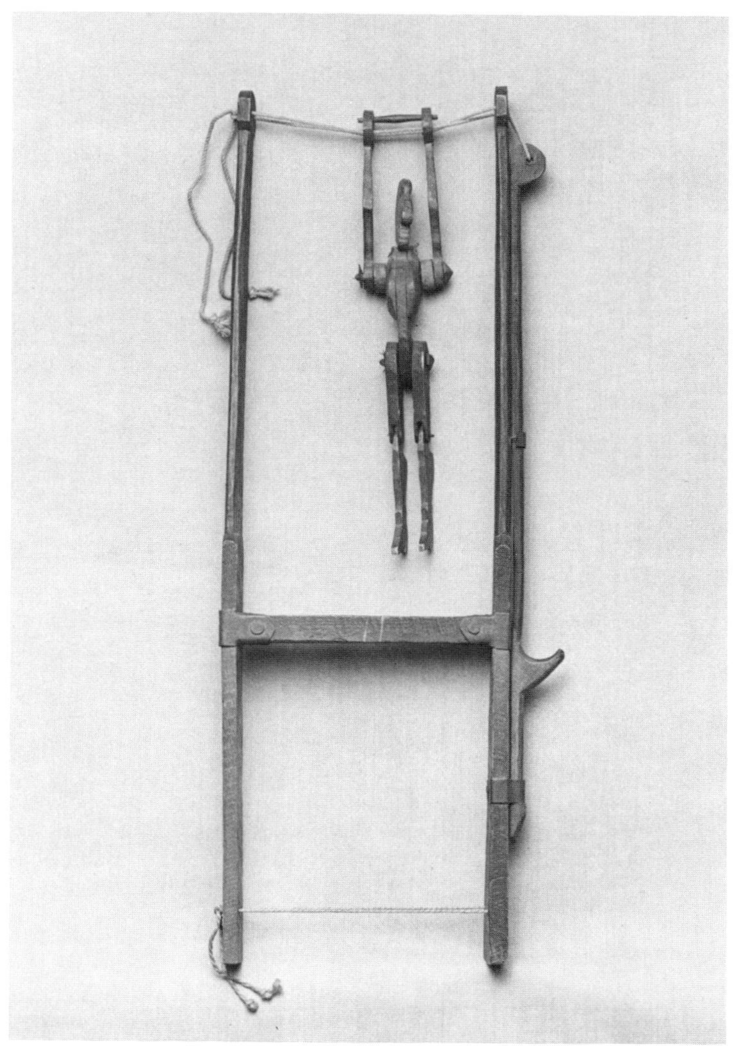

285 Rolling Pin

Halifax County

Original turned, carved and painted or stained hardwood

Artist unknown

Dimensions: diameter — 5.0 × length 32.0 cm (1$^{15}/_{16}$ × 12$^{5}/_{8}$ inches)

Circa 1890

Collection of Mr and Mrs Francis Coutellier, Moncton, New Brunswick

A small rolling pin used in the kitchen for making dough. The carved surface would create interesting patterns in the baked goods, adding design and decoration to everyday food preparation and consumption.

Structure: The rolling pin was first turned from a single block of hardwood, and then carved to create a checkered pattern.

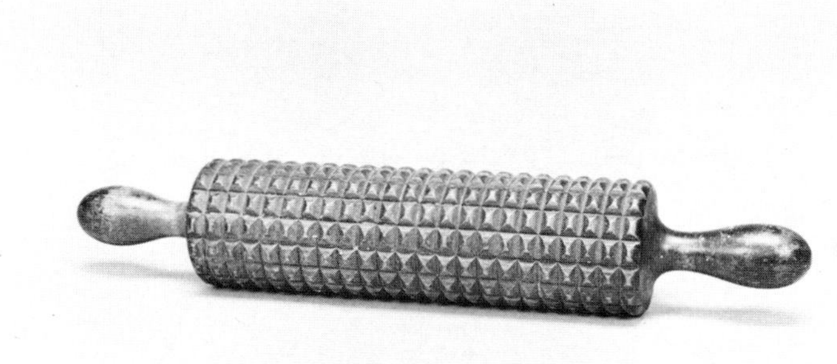

286 Carved Star

Queens County
Original carved and painted softwood
Artist unknown, but the name Elaine Hiltz is pencilled on the reverse
Circa 1890-1910
Dimensions: 14.0 × 1.0 cm (5½ × ⅜ inches)
Collection of Murray E. Stewart, Berwick, Nova Scotia

This carved and painted star is probably a remnant of a decorative ornament used in the home, or perhaps on board a ship. The star is carved in relief and painted green and white, while the rest of the area is painted dark red.

Structure: The star is carved from a single piece of softwood which has been shaped to form a circle. The rough outline of a star is partially carved and incised on the reverse unpainted side which was either a practice attempt or abandoned effort on the part of the maker.

287 Candle Holder

Digby County
Painted and turned softwood and hardwood
Artist unknown
Circa 1890-1920
Dimensions: Measured at base — 14.0 × 23.5 × 14.6 cm (5½ × 9¼ × 5¾ inches)
Collection of the National Museum of Man, Canadian Centre for Folk Culture Studies, Ottawa, Ontario

This candle holder strongly reflects the Acadian Catholic tradition of the French Shore of Nova Scotia where it was found. The actual holder is turned from hardwood while the box is made from softwood and painted. A wooden cross has been applied to the front of the box.

Structure: Plank construction with butt joints that are round nailed. The candle holder is turned and pegged into the top of the box. The cross is applied with round nails.

288 Magazine Rack

LaHave Islands, Lunenburg County

Original carved and painted hardwood

Artist unknown, but the name Fran Tumblin is written twice on the reverse

Circa 1900-1920

Dimensions: 45.7 × 70.5 × 23.5 cm (18 × 27¾ × 9¼ inches)

Private collection

A magazine rack which was hung on a wall or door to hold monthly journals or newspapers. Several similar examples with pierced hearts, stars, diamonds and other geometric motifs, and a serrated edge on the cross support, have been found in Lunenburg County. The name Fran Tumblin and the place LaHave Islands is written on the reverse of the slats.

Structure: The rack is painted red and blue with the slats of hardwood held together with brass headed tacks.

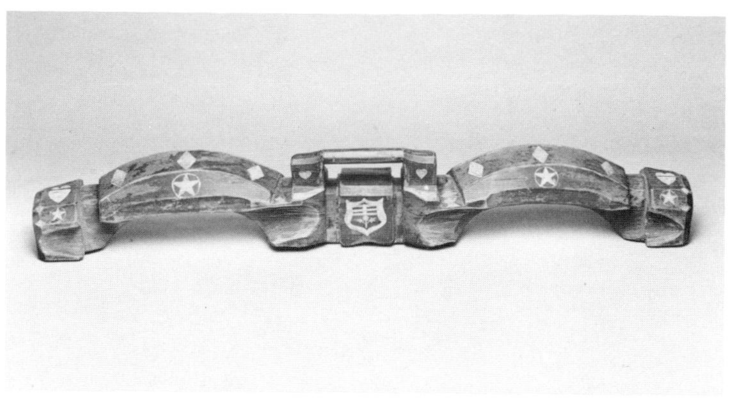

289 Gallows Yoke*

Lapland, Lunenburg County

Carved and painted hardwood

Artist unknown

Circa 1900-1920

Dimensions: 109.2 × 12.7 × 17.8 cm (43 × 5 × 7 inches)

Collection of Richard Henning Field and Deborah Field, Halifax, Nova Scotia

In the early nineteenth century estate inventories from Lunenburg County, pairs of oxen and yokes are often included in the listing of farm animals and implements,[1] teams of oxen being the draft animals used for plowing and for other heavy chores around the farm. Right up until the Second World War oxen were being used in Lunenburg County, and were often entered in oxen pull competitions on festival days. Although the oxen have given way to tractors, ox pulls are still a part of the summer exhibition held in Lunenburg. This particular yoke was probably used for just such a competition judging by its painted decoration. It was custom to make and decorate yokes specifically for such oxen pulls, not only to show off one's skills and craftsmanship, but to add decoration and adornment, sometimes as a mark of the competitor, to the occasion.

This particular example has a series of motifs painted in white on a red ground, including hearts, diamonds, five-pointed stars in circles, and the basic outline of the Nova Scotia coat-of-arms in the middle of the yoke.

Structure: The yoke is carved from a solid block of hardwood, probably maple.

1. This is based on my doctorial research into the estate inventories of Lunenburg County, on microfilm at the Public Archives of Nova Scotia.

*This piece will be on view in Halifax only

290 Tobacco Cutter
Guysborough County
Painted hardwood and forged iron cutter
Artist unknown
Circa 1870-1880
Dimensions: 31.0 × 6.0 × 7.0 cm (12³⁄₁₆ × 2⅜ × 2¾ inches)
Collection of Pascal and Angela Dinaut, Great Village, Nova Scotia

Tobacco cutters were often made and used by farmers who grew their own tobacco. This particular example has an elegant simplified form which understates the best in folk art. The forged iron blade, used to cut the plugs of tobacco which were kept handy in the carved recess, has a handsome skate tail shape that adds to the beauty of this piece.

Structure: The base is hollowed out from a single block of hardwood. The blade with handle pivots through a slot cut to one side of the block and is attached with a forged nail.

291 Wooden Spoon
Probably Lunenburg County
Unpainted and carved hardwood
Artist unknown
Circa 1850-1870
Dimensions: 4.5 × 23.5 × 5.0 cm (1¾ × 9¼ × 1¹⁵⁄₁₆ inches)
Private collection

Possibly of Micmac origin, this spoon is carved with a series of X or cross patterns and has a sweeping curved handle.

Structure: The spoon is carved from a solid block of hardwood.

292 Hanging Cupboard*

Pictou, Pictou County
Carved and painted softwood
Artist unknown
Circa 1820-1840
Dimensions: 64.0 × 97.7 × 17.6 cm (24³⁄₁₆ × 38½ × 7 inches)
Collection of Chris Huntington, Hamms Hill, Nova Scotia

This is without a doubt the greatest hanging cupboard presently known from Nova Scotia. It is a fine example of the type of furnishings that were once used in the early nineteenth century houses of Nova Scotia. Although the door is of great interest, with its arched panels, it is the decorated interior, with its pierced designs, that is simply stunning. One would only like to know what other furnishings were to be found in the interior of the house where this cupboard was used.

Structure: Plank construction with dovetailed joints. The two backboards are attached with forged nails. The paint was originally red and gold. There is a lock, clasp and ivory escutcheon on the left side of the case. The prints which are set in the door seem to be original. The wooden panels behind them are nailed in place with small square brads, and the exposed surface of the panels unfinished, suggesting that some sort of print or paper was used, and not glass.

*This piece will be on view in Halifax only

293 Desk*

Glen Haven, Halifax County
Painted softwood and hardwood with applied decorations
Made by John Awald
Circa 1860-1880
Dimensions: 100.0 × 90.0 (height at front) × 50.0 cm ($39\frac{3}{8}$ × $29\frac{1}{16}$ (height at front) × $19\frac{11}{16}$ inches)
Collection of Chris Huntington, Hamm's Hill, Nova Scotia

This desk illustrates the fanciful and traditional design and decorative treatment often found on late nineteenth century objects from Nova Scotia. The desk is painted a deep plum-brown with red applied motifs, drawer pulls and case molding, and red and black turned legs, and green drawer fronts.

Structure: Frame and plank construction with butt joints in desk and drawer sections. Sloped lid has applied molding along front edge and sides. Unpainted interior has two compartments under a single shelf. Legs turned in typical Lunenburg-German fashion with upper rings over a long unturned section of leg.

Exhibited: Decorated Nova Scotia Furnishings, Dalhousie University Art Gallery, Halifax: Nova Scotia, July 5-August 6, 1978.

Published: Tom Lackey, *Decorated Nova Scotia Furnishings,* (Halifax: Dalhousie University Art Gallery, 1978), pp. 15, 34.

*This piece will be on view in Halifax only

294 Armchair*

Country Harbour, Guysborough County
Original painted and chip-carved hardwood
Artist unknown
Circa 1860-1880
Dimensions: 56.0 × 92.5 × 42.0 cm ($22\frac{1}{16}$ × $36\frac{7}{16}$ × $16\frac{9}{16}$ inches)
Collection of Jerry and Debbie Vidito, Kentville, Nova Scotia

This chip-carved decorated armchair exhibits a certain East Lake influence popular at the turn of the century. The decorative motifs include a series of vine and leaf motifs combined with cross-hatched squares and incised X designs.

Structure: Pegged tenon construction with some secondary round nails. Front and back leg construction and arm supports made from single blocks of hardwood. Verticle and horizontal slats are pegged and tenon construction. The seat base is softwood and the slip cushion a recent replacement. The small brass knob located in the centre of the front seat stretcher was probably used to tie the original seat cushion in place. The paint was originally a dark brown.

*This piece will be on view in Halifax only

295 Plant Stand*

Lunenburg County

Original painted, carved and decorated softwood

Artist unknown

Circa 1890-1910

Dimensions: 98.0 × 59.0 (height at front) × 130.0 (height at rear) × 52.0 cm (38 9/16 × 23 3/16 (height at front) × 51 3/16 (height at rear) × 20 7/16 inches)

Collection of Pascal and Angela Dinaut, Great Village, Nova Scotia

This ornately decorated and painted stand was originally used for plants or to display other household or personal objects. This particular example is in its original red paint with gold painted finials.

Structure: Plank construction with butt, rabbet, mortise and tenon joints and corners.

*This piece will be on view in Halifax only

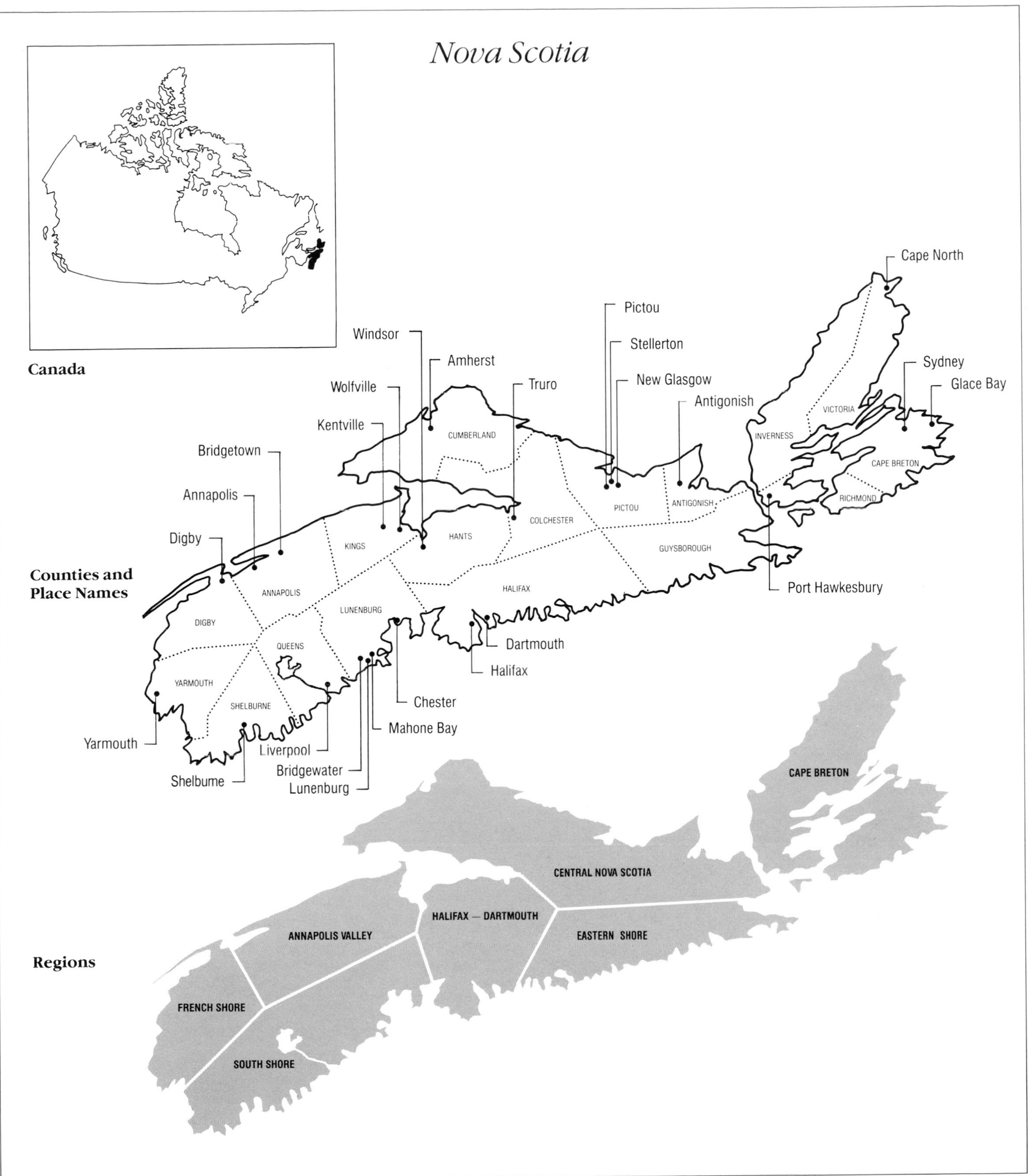
Nova Scotia
Canada
Counties and Place Names
Cape North
Pictou
Stellerton
New Glasgow
Antigonish
Sydney
Glace Bay
Windsor
Amherst
Truro
Wolfville
Kentville
Bridgetown
Annapolis
Digby
Yarmouth
Shelburne
Liverpool
Bridgewater
Lunenburg
Mahone Bay
Chester
Halifax
Dartmouth
Port Hawkesbury
CUMBERLAND
COLCHESTER
PICTOU
ANTIGONISH
GUYSBOROUGH
INVERNESS
VICTORIA
CAPE BRETON
RICHMOND
KINGS
HANTS
HALIFAX
ANNAPOLIS
LUNENBURG
DIGBY
QUEENS
YARMOUTH
SHELBURNE
Regions
CAPE BRETON
CENTRAL NOVA SCOTIA
HALIFAX — DARTMOUTH
EASTERN SHORE
ANNAPOLIS VALLEY
FRENCH SHORE
SOUTH SHORE

Selected Bibliography

Folk Art *General*

Ames, Kenneth L. *Beyond Necessity: Art in the Folk Tradition.* Winterthur, Delaware: Winterthur Museum, 1977.

Ayres, James. *British Folk Art.* Woodstock, New York: The Overlook Press, 1977.

Bird, Michael S. *Canadian Folk Art: Old Ways in a New Land.* Toronto: Oxford University Press, 1982.

Bird, Michael, and Terry Kobayashi. *A Splendid Harvest: Germanic Folk and Decorative Arts in Canada.* Toronto: Van Nostrand Reinhold, 1981.

Cuisenier, Jean. *French Folk Art.* Tokyo: Kodansha International, 1976.

Dewhurst, C. Kurt; MacDowell, Betty; and MacDowell, Marsha. *Artists in Aprons: Folk Art by American Women.* New York: Dutton Paperbacks, 1979.

Harper, Russell J. *A People's Art: Primitive, Naive, Provincial and Folk Painting in Canada.* Toronto: University of Toronto Press, 1974.

Lipman, Jean and Alice Winchester. *The Flowering of American Folk Art, 1776-1876.* New York: Viking Press, 1974.

Mattie, Wesley, (et al). *From the Heart: Folk Art in Canada.* Toronto: McClelland and Stewart, 1983.

McKendry, Blake. *Folk Art: Primitive and Naive Art in Canada.* Toronto: Methuen, 1983.

Twas Ever Thus: A Selection of Eastern Canadian Folk Art. Toronto: M. F. Feheley, 1979.

Schlee, Ernst. *German Folk Art.* Tokyo: Kodansha International, 1980.

Material History *General*

Demos, John. *A Little Commonwealth: Family Life in Plymouth Colony.* London: Oxford University Press, 1970.

Glassie, Henry. *Pattern in The Material Folk Culture of the Eastern United States.* Philadelphia: The University of Pennsylvania Press, 1968.

Quimby, Ian M. (Ed.), *Material Culture and the Study of American Life.* New York: W. W. Norton and Company, 1978.

Quimby, Ian M., and Scott Swank, (Eds). *Perspectives on American Folk Art.* New York: W. W. Norton and Company, 1980.

Schlereth, Thomas (Ed.), *Material Culture Studies in America.* Nashville, Tennessee: American Association for State and Local History, 1982.

Schlereth, Thomas. *Artifacts and the American Past.* Nashville, Tennessee: American Association for State and Local History, 1980.

Textiles

Bishop, Robert. *New Discoveries in American Quilts.* New York: Dutton Paperbacks, 1975.

Bolton, Ethel Stanwood, and Coe, Eva Johnston. *American Samplers.* Boston: The Massachusetts Society of Colonial Dames of America, 1921. Reprint, New York: Dover Publications, 1973.

Brett, K. B. *Ontario Handwoven Textiles.* Toronto: Royal Ontario Museum, 1956.

Burnham, Dorothy K. *Pieced Quilts of Ontario.* Toronto: Royal Ontario Museum, 1975.

Burnham, Dorothy K. *The Comfortable Arts: Traditional Spinning and Weaving in Canada.* Ottawa: National Museum of Canada: 1981.

Burnham, Harold B., and Dorothy K. Burnham. *Keep Me Warm One Night: Early Handweaving in Eastern Canada.* Toronto: University of Toronto Press, 1972.

Conroy, Mary. *Canada Quilts.* Toronto: Griffin Press, 1976.

Dwyer, Ruth. *Eastern Canadian Quilts and Hooked Rugs of the 19th and Early 20th Centuries.* Uxbridge: Uxbridge-Scott Historical Society, 1978.

Fennelly, Catherine. *Textiles in New England 1790-1840.* Sturbridge: Old Sturbridge Village Booklet Series, 1961.

Frost, Edward Sands. *Hooked Rug Patterns.* Dearborn, Michigan: Greenfield Village and Henry Ford Museum, 1970.

Holstein, Jonathan. *The Pieced Quilt: A North American Tradition.* Toronto: McClelland and Stewart, 1973.

Kent, William Winthrop. *The Hooked Rug.* New York: Tudor Publishing Company, 1930.

Kopp, Joel, and Kopp, Kate. *American Hooked and Sewn Rugs: Folk Art Underfoot.* New York: Dutton Paperbacks, 1975.

Krueger, Glee. *A Gallery of American Samplers: The Theodore H. Kapnek Collection.* New York: Dutton Paperbacks in Association with the Museum of American Folk Art, 1978.

Little, Nina Fletcher. *Floor Coverings in New England Before 1850.* Sturbridge, Massachusetts: Old Sturbridge Village, 1967.

McKendry, R., *Quilts and Other Bed Coverings in the Canadian Tradition.* Toronto: Van Nostrand, 1979.

Montgomery, Florence M. *Textiles in America, 1650-1870.* New York: W. W. Norton and Company, 1985.

Orlofsky, Patsy, and Orlofsky, Myron. *Quilts in America.* New York: McGraw-Hill, 1974.

Swan, Susan Burrows. *Plain and Fancy; American Women and Their Needlework, 1700-1850.* New York: Holt, Rinehart & Winston, 1977.

Sculpture

Barber, Joel. *Wildfowl Decoys.* New York: Dover Publications, 1934.

Bishop, Robert. *American Folk Sculpture.* New York: E. P. Dutton, 1974.

Bishop, Robert and Coblentz, Patricia. *A Gallery of American Weathervanes and Whirligigs.* New York: E. P. Dutton and Company, 1981.

Cahill, Holger. *American Folk Sculpture.* Newark, New Jersey: The Newark Museum, 1931.

Fitzgerald, Ken. *Weathervanes and Whirligigs.* New York: Clarkson N. Potter, 1967.

Guyette, Gary and Dale Guyette, *Decoys of Maritime Canada.* Exton, Pennsylvania: Schiffer Publishing Ltd., 1983.

Klamkin, Charles. *Weathervanes: The History, Manufacture, and Design of an American Folk Art.* New York: Hawthorn Books, 1973.

Lipman, Jean. *American Folk Art in Wood, Metal and Stone.* New York: Pantheon Books, 1948.

Ludwig, Allan I. *Graven Images: New England Stonecarving and Its Symbols, 1650-1815.* Middletown, Connecticut: Wesleyan University Press, 1966.

Starr, George R. *Decoys of the Atlantic Flyway.* New York: Winchester Press, 1974.

Trask, Deborah. *Life How Short, Eternity How Long: Gravestone Carving and Carvers in Nova Scotia.* Halifax: Now Scotia Museum, 1978.

Paintings, Watercolours and Drawings.

Armour, Charles A., and Lackey Thomas. *Sailing Ships of The Maritimes.* Toronto: McGraw-Hill Ryerson, Limited, 1975.

Black, Mary C., and Lipman, Jean. *American Folk Painting.* New York: Clarkson N. Potter, 1966.

Borneman, Henry S. *Pennsylvania German Illuminated Manuscripts.* New York: Dover Publications, 1964.

Cahill, Holger. *American Primitives, An Exhibit of the Paintings of Nineteenth Century Folk Artists.* Newark, New Jersey: The Newark Museum, 1930.

Ebert, John, and Ebert, Katherine. *American Folk Painters.* New York: Charles Scribner's Sons, 1975.

Flexner, James Thomas. *The Light of Distant Skies, 1760-1835.* New York: Harcourt, Brace and Co., 1954.

Lipman, Jean. *American Primitive Painting.* New York: Oxford University Press, 1942. Reprint, New York: Dover Publications, 1972.

McGraw, Myrtle B. *The Child in Painting.* New York: The Greystone Press, 1941.

Miles, Ellen, (Ed.), *Portrait Painting in America* (Antiques Magazine Library). New York: Universe Books, 1977.

Rumford, Beatrix T. (Ed.), *American Folk Portraits.* Boston: New York Graphic Society in Association with the Colonial Williamburg Foundation, 1981.

Shelley, Donald A. *A Catalogue of American Portraits in the New York Historical Society.* New York: The New York Historical Society, 1941.

Shelley, Donald A. *The Fraktur: Writings or Illuminated Manuscripts of the Pennsylvania Germans.* Allentown, Pennsylvania: Pennsylvania German Folklore Society, 1961.

Tillou, Peter H. *Nineteenth Century Folk Painting: Our Spirited National Heritage,* Works of Art from the Collection of Mr. and Mrs. Peter Tillou (exhibition catalogue). Storrs, Connecticut: The University of Connecticut, The William Benton Museum of Art, 1973.

Weiser, Frederick S., and Heaney, Howell J., comps. *The Pennsylvania German Fraktur of the Free Library of Philadelphia.* 2 vols. Breiningsville, Pa.: The Free Library of Philadelphia, 1976.

Decorated Utilitarian Objects

Dobson, Henry and Barbara Dobson. *The Early Furniture of Ontario and the Atlantic Provinces.* Toronto: M. F. Feheley Publishers Ltd., 1974.

Fabian, Munroe H. *The Pennsylvania-German Decorated Chest.* New York: Universe Books, 1978.

Fales, Dean A., and Bishop, Robert. *American Painted Furniture, 1660-1880.* New York: Dutton Paperbacks, 1979.

Ferguson, Bruce W. *Decorated Nova Scotia Furnishings.* Halifax: Dalhousie Art Gallery, 1978.

Field, Richard. *An Exhibition of Canadian Gameboards of the Nineteenth and Twentieth Centuries from Ontario, Quebec and Nova Scotia.* Halifax: Art Gallery of Nova Scotia, 1981.

Flayderman, E. Norman. *Scrimshaw and Scrimshanders: Whales and Whalemen.* New Milford, Connecticut: N. Flayderman & Co., 1972.

Lichten, Frances. *Folk Art Motifs of Pennsylvania.* New York: Hastings House, 1954.

McClintok, Inez, and McClintok, Marshall. *Toys in America.* Washington, D.C.: Public Affairs Press, 1961.

Pain, Howard. *The Heritage of Upper Canadian Furniture.* Toronto: Van Nostrand Reinhold, 1978.

Ravenswaay, Charles Van. *The Arts and Architecture of German Settlements in Missouri.* Columbia, Missouri: University of Missouri Press, 1977.

Stoudt, John Joseph. *Early Pennsylvania Arts and Crafts.* Cranbury, New Jersey: A. S. Barnes, 1964.

Whitehead, Ruth Holmes. *Micmac Quillwork.* Halifax: The Nova Scotia Museum, 1982.